# INTERPERSONAL COMMUNICATION

## A Handbook for Health Professionals

**George M. Gazda, Ph.D.**
University of Georgia
Athens, Georgia

**William C. Childers, Ph.D.**
University of Georgia
Athens, Georgia

**Richard P. Walters, Ph.D.**
Pine Crest Christian Hospital
Grand Rapids, Michigan

AN ASPEN PUBLICATION®
Aspen Systems Corporation
Rockville, Maryland
Royal Tunbridge Wells
1982

Library of Congress Cataloging in Publication Data

Gazda, George Michael, 1931-
Interpersonal communication.

Includes bibliographies and index.
1. Interpersonal communication. 2. Medical personnel
and patient. 3. Medical personnel. I. Childers,
William C., 1947- . II. Walters, Richard P.
III. Title.
R727.3.G39      610.69'6      82-6755
ISBN: 0-89443-655-4      AACR2

Publisher: John Marozsan
Editorial Director: R. Curtis Whitesel
Managing Editor: Margot Raphael
Editorial Services: Jane Coyle
Printing and Manufacturing: Debbie Swarr

Library of Congress Catalog Card Number: 82-6755
ISBN: 0-89443-655-4

*Printed in the United States of America*

2   3   4   5

# Table of Contents

# Preface

This handbook presents a model for the development of interpersonal communication. Interpersonal communication is one of the most important of all of the generic life skills. Effective interpersonal communication is a prerequisite to the development of the other life skills. In no other profession is it more important than in the health services, especially for nursing and related professionals and paraprofessionals. Effective nursing and health care delivery, therefore, are dependent upon high levels of interpersonal communication.

This handbook is organized so that users can increase their interpersonal communication skills by performing a series of carefully developed exercises leading to the mastery of an effective model. Therefore, it should be read and the exercises completed in order from Chapters 1 through 17. Additional chapters and appendixes provide supplementary material. In addition to independent study, the book also may be used as the basic text for training in small groups or classes led by an expert trainer. It is appropriate for both preservice and inservice training.

This interpersonal communications model has been developed over a period of 10 years. It has been used successfully with hundreds of nurses and related health care professionals. Research studies have shown increased staff morale and patient improvement.

Throughout, *helping* and *facilitating* are used interchangeably and *helper* and *helpee* comprehensively. *Helper* may mean someone who simply gives another person some requested but useful information, or on another occasion may refer to someone who is providing psychotherapeutic assistance over several months. Helper and caregiver also are used interchangeably. *Helpee* denotes a person who is the passive recipient of assistance as well as the individual who is actively seeking aid with minor and major problems. Health care professionals (HCPs) refers to nurses and the many related professionals and paraprofessionals with whom they interact.

The authors wish to acknowledge the many individuals who have contributed directly or indirectly to the development of this handbook. First, the pioneering work of Carl Rogers, Charles Truax, Robert Carkhuff, and their associates gave us an empirically sound rationale for the model we have adapted. Next, we wish to thank Angie Echols, Jean Nash-Pullian, and David Brooks for their assistance in typing and assembling the manuscript.

Portions of this book appeared previously in *Human Relations Development: A Manual for Health Sciences* by these same three authors—George M. Gazda, Richard P. Walters, and William C. Childers—and published by Allyn & Bacon, Inc., in 1975.

Chapter 2, "Learning How to Learn," was written by Nancy A. Haynie, Ph.D. She also wrote Appendix B, "Sensory Modality Checklist." Both appear with her permission as copyright holder.

In Chapter 9, the section on "Attending Skills" is adapted from *Amity: Friendship in Action* by Richard P. Walters, published by C.H.I., Kentwood, Michigan (1980).

Chapter 18, "Anger: Friend and Foe," is adapted from *Anger: Yours, Mine and What to Do About It* by Richard P. Walters, published by Zondervan Publishing House, Grand Rapids, Michigan (1981). A soundstrip on anger is available from C.H.I., 5500 Waterbury Place, S.E., Kentwood, Michigan 49508.

In Chapter 19, Exhibit 19–1, "Protocol: Effective Helper (Responding to the Wife of a Terminally Ill Patient)" was developed by Ms. Frances Knapp, B.S.N., Nursing Supervisor, Eugene Talmadge Memorial Hospital, Augusta, Georgia. The discussion is by George M. Gazda.

*George M. Gazda*
*William C. Childers*
*Richard P. Walters*

# Chapter 1

# Rationale and Model for the Development of Interpersonal Communications

To be effective health care professionals (HCPs), individuals must have effective life skills. But what are life skills? To date no one has systematically or scientifically isolated the generic ones. However, research is under way by the senior author and his students to determine what they are. The National Assessment of Educational Progress (NAEP) (1975), a division of the Commission on the Education of the States, cites the following seven areas that were recommended by a planning committee as basic skills:

1. consumer
2. health maintenance
3. interpersonal
4. citizenship
5. family relationship
6. community resource utilization
7. career and occupational development.

In 1918 the seven cardinal principles of education were outlined as:

1. health
2. command of fundamental processes
3. worthy home membership
4. a vocation
5. good citizenship
6. worthy use of leisure time
7. ethical character.

Shane (1977) contends that the seven cardinal principles "have retained their usefulness and importance even after the passage of 60 years."

A comparison of these two lists of skill areas shows considerable similarity between them. One area that repeats itself (though not in those precise words) is the interpersonal (relationship/communication). It is cited specifically by the NAEP and it is contained in several of the seven cardinal principles, especially in the "command of fundamental processes." In this text, this life skill is referred to as interpersonal communications. The rest of the book is devoted to the development of the rationale for this skill and procedures for its mastery.

## COMMUNICATION SKILLS

It is not necessary to reflect very long on how communication skills are taught in school to conclude that only the rudimentary ones in English grammar and composition and speech are presented. If learning these basics were sufficient, it would not be necessary to complain, "The problem is poor communication." The fact is that learning these basics does not prepare the majority of the population to be effective interpersonal communicators in the fullest sense of the word. What more is needed, then?

The position taken here is that interpersonal communication is only one of perhaps a dozen generic life skills. Some others include physical fitness/health maintenance, family relationship, self-evaluation, purpose/meaning in life (establishment of personal identity and values), decision making/problem solving, organizational/institutional functioning, career development, and the like.

Generic life skills refer to a family of related skills. For example, within the family relationship are separate subskills involving marriage relationship, parenting (if there are children), and sibling relationship (if there are siblings). Generic interpersonal communications skills include such subskills as attending, listening, perceiving, verbal responding, nonverbal responding, and problem solving.

Interpersonal communication skills are identified most clearly in the area of psychosocial development as outlined by such developmental psychologists as Havighurst (1953, 1972) and Erikson (1963). If the development of the whole person is to be understood, however, all other areas of human development must be conceptualized, as outlined in Figure 1–1.

This figure demonstrates that the whole person consists of skills in the following areas of human development: psychosocial (Erikson, 1963; Havighurst, 1953, 1972), physical-sexual (Gesell, Ilg, & Ames, 1956; Gesell, Ilg, Ames, & Bullis, 1946), cognitive, of Jean Piaget (Flavell, 1963; Wadsworth, 1971), moral (Kohlberg, 1973; Kohlberg & Turiel, 1971), ego (Loevinger, 1976), emotional (Dupont, 1976), and vocational (Super, 1963; Super, Crites, Hummel, Moser, Overstreet, & Warnath, 1957).

**Figure 1–1** Seven Developmental Modalities and Illustrative Life Skills

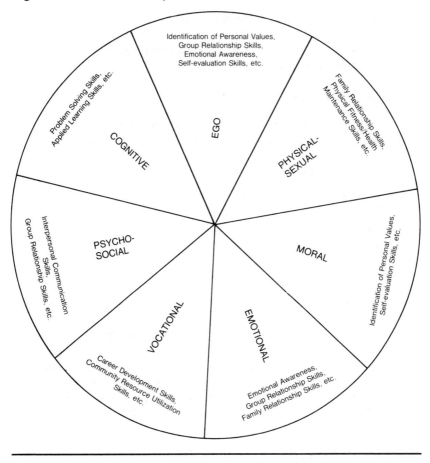

To function effectively in life, individuals must develop effective skills in all seven of these areas. This book presents a model for the development of effective skills in interpersonal communication that are prerequisites to the others because without them the others are unlikely to be developed.

An attempt by Flanagan and the American Institute for Research (1978) to define the quality of life for Americans produced 15 categories grouped under five headings:

*Physical and Material Well-Being*

Material well-being and financial security
Health and personal safety

*Relations with Other People*

Relations with spouse (girlfriend, boyfriend)
Having and rearing children
Relations with parents, siblings, and other relatives
Relations with friends

*Social, Community, and Civic Activities*

Activities related to helping or encouraging other people
Activities relating to local and national governments

*Personal Development and Fulfillment*

Intellectual development
Personal understanding and planning
Occupational role (job)
Creativity and personal expression

*Recreation*

Socializing
Passive and observational recreational activities
Active and participatory recreational activities (p. 141)

The importance of effective interpersonal communication skills is apparent in this list. One entire category is devoted to interpersonal activities (Relations with Other People) and the remaining four could not be fulfilled without effective interpersonal communication skills.

## THE USE OF MODELS

To master any life skill, the most effective approach is to develop a model. When separate skills are taught willy-nilly and there is no complete rationale for showing relationship among them nor an ordering for teaching them, they soon are lost or atrophied. However, when a sound model provides a logical and scientific defense for its use, learners are presented with the whole picture and are motivated to master the component parts because they fit together like a carefully machined group of gears. If one cog is imperfect the gears will not mesh and the machine will not function, or it will function imperfectly.

This essentially involves what Egan and Cowan (1979) describe as working models:

Working models (as opposed to models devised primarily to *understand* social phenomena) do the following:

- they provide vehicles for translating theory and research into visualizations of how things work;

- they constitute a framework for action or intervention (delivery) by practitioners;

- they suggest programs and the technologies needed to implement these programs;

- they suggest areas of action-based research with "delivery" potential; and

- they remain open to modification and development as they are influenced by new theory, research, and ongoing practice. (p. 15)

The model for interpersonal communications training outlined in this chapter has evolved from hundreds of studies based on research of numerous specialists. From these divergent theories and therapies, a common thread was discovered. Truax and Carkhuff (1967), who have carefully traced this thread, describe it as consisting of certain particular characteristics of the therapist: accurate empathy, nonpossessive warmth, and genuineness.

Rogers (1957) served as the impetus to focus renewed interest on these and similar characteristics. Working with Rogers at the University of Wisconsin, Truax, Carkhuff, and a host of others began to investigate the effect of the presence of that common thread in the therapist-client relationship. They discovered that certain conditions or dimensions offered by the therapist, when present in high levels, led to client growth and when absent or present only in low levels led to client deterioration. The accumulated evidence of the validity of the core conditions, or dimensions, as they were to be called, can be found in Rogers, (1957), Truax and Carkhuff (1967), Carkhuff and Berenson (1967), Berenson and Carkhuff (1967), Carkhuff (1969a, 1969b, 1971a, 1971b), and Rogers, Gendlin, Kiesler, and Truax, (1967).

As the research progressed, several new dimensions were discovered and scales for rating them were developed (Carkhuff 1969a, 1969b; Carkhuff & Berenson, 1967; Truax & Carkhuff, 1967). Eventually Carkhuff (1969a, 1969b) renamed and standardized the scales of the core dimensions and added a rationale that seemed to complete the model for a helping relationship. Although further refinement of existing dimensions and scales and the search for new dimensions continues, there is now available a substantial body of research and knowledge that supports the model presented in this chapter and throughout this manual.

No other model for interpersonal communications training has been so thoroughly researched, so it is offered with considerable confidence in its validity. The outline of rationale is presented as interpreted from the authors' personal contacts, their research and writings, and their application of the constructs to the training of health care professionals.

Although this model was developed originally from research on the therapist-client relationship, it has been adapted for training in effective interpersonal communication in general. The authors have adapted it to teachers/educators (Gazda, Asbury, Balzer, Childers, & Walters, 1977), health practitioners (Gazda, Walters, & Childers, 1975), secondary school students (Gazda, Walters, & Childers, 1981), and criminal justice personnel (Sisson, Arthur, & Gazda, 1981). In their 1975 version, Gazda, Walters, and Childers developed a text that was used successfully with nurses, physicians, and dentists and their support personnel. What originally was found to be an effective model for psychotherapy has now been translated into an equally effective model for teaching facilitative interpersonal communication skills—the emphasis is on the facilitative or helpful.

(At this point it would be useful to take the *Nursing Index of Responding* in Appendix A. A key for scoring the index follows it. Completing this index as a pretest will help determine current levels of functioning; taking it again after completing this text will show the extent of growth.)

## THE CYCLE OF HELPING

Self-exploration usually leads to a better understanding of helpees' concerns which, in turn, makes possible a more successful course of action. The action itself provides the ultimate feedback to helpees. Often they will need to refine or alter their responses to arrive at the preferred behavioral outcome. Helpers repeat the cycle as often as necessary to lead them toward their goal.

The three-phase cycle that Carkhuff (1971a) has outlined for problem solving (self-exploration → better self-understanding → more appropriate action or direction) works for most people; however, there are exceptions. With individuals who are not in good contact with reality, it usually is necessary to reverse the cycle and first do something to get them back in contact with reality before understanding can occur. This generally describes the mentally ill, and since only specialized health care workers are expected to deal extensively with such dysfunctional individuals, this type of helping is not the primary focus here.

## THE PROCESS OF HELPING

Exhibit 1–1 contains the key concepts in the helping model developed by Carkhuff (1969a, 1969b, 1971b, 1972). The starting point is the procedural goals for basically normal individuals of all age levels. Of course, when dealing with very young children, the adult communicates through direct action. For example, the adult communicates directly by cuddling, squeezing, feeding, cleansing, hugging, rocking, and spanking them. The adult may add words to describe the action even when the children cannot

**Exhibit 1–1** Outline of the Key Concepts of a Helping Relationship

| FACILITATION PHASE | TRANSITION PHASE | ACTION PHASE |
|---|---|---|
| Helpee describes symptoms. Helper suspends acting on evaluations. Helper's tenderness emphasized; helper "earns the right" to risk conditionality. | Helpee defines problem and accepts responsibility for its change. Helper gently presses the helpee toward recognizing helpee's role. Helper cautiously and tentatively becomes more evaluative. | Helpee takes appropriate actions to solve problem. Helper may be conditional (judgmental). Helper's self-confidence and knowledge are emphasized. |
| Procedural Goals: Self-Exploration | Better Self-Understanding & Commitment to Change | More Appropriate Action or Direction |

| **Facilitative Dimensions*** | **Transition Dimensions*** | **Action Dimensions*** |
|---|---|---|
| *Empathy* (depth, understanding) | *Concreteness* (ability to be specific) | *Confrontation* (pointing out discrepancies) |
| *Respect* (belief in) | *Genuineness* (honesty, realness) | *Immediacy* (helper and helpee telling it like it is in the "here and now") |
| *Warmth* (caring, love) (nonverbal) | *Self-disclosure* (ability to convey appropriately "I've been there too.") | |

* Each of the eight dimensions involves the act of perceiving (becoming aware of) and the act of responding (acting on awareness).

understand them, and respond to the youngsters with verbal and nonverbal media that express the way the individual feels about the children at the moment.

The first phase of helping is directed toward establishing a base or building a good relationship with the helpees. This can entail verbal expression, nonverbal expression, direct physical action, or a combination of all of these modes depending upon the helpee's age, intelligence, and degree of contact with reality.

Preparing for a space shot and firing the rocket are analogous to the two basic phases of helping: facilitation and action. Before a rocket can be fired, many preparations must be made. A very strong base must be built to hold it and to sustain the backward thrust when it is fired. Similarly, in a helping relationship, helpers first must use the less threatening (facilitative) dimensions to prepare and sustain the helpees for the more threatening but often necessary action or initiative dimensions. If the helpers carefully build their base with these individuals, they will help ensure success when the caregivers become more direct with the helpees at a later action period. Carkhuff (1971a) succinctly states the importance of the facilitation phase of helping: "Even if you have just 15 minutes to help, you must use five minutes or so responding (facilitating) to the helpee in order to find out for sure where the helpee is before starting to put the picture together (initiating) and acting upon that picture" (p. 22). The helping process consists of eight dimensions divided into three stages. Each dimension is defined by four levels. A discussion of this process follows.

2

## FACILITATION DIMENSIONS

Helpers begin to build their base with helpees by first emphasizing empathy, respect, and warmth in their responses. (Concreteness and genuineness, though not emphasized during this phase [Exhibit 1–2] can hardly be excluded from the interaction.) The exhibit shows how responding with the facilitative dimensions leads to increased helpee exploration (the first goal of helping.)

To achieve success in the first goal of helping, helpers must be able to refrain from acting on their judgments of the individuals. Virtually no one can refrain from making evaluations or judgments about others, but a helper can refrain from acting on those reactions. This is especially important if early evaluations or judgments are negative. For example, helpers may initially be repulsed by a helpee for a number of reasons; nevertheless, if they can suspend acting on those feelings, they usually can discover something good or likeable about the person. At that point they can begin to invest in the helpee and build a base from which to work. If, after a reasonable time, helpers are unable to develop some interest in, or positive feelings toward, the helpee, they should refer the person to someone more likely to be able to help or refrain from assuming the "helping" role, whichever is relevant.

"Putting oneself in the shoes of another" and "seeing through the eyes of another" are ways of describing empathy. Empathy appears to be the most important dimension in the helping process (Carkhuff, 1969a). If helpers cannot understand (empathize with) helpees, they cannot help them, i.e., assist in the problem-solving sense of this model.

Another facilitative dimension is respect. Helpers cannot help if they have no faith in helpees' ability to solve their own problems. Respect develops as caregivers learn about the uniqueness and the capabilities of helpees. It grows as helpers observe these individuals' efforts in many aspects of their lives.

Warmth or caring, the third facilitative dimension, is closely related to empathy and respect. People tend to love or have concern for those they know (understand) and believe in (respect). It is difficult to conceive of being able to help someone the helpers do not care for. ("Help" here means to "make a significant investment in.") This model emphasizes the communication of warmth primarily through nonverbal means.

## TRANSITION DIMENSIONS—HELPER ORIENTED

As helpers begin to develop a base with the helpee through emphasizing empathy, respect, and warmth, the latter self-explores in greater and greater depth. In fact, the clue to whether or not the helpers are successful in the early phase is based on the degree to which the helpee uses their responses to make deeper and more thorough self-explorations.

With repeated interchangeable helper responses (level 3)—responses that give back essentially what the helpees have given to the helpers—the helpees often begin to repeat themselves and "spins their wheels" or reach a plateau of self-exploration and understanding. It is at this point that helpers need to draw upon some new dimensions to encourage the helpees to risk more self-exploration.

The dimensions of concreteness, genuineness, and self-disclosure are carefully implemented next (Exhibit 1–2, earlier). When helpers press for greater concreteness or specificity on the part of the helpee, the resulting disclosure can be threatening to the helpee unless a strong base has been previously established. (This dimension is sometimes the exception to the general progression from level 3 to 4 across phases. With some individuals,

**Exhibit 1–2** Phases of the Helping Relationship

Helper-Offered Levels of Core Dimensions and Helpee Behaviors in the Phases of Helping

| Dimensions | Facilitation | Transition | Action |
|---|---|---|---|
| Empathy | Level 3 (reflective interchangeable affect/meaning) | Level 4 (interpretation of underlying feelings/meaning) | Level 4 (emphasizes periodic feedback) |
| Respect | Level 3 (belief in helpee's worth and potential) | Level 4 (deep valuing and commitment to helpee's growth) | Level 4 (deep valuing and commitment to helpee's growth) |
| Warmth | Level 3 (shows attention and interest clearly) | Level 4 (wholly, intensely attentive and supportive) | Level 4 (wholly, intensely attentive and supportive) |
| Concreteness | Level 3 (specific, concrete expressions) | (Concreteness may be deemphasized; abstract exploration is sometimes necessary) | Level 4 (specificity plus solicitation of specificity for plans and programs of action) |
| Genuineness | Level 3 (controlled expression of feelings; absence of phoniness) | Level 3 (controlled expression of feelings; absence of phoniness) and Level 4 (congruence between verbal and nonverbal messages; spontaneity) | Level 4 (congruence between verbal and nonverbal messages; spontaneity) |
| Self-Disclosure | | Level 3 (volunteers own general material) and Level 4 (volunteers own specific material) | Level 4 (volunteers own specific material; and may risk exposing own fear; hang-ups, etc.) |

The helper's communication, having these dimensions, serves as a stimulus and elicits

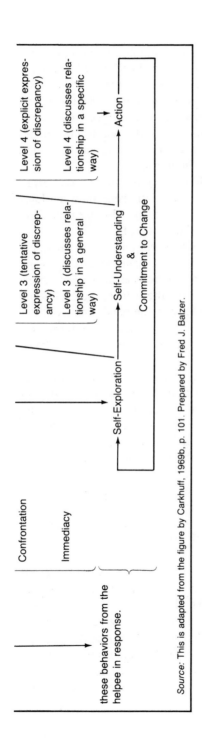

Confrontation

Immediacy

these behaviors from the
helpee in response.

Level 3 (tentative
expression of discrep-
ancy)

Level 3 (discusses rela-
tionship in a general
way)

Level 4 (explicit expres-
sion of discrepancy)

Level 4 (discusses rela-
tionship in a specific
way)

Self-Exploration

Self-Understanding
&
Commitment to Change

Action

*Source:* This is adapted from the figure by Carkhuff, 1969b, p. 101. Prepared by Fred J. Balzer.

less concreteness may be allowed in the transition phase than in the facilitative phase because they may need to "free associate" in order to elicit relevant material.) Greater threat also occurs when helpers become more genuine and set the stage (by their modeling of genuineness) for the helpee to become more genuine. Helper self-disclosure encourages greater intimacy in the relationship, which can lead to increased threat to the helpee. In other words, these three dimensions increase the threat level for the helpee and thus are similar to the action dimensions.

Because they may be facilitating as well as initiating, these are referred to as transition dimensions. In addition to the relationship between level of threat and the action phase, these three dimensions also are utilized in the problem-solving or planning stages of the action phase.

Specifically, concreteness refers to the helpees' pinpointing or accurately labeling their feelings and experiences. Helpers facilitate this by being specific themselves, or at least as specific as the helpees have been (interchangeable). When they are more specific than the helpee, they are going beyond where the helpee is, or are additive. If the helpers' timing of their use of additive concreteness is correct, helpees can achieve greater understanding than when the helpers were more vague about their problem or concern.

Genuineness refers to the helpers' ability to be real or honest with the helpee. Their verbalizations are congruent with their inner feelings. Whether or not the helpers' genuineness is useful to the helpee often will depend upon the helpers' ability to time their level of honesty so as to lead to greater trust and understanding. As Carkhuff (1971a) says, "Helping is for the helpee." If the helpees cannot utilize the helper genuineness, it may be useless or even damaging. The adage "Honesty is the best policy" is not always correct, especially if brutal honesty is used and the recipients are not capable of dealing with it to improve themselves. To illustrate, encounter groups can be harmful to certain persons, especially when, as is sometimes the case, frankness precedes the establishment of a solid base or relationship.

Self-disclosure by helpers can lead to greater closeness with helpees if it is appropriate or relevant to the problem. If the helper "has been where the helpee is at" and has found a solution, this can be reassuring to the helpee. Furthermore, the helpee's potential solution may even be similar to the one employed by the helper. The success of Alcoholics Anonymous (AA) and other self-help groups is related to this dimension. Drinking alcoholics for example, look to the "dry alcoholic" of AA for the solution to their own problem. The "speaker" phase of AA thus uses the self-disclosure dimension.

When helper self-disclosure is premature or irrelevant to the helpees' problem, it tends to confuse the latter or transfer the focus to the helpers. There is a danger of stealing the spotlight when the helpers self-disclose prematurely and inappropriately; therefore this tactic should be used sparingly and only when it can be predicted with a high degree of certainty that it will be relevant to helpees' concerns, increase their understanding of their problem, or identify the potential action needed in its resolution.

## TRANSITION DIMENSIONS—HELPEE ORIENTED

The transition dimensions of concreteness, genuineness, and self-disclosure can be used to predict the degree of success of the helpees' help-seeking. The degree to which helpees can be concrete about their problem (can label it accurately, for instance), can be honest and open with the helpers, and can self-disclose at high levels will determine whether or not they will, in fact, receive help. Of course, the other important factor in the help-seeking equation is the helper. If helpees choose to be concrete, genuine, and to self-disclose to persons who are incapable of helping them, the helpees may become disillusioned or, worse still, damaged. Helping can be for better or for worse (Truax & Carkhuff, 1967).

The prospective helper (health care professional) can predict the relative success that might be achieved with a given individual. For example, the helper can rate the helpee on the scale for help-seeking, e.g., ability to be concrete about needs and problem, ability to be genuine with the helper, and ability to disclose personally relevant material.

If the prospective helpee talks about concerns in vague and general terms (not concrete), is observed to be playing a role or relating in a superficial manner (not genuine), and does not make personally relevant disclosures, the helper is relatively safe in predicting that the person will be difficult to assist. Also, the process might require a relatively long period of time in developing the base—the first phase of helping—before any positive action may occur.

## ACTION DIMENSIONS

The action or initiative phase of helping may be considered as the most important. It is in this phase that tough decisions are made and that hard work must be done. It is the ultimate test of whether or not the helpers are, in fact, the "more knowing" individuals and are tough and confident enough to believe both in their own and their helpees' ability to come up with a plan of action (strategy) and follow through on it when difficulties arise. Helpers must be capable of assisting in the development of a plan or strategy for helpees that will lead to the successful resolution of their current problem and provide them at the same time with a method for attacking future problems.

If the helpers have not resolved the particular problem or concern in question, it is highly unlikely they can assist the helpees. A maxim all helpers must use to guide their helping attempts is that they cannot help someone else solve a problem that they have failed to resolve themselves. If the helpers know themselves, they will be unlikely to enter into a helping relationship in a problem area that remains unresolved.

There is another cardinal rule in helping. Helpers do not confront nor emphasize the action dimensions until they have earned the right, that is, have built the base. It often is said, especially by young people, "Tell it like it is." Telling it like it is often is tantamount to confronting someone. It must be emphasized once more that people can be most punitive or harmful when they are being brutally honest and confronting. Confrontation, a key action dimension, can be extremely helpful when the helpees have learned, from earlier experience, that the helpers are concerned about their welfare and care enough even to risk the relationship to "level" with them.

Frequently, confrontation refers to dealing with a discrepancy between what helpees have been saying about themselves and what they in fact have been doing. A common confrontation occurs when assisting helpees to face the reality of a situation. The most threatening type of confrontation is one that does not allow helpees to "save face." This is the type of confrontation that deals with the present. When individuals are caught behaving contrary to the way they claim to behave and they are confronted directly with it, it is difficult for them to deny it. They have few good means of defense and may use denial and other inappropriate short-term mechanisms that have long-term disadvantages. For example, if a mother catches her child with a hand in the cookie jar and accuses the youngster of stealing cookies, the child may actually deny it. This often happens; the child denies reality when the external threat is great enough. Parents, teachers, and other adults often unknowingly teach children to lie and deny reality by their use of threats. Similarly, supervisors or other authorities may inadvertently create a degree of fear or threat that leads their employees to deceitful behavior.

The last dimension, immediacy, often is related to confrontation. It refers to what is really going on between helpers and helpees. When the helpees are unaware of their reactions toward the helpers, the latter may need to describe or explain them. It includes "telling it like it is" between helpers and helpees. The helpees can gain a better understanding of themselves, especially how their actions affect others (in this case the helpers), when the helpers appropriately use the immediacy dimension. Once again, they must time their employment of immediacy so that the helpees can use it productively.

The productive use of the action dimensions of confrontation and immediacy can be guaranteed by taking the position that "the customer (helpee) is always right." This simply means that regardless of how brilliant and creative the helpers' responses may appear to be, if the helpees cannot use them in solving a problem, they are worthless, if not harmful, to them.

## COURSES OF ACTION

Although confrontation and immediacy have been determined to be dimensions that tend to promote action on the part of the helpee, the action itself can take many forms. It can be attitude change and/or behavioral change. For example, following a facilitative interaction with a floor nurse, a patient/helpee may achieve a confident attitude toward impending surgery versus a previously insecure or fearful feeling. With more substantial life skill deficits, the helpee may need to enter into a training/therapy program to modify attitudes and behavior. For example, a patient who is having difficulty parenting may need to enroll in an "effective parenting class" to resolve personal deficits. In such a situation the helper could serve two important functions: (1) to facilitate the helpee's awareness and commitment to change and (2) to refer the helpee to an appropriate parenting class. Obviously, not all health care professionals would know of such classes and may need to obtain the information from other professionals.

## IMPLEMENTING A COURSE OF ACTION

Chapter 12 illustrates a method for arriving systematically at a course of action. Most health care professionals will not be in a position to apply this method as thoroughly as it is outlined; however, it provides some basic guidelines. An important consideration is to consider the whole person when facilitating problem solving. The whole person is considered when a life skills philosophy is assumed, i.e., all aspects of human development (or lack thereof) are considered, viz., psychosocial, physical-sexual, moral, vocational, emotional, ego, and cognitive.

The principles involved in implementing a course of action recommended by Carkhuff (1969a) are summarized as follows:

1. The helper must check with the helpee at all stages of development and implementation to be sure that what is planned or performed is relevant to the helpee's functioning.
2. The focus of change usually should be on the helpee first and only secondarily on the helpee's relationships with others.
3. The only measures or procedures used are those that ensure the highest probability of constructive change.
4. The emphasis is on outcomes and the achievement of attainable goals. The actions of the helper and helpee are affected by the feedback that they receive.

Often the real test of helpers, as stated earlier, is whether or not they and the helpees together can develop appropriate plans of action or programs. Frequently the helpees will be unable to develop their own course of action completely and will require help in structuring their program. When the helpees cannot participate fully, Carkhuff (1969a) cautions the helpers to develop programs that will "enable the helpee to carry some of the burden of responsibility for his own life."

General health care professionals who can master the basic dimensions of the helping relationship outlined in this chapter can prevent the development of many problems. Even when these generalists function at higher levels, other external factors such as home, school, community, and hospital environment will produce casualties. The general professionals therefore will need the assistance of specialists such as psychiatrists, psychologists, social workers, and the clergy to deal more intensely with these casualties.

**HELPING IS LEARNING**

As helpers show empathy, respect, and warmth, helpees explore their behavior and problem. As helpers continue these attitudes and display appropriate levels of concreteness, genuineness, self-disclosure, and confrontation, the helpees begin to understand themselves and their problem. After the base is built, the helpers use high levels of confrontation and immediacy to help the helpees take action or find direction.

This description is oversimplified, but generally this is the pattern of helping. An important understanding is that during this process the helpers really are reinforcing certain behaviors and extinguishing others. Showing empathy, respect, and warmth generally reinforces whatever the helpees say or do, which increases the probability of self-exploration and problem exploration.

Responding with appropriate levels of concreteness, genuineness, self-disclosure, and confrontation (only about discrepancies in what the helpees are saying) results in more selective reinforcement. The helpers no longer are speaking strictly from the helpees' point of view. They begin to focus on the aspects of helpee behavior that they think will be more productive, begin to relate more of their own feelings that reinforce in a certain direction, and point out discrepancies in helpee behavior. These helper behaviors increase the probability that the helpees will understand themselves and their problem.

If an adequate relationship has been established, high levels of confrontation clearly reinforce certain kinds of behavior and extinguish others, as noted. These helper responses increase the probability that the helpees will act on their problems and try to find some direction to follow that may solve them.

The art of helping includes first knowing how to respond helpfully and then knowing when to use interchangeable responses or to use higher level replies employing the various core dimensions. Many beginning helpers learn to show interchangeable empathy, respect, and warmth but never become capable of displaying other, more action-oriented dimensions. They often say, "I don't want to be responsible if they make the wrong decision so I always make sure it's their decision" or "I don't want them to become dependent on others to make their decisions." These are legitimate concerns but they must be kept in perspective.

Helpers who display only interchangeable empathy, respect, and warmth are not very selective in what they reinforce. This often results in helpees accepting their problem as a permanent part of themselves instead of solving it. If they are rewarded for discussing their problem over and over without moving toward some conclusion, they become desensitized to it and begin to think it's OK to have this kind of situation. It's like the 30-year-old man who went to a psychotherapist for his bed-wetting problem. For several months the therapist displayed much empathy and respect. Later, when asked whether he had quit wetting the bed, the man exclaimed, "No, but I feel a lot better about it now!"

It is extremely important for helpers to be aware of what behaviors they are reinforcing. The art of helping includes knowing what behaviors to reinforce at a given time and how to do it, as well as knowing what behaviors to extinguish and how to extinguish them effectively. (See Chapter 2 for a more complete discussion of learning.)

## REFERENCES

Berenson, B. G., & Carkhuff, R. R. *Sources of gain in counseling and psychotherapy: Readings and commentary.* New York: Holt, Rinehart & Winston, 1967.

Carkhuff, R. R. *Helping and human relations: A primer for lay and professional helpers,* Vol. 1, *Selection and training.* New York: Holt, Rinehart & Winston, 1969(a).

Carkhuff, R. R. *Helping and human relations: A primer for lay and professional helpers,* Vol. 2, *Practice and research.* New York: Holt, Rinehart & Winston, 1969(b).

Carkhuff, R. R. Helping and human relations: A brief guide for training lay helpers. *Journal of Research and Development in Education,* 1971, *4*(2), 17–27 (a).

Carkhuff, R. R. *The development of human resources: Education, psychology, and social change.* New York: Holt, Rinehart & Winston, 1971(b).

Carkhuff, R. R. Rejoinder: What's it all about anyway? Some reflections on helping and human resource development models. *The Counseling Psychologist,* 1972, *3*(3), 79–87.

Carkhuff, R R., & Berenson, B. G. *Beyond counseling and therapy.* New York: Holt, Rinehart & Winston, 1967.

Dupont, H. Meeting the emotional-social needs of students in a mainstreamed environment. *Counseling and Human Development,* 1976, *10,* 1–12.

Egan, G., & Cowan, M. *People in systems: A model for development in human service professional and education.* Monterey, Calif.: Brooks/Cole Publishing Co., Inc., 1979.

Erikson, E. H. *Childhood and society* (2nd ed.). New York: W. W. Norton & Company, Inc., 1963.

Flanagan, J. C. A research approach to improving our quality of life. *American Psychologist,* 1978, *33,* 138–147.

Flavell, J. H. *The developmental psychology of Jean Piaget.* Princeton, N.J.: D. Van Nostrand Co., Inc., 1963.

Gazda, G. M., Asbury, F. R., Balzer, F. J., Childers, W. C., & Walters, R. P. *Human relations development: A manual for educators* (2nd ed.). Boston: Allyn & Bacon, Inc., 1977.

Gazda, G. M., Walters, R. P., & Childers, W. C. *Human relations development: A manual for health sciences.* Boston: Allyn & Bacon, Inc., 1975.

Gazda, G. M., Walters, R. P., & Childers, W. C. *Realtalk: Exercises in friendship and helping skills.* Atlanta: Humanics Limited, 1981.

Gesell, A., Ilg, F. L., & Ames, L. B. *The years of ten to sixteen.* New York: Harper & Brothers, 1956.

Gesell, A., Ilg, F. L., Ames, L. B., & Bullis, G. E. *The child from five to ten.* New York: Harper & Brothers, 1946.

Havighurst, R. J. *Human development and education* (2nd ed.). New York: Longmans, Green, 1953.

Havighurst, R. J. *Human development and education* (3rd ed.). New York: Longmans, Green, 1972.

Kohlberg, L. Continuities and discontinuities in childhood and adult moral development revisited. In P. L. Baltes & K. W. Schaie (Eds.), *Lifespan development psychology: Personality and socialization.* New York: Academic Press, 1973.

Kohlberg, L., & Turiel, P. Moral development and moral education. In G. Lesser (Ed.), *Psychology and education practice*. New York: Scott, Foresman, & Co., 1971.

Loevinger, J. *Ego development*. San Francisco: Jossey-Bass, Inc., 1976.

National Assessment of Educational Progress. *Draft of basic skills objectives*. Denver: National Assessment of Educational Progress, A Division of the Commission on the Education of the States, August, 1975.

Rogers, C. R. The necessary and sufficient conditions of therapeutic personality change. *Journal of Consulting Psychology*, 1957, *21*, 95–103.

Rogers, C. R., Gendlin, E. T., Kiesler, D. J., & Truax, C. B. *The therapeutic relationship and its impact: A study of psychotherapy with schizophrenics*. Madison, Wis.: University of Wisconsin Press, 1967.

Shane, H. G. *Curriculum change toward the 21st century*. Washington, D. C.: National Education Association, 1977.

Sisson, P. J., Arthur, G. L., & Gazda, G. M. *Human relations for criminal justice personnel*. Boston: Allyn & Bacon, Inc., 1981.

Super, D. E. Vocational development in adolescence and early adulthood: Tasks and behaviors. In D. E. Super, *Career development: Self-concept theory*. New York: College Entrance Examination Board, 1963.

Super, D. E., Crites, J., Hummel, R., Moser, H., Overstreet, C. B., & Warnath, C. *Vocational development: A framework for research*, Monograph No. 1. New York :Teachers College Press, 1957.

Truax, C. B., & Carkhuff, R. R. *Toward effective counseling and psychotherapy: Training and practice*. Chicago: Aldine Publishing Co., 1967.

Wadsworth, B. J. *Piaget's theory of cognitive development*. New York: David McKay Company, Inc., 1971.

## Chapter 2

# Learning How to Learn

Marilyn Ferguson in *The Aquarian Conspiracy* (1980) writes that the transforming teacher senses readiness to change and helps the student respond to more complex needs, transcending the old levels again and again:

> Research confirms what observant parents and teachers have always known: We learn in different ways. Of our assorted brains, some are left-dominant, some are right-dominant, some are neither. Some of us learn better by hearing, others by seeing or touching. Some visualize easily, others not at all. Some recall odometer readings, telephone numbers, dates; others remember colors and feelings. Some learn best in groups, others in isolation. Some peak in the mornings, others in the afternoon. No single educational method can draw the best from diverse brains. (p. 299)

Professional educators and coping skill trainers have a continuing need to make explicit the rules of how people learn, of how people represent their feeling states, of how behavior changes. Do they prefer to seek meaning through listening or reading? Are they concerned with their own points of view or are they influenced by family or peers? Do they react to their environment with thoughtful awareness or do they use physical activity and practice to gain skill?

These questions, as well as others, confront educators and trainers as they focus on the design and implementation of instruction. The identification and utilization of people's cognitive strengths for success in learning is a coping tool and skill of signal importance to individuals as students and as educators or service providers.

## THROUGH THE SENSORY MODALITIES

Recognizing that the sensory modalities are important variables in the individual's learning style, several educators have addressed the question of techniques and strategies of teaching that would coordinate with the student's most highly valued input channel for processing information (Bandler & Grinder, 1975, 1979; Dunn & Dunn, 1978; Grinder & Bandler, 1976; Laosa, 1977; Raskin & Baker, 1975). The most salient sensory modalities are the visual, auditory, and kinesthetic. Individuals may process information most efficiently in just one of these channels, or all of them. When two or more sensory channels are equally efficient, the result is a mixed modality strength.

Goldman (1967) conducted a well-designed experimental study comparing individual preferences for a sensory modality: visual, auditory, or haptic (defined as a combination of kinesthesis, pressure, and tactile sensation). He concludes that adults, and first and third grade children, preferred an auditory modality; the adults chose the visual over the haptic; the children were equally divided between the haptic and the visual.

More recently, children have shown a developmental sequence of modality strengths (Barbe & Milone, 1980). In the early grades, children have more well-defined strengths and tend to be auditory rather than visual or kinesthetic. As they progress through elementary school, their modalities become mixed and interdependent, shifting toward the visual and kinesthetic. By adulthood, many people have a mixed modality strength. Other researchers have implied that vision is the dominant modality of the species (MacLean, 1973).

All of the senses work together, of course, in the information processing of the brain. A clear delineation of strengths and weaknesses may be impossible in the average individual. The *Sensory Modality Checklist* (Appendix B) is a quick and general assessment of preferred sensory modalities for learning and self-expression. A study of the sensory modalities is one approach to the analysis of cognitive style for learning and problem solving.

Health care providers, teachers, or service workers have preferred modality strengths that can be identified, in many cases, by an assessment of these individuals' classroom styles, management techniques, and recreational habits. Modality matching of teacher or trainer and students is not a reasonable procedure, however, since no teaching method is modality pure. It is best to train students to use a variety of strategies and combinations of cognitive learning styles (Entwistle, 1977).

## TO THE HEMISPHERES OF THE BRAIN

Information processing in the brain is concerned with two types of symbols: (1) language-related elements or the theoretical symbols and (2) thought-related elements or the qualitative symbols (Mullally, 1977). Processing the different types of symbols is dependent upon functions occurring within the left and right hemispheres of the brain.

The theoretical symbols, such as visual linguistic elements or the written word, auditory linguistic elements or the spoken word, visual quantitative or written numbers, and auditory quantitative or spoken numbers, are processed primarily in the left hemisphere of the brain. Qualitative symbols of a sensory nature such as sounds, taste, or visual pictures, are associated with cultural codes or the meanings received from observing nonverbal expressions, role playing, social distance, or time constraints. These symbols are processed primarily in the right side of the brain.

The bilateral symmetry of the brain provides that sights and sounds bringing in information from the external environment are processed by using both hemispheres together. The two hemispheres are connected by the corpus callosum for the transfer of information of different sensory modalities (Brodal, 1981). In the normal brain it appears that any information reaching one hemisphere is communicated regularly to the other, largely to corresponding regions.

Scientists and researchers have reported anatomical, physiological, and behavioral discoveries about the specialization of the cerebral hemispheres. Bakan (1971) discusses the directions of conjugate lateral eye movement (CLEM) and the inherent duality of humans' behavior and experience. The neurological pathways that come from the left side of both eyes (left visual field) are represented in the right cerebral hemisphere. When parts of the left cerebral hemisphere are stimulated, the eyes move to the right; when parts of the right hemisphere are stimulated, the eyes shift to the left.

Day (1964) associates CLEMs and thought processes, identifying right-movers and left-movers, persons who tend to look to the right or left while reflecting, respectively. Right-movement presumably activates the left cerebral hemisphere and its specialized functions that are verbal, analytic, digital, and objective. Left-movement is presumed to activate the right cerebral hemisphere with its special functions: preverbal, synthetic, analogic, and subjective.

Individuals tend to look up and away when a question has been posed and the answer must be retrieved (Gur, 1975). Singer (1976) reports experimental research findings to support the conclusion that if an individual is involved primarily in attending to visual images and fantasies (i.e., for the answer to the question above), the person is less likely to be accurate in detecting external visual cues. Similarly, if internal processing is primarily oriented around auditory fantasies, that is, imagined conversations or music, then the person is less likely to be accurate in detecting external auditory signals.

In both cases, the individual is better at detecting external cues in the modality other than the one in which the person is attending to internal images and fantasies. Such experiments suggest that a private internal image or fantasy in a given modality uses the same brain structures or pathways as does the processing of an external stimulus in that same modality.

Individuals look up, to the side, or down to eliminate visual stimuli, especially the meaningful and reinforcing face of another person, that might interfere with a train of thought. Dilts, Grinder, Bandler, DeLozier, and Cameron-Bandler (1979) in *Neurolinguistic Programming* illustrate the eye positions for visual, auditory, and kinesthetic accessing of information. Dilts identifies each eye position with its particular body posture, breathing pattern, and hemispheric specialization (Figure 2–1).

**Figure 2–1** Eye Positions for Accessing Information

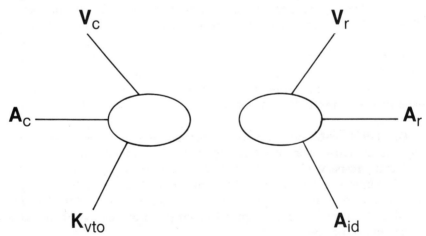

Visual accessing cues for a normally organized right-handed person: $V_c$ = visual constructed; $A_c$ = auditory constructed; $K_{vto}$ = kinesthetic visceral, tactile, or olfactory; $V_r$ = visual remembered; $A_r$ = auditory remembered, $A_{id}$ = auditory internal dialogue.
*Source:* Adapted from *Neurolinguistic Programming I* by R. B. Dilts, J. Grinder, R. Bandler, J. DeLozier, & L. Cameron-Bandler, Meta Publications © 1979.

The right-movements of the eyes access the left hemisphere for constructed images ($V_c$), for visualization of novel and abstract patterns, or
for constructed auditory ($A_c$), putting an idea into words. The eyes looking
down and to the right access an awareness of body sensations ($K_{vto}$) and
kinesthetic information including the visceral, tactile, and olfactory. The
left-movements of the eyes access the right hemisphere for remembered
images ($V_r$), for visualization of eidetic patterns from past experiences, or
for remembered auditory experiences ($A_r$), and sounds and tape loops of
messages from past activities. The eyes looking down and to the left are
representative of an internal auditory dialogue ($A_{id}$), talking to oneself,
probably in short cryptic commands and suggestions and simple sentence
messages.

The left cerebral hemisphere is associated with the development of speech
and language. The temporal lobe is larger on the left side than on the right
in about two-thirds of the brains examined (Geschwind & Levitsky, 1968;
Witelson & Pallie, 1973). The left side is best developed in the brain of
the fetus and newborn infants, suggesting that asymmetry does not result
from environmental or developmental factors after birth.

Electrophysiological experiments using auditory (click) and visual (flash)
stimuli were designed to measure the evoked responses in the brains of
both adults and 5-week-old infants (Wada, 1977). The results show that
auditory responses are significantly greater in the left hemisphere and visual
in the right. It appears that the fundamental auditory neurocircuitry needed
for the growth of speech and language is biologically and asymmetrically
designed for their acquisition and development.

The right ear outperforms the left ear in hearing and identifying com-
peting digits, a reflection of left-brain dominance for language (Kimura,
1961). The right ear has better access to the left hemisphere because of
the crossed auditory pathways. While the right ear connects directly to the
left hemisphere (language area), the left ear's route to the same area first
must go to the right hemisphere and then cross over to the left side and
the language area. However, a clear left ear advantage was found for all
melodies and environmental sounds (Krashen, 1977). The left ear has direct
access to the right hemisphere and the right brain is dominant for music,
chords, and nonverbal sounds.

It is evident from studies with patients who have suffered brain damage
to the right hemisphere that the right brain makes an important contribution to human performance, having functions complementary to those
of the left hemisphere. The right side of the brain probably processes
information differently from the left, relying more on visual imagery than
on language and being more synthetic and holistic than analytical and
sequential in handling data. The right hemisphere specializes in perceiving

and remembering faces, unfamiliar and complex shapes for which there are no ready names, and drawings of incomplete gestalts in which part of the contour is missing. Its importance to spatial orientation and visuospatial relationships is well documented. It also probably provides the neurological basis for the ability to take the fragmentary sensory information received and to construct from it a coherent concept of the spatial organization of the outside world—a sort of cognitive spatial map by which individuals plan their actions (Nebes, 1977).

## FROM INTERNAL SENSORY INFORMATION

Deep within the structures of the brain lies another lobe that is proportionately larger in humans than in other species. It is a convolution called the fusiform gyrus (Ariëns Kappers, Huber, & Crosby, 1936) that lies between the structures associated with visual and with emotional processing. Stimulation deep within this lobe results in visual illusions, evocation of memories, and many forms of intense emotional experience. There may be a feeling of familiarity or déjà vu with the conviction that the person is reliving an experience; in contrast, there may be feelings of strangeness and things may appear altered and unreal. Among the reported effects is a feeling of sadness and of wanting to cry.

MacLean (1973) identifies this enlarged lobe as the connecting structure between the visual system and the limbic system of emotional behaviors. He suggests that the fusiform gyrus gives rise to the weepy feelings that people may experience upon witnessing an altruistic act:

> Primates, above all other animals, have developed a social sense which in man becomes conspicuous for its altruistic manifestations. As evidence that a charitable social sense is still in evolution we need only recall that the word *altruism* was coined as lately as 1853 by the philosopher Comte . . . and that the word *empathy* was introduced into our language by Lipps . . . about 1900. Altruism depends not only on feeling one's way into another person in the sense of empathy. It also involves the capacity to *see with feeling* into another person's situation (p. 42).

Emotional behavior may be understood in part by studying the basic consummatory behaviors necessary for self-preservation and procreation. One list of such behaviors (modified from Denny & Ratner, 1970) is resting, eliminating, water balance, thermoregulation, feeding, aggressive-defensive behaviors, sexual behaviors, and care of the young (Thomas, 1980).

Animals, including humans, fulfill their basic needs in cycles that include an appetitive phase, a consummatory phase, and a postconsummatory phase (Denny & Ratner, 1970). Feeding is an example of the process. Thomas (1981) describes it this way:

When individuals have not eaten for a time, they begin to be aroused and behaviors become directed toward acquiring food; this is the appetitive phase. This phase continues and merges with the consummatory phase when food actually is eaten. Individuals then engage in behavior that terminates the feeding process (e.g., belching, going for a walk, etc.); this is the postconsummatory phase. Ordinarily, eating behavior is not thought of as particularly emotional, but it is possible to imagine situations where eating (or lack thereof) may be very emotional (e.g., lost in the woods).[11]

Even under the most normal circumstances there is a rise and fall in bodily activities (brain, digestive system, senses of taste and smell, etc.). This cyclical rise and fall is referred to as facilitation or inhibition, respectively; emotional behavior may be represented as exceptional states of facilitation or inhibition. Each of the several basic consummatory behaviors has its own normal range of arousal and also may show a range of overreaction (extreme facilitation) and underreaction (extreme inhibition). The language used to describe feelings and emotions usually refers to these extremes. Examples of inhibitory words for underreaction are "depressed, helpless, lonely, discouraged;" facilitory words for overreaction are "excited, angry, panicked, passionate."

The limbic system is said to consist of the structures in the brain that are essential to emotion. It has been described as a response-modulation system on a continuum of inhibition to facilitation for consummatory behaviors to meet physiological needs (McCleary, 1966). The visual structures of the brain have connections to the limbic system through the prefrontal cortex and in the occipitotemporal lobe and the fusiform gyrus. There is evidence that these connections function to help individuals gain insight into the feelings of others, to see with feeling. MacLean (1962) writes that in the complex organization of these evolving structures "we presumably have a neural ladder, a visionary ladder, for ascending from the most primitive sexual feeling to the highest level of altruistic sentiments" (p. 300).

MacLean (1973) also suggests that these large evolving territories of the brain may be incapable of being brought into full operation until the hormonal changes of adolescence occur. If this is so, it would weigh heavily against the claims of those who contend that the personality is fully developed and rigid by adolescence, if indeed not by the age of 5 or 6.

Each individual learns to depend on one sensory system or another as a means of perceiving and understanding the world. This dependence upon particular sensory modalities is characteristic of human beings and generates patterns of experience that differ between and within individuals.

All normal humans are endowed with essentially equivalent sensory organs and structures, both anatomically and physiologically. The neurological pathways and projection areas that serve the sensory mechanisms also are presumed to be similar in all human brains. Yet despite the similar equipment, no two individuals understand a particular occurrence in exactly the same way. It is the differences that are learned through selective attention to sensory input channels and with variations of experience with the senses (Bandler & Grinder, 1975; Bateson, 1972; Korzybski, 1958).

"Selective attention to sensory input" means that at any one time individuals usually attend to (are conscious of) one, or possibly two, of their sensory channels and their attention is limited to only seven "bits" of information. Miller (1956) reports that the span of absolute judgment and the span of immediate memory impose severe limitations on the amount of information people are able to receive, process, and remember.

"Bits" and "chunks" of information have been measured and quantified by several researchers to ascertain how much individuals can know at any one time. The number of bits of information ($7 \pm 2$) is constant for the absolute judgment of inputs into one sensory channel. The number of chunks of information (also $7 \pm 2$) also is constant for immediate memory. Immediate memory is limited to $7 \pm 2$ chunks at any moment but the number of bits that each chunk contains, up to $7 \pm 2$, can be increased simply by building larger and larger chunks, each chunk containing more information than before.

Since the bits are received through sensory channels, it is advantageous to attend primarily to the input from one critically important channel. The research indicates that the channel for making visual judgments is more accurate than those for auditory and gustatory judgments. However, each individual learns to depend on one sensory system or another as a means of perceiving the world and recoding an understanding of it into language and memory. Information from the other sensory systems may be ignored temporarily as irrelevant. This ability to focus attention in $7 \pm 2$ chunks protects the brain from the bombardment of too much information and a resulting state of confusion.

Learning from internal sensory representations includes how to pay attention to the feeling states of emotion, the visceral and proprioceptive cues for breathing and digestion, and the visual imageries of day and night dreams. Individuals "turning on" to their own bodies are knowing themselves through internal kinesthetic sensory information ($K^i$). People can pay selective attention periodically to the responses occurring in the deeper recesses of the brain. They can monitor the rise and fall of emotional responses connected with consummatory acts, particularly aggressive-defensive or sexual behaviors. They can identify gut reactions and catching the breath as kinesthetic sensory responses to stimuli. They can develop a facility for remembering night dreams and embroidering daydreams into useful visual information emanating from the deep internal gyruses of the brain ($V^i$). By "listening" to messages and melodies that are still being played on the internal auditory tape loops ($A^i$), individuals can learn how to erase any harmful or outdated messages and how to magnify the comforting and useful sounds.

So, one reason that individuals have different experiences despite similar genetic endowments of brain and body and despite similar environments is that characteristically each one attends to different aspects of the self and of the environment. "It is something like a cooking class. Since each of us selects some similar and some different ingredients in similar and varying proportions, we each end up with something different to put into the oven" (Gordon, 1978, p. 215).

An inside look at the brain can help clarify the terms and concepts described here (Figure 2–2). The basic diagram shows a medial view of the human brain, spinal cord, and the projection areas for the sensory modalities. The temporal lobe is part of the surface cortex; it lies within the dotted lines.

## FROM EXTERNAL SENSORY INFORMATION

The face of another person is the single most intriguing and meaningful stimulus in a human's physical environment (Singer, 1976). This understanding derives from extensive work by Prof. Silvan Tomkins of Rutgers University, who has developed an important theory about the major role that facial expression plays in the communication of emotion and in the feedback to individuals of their own continuing emotions and motives. Watching the facial responsiveness and the body language of other individuals is an important contribution to understanding of the world through the visual external sensory modality ($V^e$).

Learning to notice and pay attention to the physiological cues expressed in another person's visage and physique is a way of identifying emotional responses that that other individual is experiencing internally. Bandler and Grinder (1979) identify four cues that reflect the internal emotional processes and the physiological changes attendant to those feelings: muscle tone, skin color, breathing, and lip size. By watching the subtle changes

**Figure 2–2** Medial View of Brain and Spinal Cord

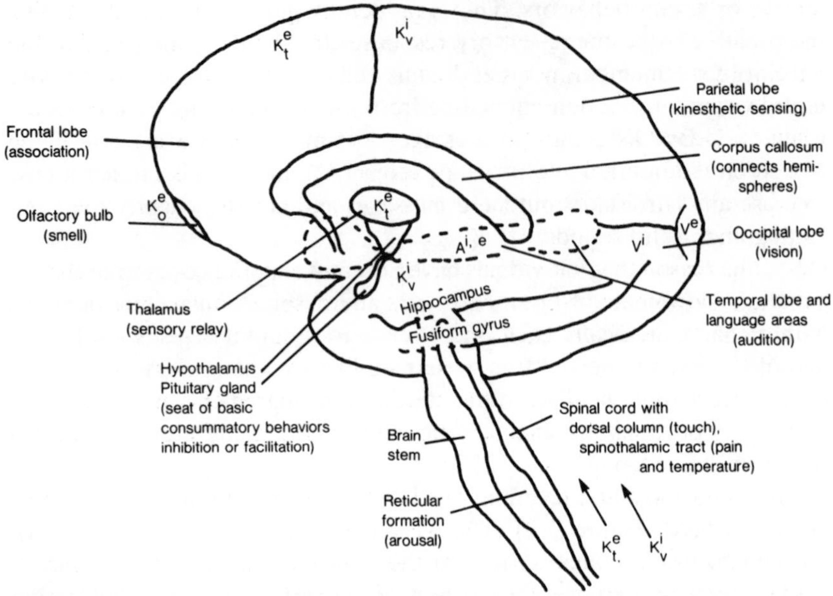

This medial aspect of the brain and spinal cord of the central nervous system includes a surface view of the temporal lobe, with language areas illustrated in dotted lines. Projection sites for receiving information through the sensory modalities are plotted with the following abbreviations:

$A^{i,e}$ = auditory input, both internal and external.

$V^e$ = visual input in the occipital lobe, external.

$V^i$ = visualization in the deeper striate layers of the occipital lobe or temporal lobe.

$K_o^e$ = kinesthetic input from sense of smell, external.

$K_t^e$ = kinesthetic input from touch, external. The nerve signals move up the spinal cord in the dorsal column, are relayed through the thalamus, and are projected to the sensory cortex of the parietal lobe.

$K_v^i$ = kinesthetic input from pain and temperature, internal, visceral. The nerve signals move up the spinal cord in the spinothalamic tract, are processed in the hypothalamus, and are projected to the sensory cortex of the parietal lobe.

*Source:* Nancy A. Haynie, unpublished doctoral dissertation, 1981, reprinted by permission.

in these areas, it is possible to evaluate the impact of personal interaction or other stimuli on other persons.

Skin color sometimes is expressed in language that describes the feeling state both metaphorically and physiologically: red with rage, white with fear (or pain), black with fury. Lips flush with an increased flow of blood when an individual is excited or aroused; they become narrow and white or purple with terror or tension. Muscle tone in the face causes drooping and lifting of the mouth, chin, and cheeks. Breathing patterns are rapid and shallow in states of excitement or tension, deep and rhythmic in a relaxed state, or arrhythmic in a depressed state. Fluctuations in skin temperature and moisture content are other cues. These and pulse rate are monitored by an individual's kinesthetic external sensory channels ($K^e$). Voice tone and tempo are processed through the auditory external channel ($A^e$). The physiological cue changes are expressed externally and are observable responses to the facilitory and inhibitory influences from the limbic system of the brain.

Learning from the external world "out there" through the sensory modalities is complex and unending. The many ways that are available for learning visually, auditorily, and kinesthetically cannot be itemized, much less described here. In addition to the learning to be gained from processing sensory information about another person's physiology and behavior, there are elements of social learning that are relevant for interpersonal communications training.

Modeling and role playing are two learning activities that begin as soon as an infant is maturationally capable of performing. Modeling is the imitation of others in the environment through observation ($V^e$), listening ($A^e$), and experimentation ($K^e$). Modeling, or watching someone else do something first, is a most efficient and encouraging learning activity. It involves all of the sensory modality input channels and includes the realization of the possible. The imitation of modeled behavior is the usual way that formal culture is passed on from generation to generation.

Role playing is an experimental activity of physically enacting a new behavior ($K^e$), including the language of the new role ($A^e$) and perhaps costuming and props ($V^e$). Children are natural role players, trying out every conceivable style of behavior. Commonly, as human beings adopt the cultural rules of the environmental models, they "freeze" their behavior into acceptable or stereotyped social roles. Relearning how to role-play in spontaneous or structured settings is a valuable way individuals can learn about themselves and others.

Shaw, Corsini, Blake, and Mouton (1980) enumerate four distinct concepts of role playing:

1. The theatrical role play is a dramatic presentation defined by the playwright and can be an appropriate way for experimenting with novel and unusual behaviors.
2. The sociological role play refers to the practice of usual behaviors that are essential in the formal cultural context. These are the social and behavioral skills learned primarily through modeling culturally determined patterns.
3. Dissimulative role play is an exercise in deceiving others or in creating an impression contrary to the player's real feelings.
4. Educational role play is an action-spontaneous procedure under contrived conditions. The artificial setting allows for structured and planned role rehearsal or for unstructured and developmental learning in an unrehearsed role play or psychodrama.

The purposes of role play are to inform individuals of their own behavior or of new behavioral choices, to train them in behavioral skills, to evaluate the success of a particular behavioral repertoire, and to modify and change habitual behaviors through practice. Role play involves all of the senses simultaneously: external influences bombard the eyes, ears, and body, and internal responses are generated in feelings, internal dialogues, and visual imagination. People are limited in opportunities to learn only by the limits of $7 \pm 2$ chunks of data that they can process at one moment.

Social reinforcement is an important variable in making behavior happen, solidifying the learning, and maintaining the changes. Praise, approval, and encouragement are reinforcers and usually are experienced auditorily ($A^e$) through words and sounds. Other social reinforcers can appeal to the sense of taste (kiss), sight (smile), kinesthetics (hug), or smell (clean and sweet) and provide encouragement for learning. If the reinforcement matches the preferred sensory modality of an individual, its power for facilitating learning is increased.

**THE FEEDBACK LOOP**

Three subsystems are in operation when an adaptive individual performs: (1) the input system of sensory information (internal and external), (2) the connector system in the association cortex of the brain that selects the $7 \pm 2$ chunks of data for attention, and (3) the output system of behavior and language. It is in the connector system (also called the representational system by Grinder and Bandler, 1976) that information is given meaning. Language is selected to express the meaning and thereby, in the output system, to limit perception and understanding of the world by the choice of words.

A feedback loop is part of the system whereby some of the output behaviors and language are reintroduced as information for the input system. This is referred to as positive or negative feedback. Negative feedback maintains the individual in a steady state of balance between the inhibitory and facilitory states of arousal. Positive feedback leads to change.

Interpersonal systems also can be viewed as feedback loops. The behavior of each individual affects and is affected by the behavior of each other individual (Watzlawick, Beavin, & Jackson, 1967). Within social systems, individuals receive constant information from others about the appropriateness of their behavior. The significance of the human face for feedback was described earlier.

The use of feedback is essential for learning. Other persons tell or show how the behavior appears to them and they learn how others are affected by their own behavior. Shaw et al. (1980) elevate feedback to a "basic approach to studying human problems." Feedback helps individuals to identify their blind spots and to receive the kind of information that they ordinarily fail to see or hear.

Feedback techniques depend largely on the auditory channels ($A^e$) as individuals in the social system respond by telling, explaining, describing, yelling, coaxing, and so forth. For learning, it is important that the feedback process be designed so that it creates awareness and sensitivity rather than becoming a vehicle for criticism or evaluation. Athletes, joggers, and active people receive feedback through the kinesthetic channels ($K^{e,i}$); they feel the aching muscles, monitor the exertion of heartbeats and lung capacity, judge the impact of a ball hit, and endless other physical information.

Feedback technologies are powerful reinforcers and invaluable tools for accelerating learning. In the field of interpersonal communications training, audio taping and videotaping feedback are recommended. In a study of the relative effects of role playing, video feedback, and modeling, video feedback was found to be a useful technique after modeling for instigating changes (Bailey, Deardoff & Nay, 1977). When individuals can see and hear behaviors just experienced, self-evaluation and self-improvement are enhanced. Different sensory channels for processing the same experience are available, a new selection of $7 \pm 2$ chunks of data is possible, criticism and negative evaluation from others are minimized, and learning is maximized.

Self-monitoring is the goal of practicing and learning how to obtain feedback. Individuals differ in the amount and degree of importance they attach to internal sources of information such as feeling states, attitudes, and dispositions, or to external sources such as social cues in the social situation and interpersonal specifications of appropriateness (Snyder & Monson, 1975). According to this research, scoring high on the Snyder and Monson Self-Monitoring Scale indicates that individuals make more behavioral choices based on situational information from the external environment. If they score low on this scale, they tend to guide their choices on the basis of salient information from relevant inner states. In giving or receiving feedback about behavior for self or others, it is important to remember that individual differences provide uniqueness and delight as well as conflict and confusion.

## TRANSFER OF LEARNING TO A NEW CONTEXT

The measurement of success on any training, including interpersonal communications, is individuals' performance in a new setting outside of the class, workshop, or training group. Learning the skills revolves around practice and improved ability. It is a question of "Can you do it?" Performance of the new learning is a matter of "Will you do it?" (Goldstein, Sprafkin, & Gershaw, 1976). Without social reinforcement and self-reward, trained skills often wither away with disuse.

Supplemental incentives in the real world are needed to encourage the continued performance of the learning. Goldstein et al. (1976) recommend that after individuals have practiced a new skill through role playing and have tried the behavior at home and received feedback from someone else or a group, they should continue to practice as frequently as possible. At this time in the transfer of learning, a program of self-reinforcement should be instigated. Individuals need to learn how to choose the best reinforcers for themselves—those that match their preferred sensory modality and/or their preferred source of internal or external information. Self-reinforcement means to say something complimentary and do something nice for themselves if the new skill is performed well.

## LEARNING TO COMMUNICATE WITH OTHERS

Interpersonal communications training is a way of developing these fundamental learning processes into the skill of being able to communicate with personal helpfulness toward others. The purpose of good interpersonal communication is to help others to learn about themselves and to make decisions based on this knowledge. Another purpose of good communication is so people can learn about themselves through sharing with others and through self-monitoring of their own words and actions.

Neurolinguistics may be described as a study of how people receive information through the senses, process the information in neurons and neural pathways of the brain including the language areas, and express the information in language and behaviors. When individuals' expressed messages in verbal (A) and nonverbal (V,K) language are received, understood, and expressed by other persons, communication occurs. Learning how to identify the others' preferred sensory modality provides a way of communicating more specifically and understandably to them.

Practitioners of good communication are indebted to Neurolinguistic Programming (NLP) (Bandler & Grinder, 1975; Grinder & Bandler, 1976) for identifying that the predicates people use are representative of the preferred sensory modalities. Individuals who highly value the visual system will express themselves in visual process words and predicates (verbs and adjectives) such as "clear, bright, see, perspective." Those who prefer the auditory mode will use auditory process words such as "sound, loud, hear, harmony." Kinesthetic words such as "grasp, hard, handle, feel" are used by individuals who prefer to learn through the kinesthetic system, either externally with muscle power and touch or internally with emotions and gut feelings.

In the earlier section on the feedback loop, language was described as a vehicle of the output system for expressing meaning. Individuals' perception and understanding of the world was described as necessarily limited by the $7 \pm 2$ chunks of data being processed and by the choice of words used to define their experiences. There are three transformations of grammar—nominalizations, generalizations, and deletions—that individuals use unconsciously that change the expression of the deeper meanings to surface meanings that do not communicate as understandably. Learning how to correct these three transformations improves people's ability to express themselves clearly and fully.

Nominalization is the transformation of a process (action) word or verb into an event word or noun. When the alive action of experience is changed to a passive, unmoving event, much of the power is robbed from the communication. For example, an emotional feeling expression would be: "You are feeling angry and afraid of what you might do." A nominalization of this expression might be: "You have some anger and fear about the situation." The affective energy becomes neutralized and almost static. Positive words also can be nominalized: "You had a lot of pleasure and happiness with them" is a less dynamic way of saying, "You seem pleased and happy with them." The active verbs that express most fully the vitality of individuals' experience have been changed to the passive nouns that set them apart from their real feelings.

Generalization diminishes the richness and detail of the specific and expands a particular experience, event, or feeling to the universal level. An example of generalizing is from "Tom (or Sue) doesn't like me," to "Men (or women) don't like me," to "Nobody likes me." Words that are universal quantifiers include "all, each, every, any;" negative quantifiers include "never, nowhere, none, no one, nothing, nobody." These sets of words are not specific and do not contribute to effective communication when used without further explanation.

Deletion removes portions of the original experience and of the full linguistic expression of the deep meaning. The communicated sentences are unfinished or incomplete because the full explanation has been left out or removed. By reading between the lines, listeners to other persons may be able to add the missing data for full communication. It might be known that a person who has been in a stressful situation says, "I don't know what to do." This raises the questions: Do about what? Do to whom? Do when or where? Do for self? The reply could be: "You seem upset and confused about what to do now to help yourself make some good decisions." The listener has tried to improve the communication with some reasonable guesses. However, the person who is making the deletions would need to verify (feedback) the information that the added guess was meaningful.

Effective communication and human relations can be enhanced by learning how to use neurolinguistic techniques (Haynie, 1981). Watching another person's eye patterns and noticing the choice of predicates and process words can provide clues to the individual's preferred sensory modality. By matching language to the modality, it is possible to communicate with rapport, empathy, and trustworthiness. Appreciation of the different processing styles of other persons can encourage respect for them and their responsibility and right to make their own decisions. Knowing these rules of transformational grammar can guide a facilitative individual to be more specific and honest with others.

## SUMMARY

This chapter has described the steps and processes that individuals use as they learn for themselves and in interaction with others. Communication is teaching others about oneself and learning about them.

Learning begins as information is received through the sensory modalities, primarily through the visual, auditory, and kinesthetic channels. In the association areas of the brain, this information is organized into meaningful patterns—7 ± 2 chunks of data. The specialized functions of both cerebral hemispheres are used in the selection and sharing of information: thinking.

Thinking and learning are influenced by internal sensory information— emotions and levels of arousal that fluctuate between inhibition and facilitation. External sensory information guides choices and decisions about what is important to learn and express. Through sensory channels, individuals observe cues from others, their emotional and behavioral actions and reactions. Social reinforcement from others directs learning toward specific goals.

Learning is modified by the feedback received. The feedback from behavioral expressions may be positive, which gives an impetus for change, or negative, which maintains balance in the system. Feedback from others and from modern technologies such as audio and videotaping and biofeedback, have a powerful influence on learning. Self-monitoring is a coping skill for noticing and using internal and external sensory information as feedback to oneself.

After individuals have studied the ways they learn best and easiest, they will become more aware of the variations in the ways others learn and communicate knowledge about themselves. Some specific skills for recognizing another person's best cognitive learning style can be developed through the study and understanding of neurolinguistics and nonverbal behaviors. These give cues to that person's preferred sensory modalities, cerebral hemispheric specialization, and emotional state. Individuals' knowing their own preferred cognitive learning style, and adapting it to those of others, is a coping skill par excellence for good communicators.

**REFERENCES**

Ariëns Kappers, C. U., Huber, G. C., & Crosby, E. C. *The comparative anatomy of the nervous system of vertebrates, including man* (2 vols.). New York: The Macmillan Company, 1936.

Bailey, K. S. Deardorff, P., & Nay, W. R. Students play therapist: Relative effects of role playing, video feedback and modeling in a simulated interview. *Journal of Consulting and Clinical Psychology*, 1977, *45*, 257–266.

Bakan, P. The eyes have it. *Psychology Today*, 1971, *4*(11), 64–67.

Bandler, R., & Grinder, J. *The structure of magic I.* Palo Alto, Calif.: Science & Behavior Books, 1975

Bandler, R., & Grinder, J. *Frogs into princes.* Moab, Utah: Real People Press, 1979.

Barbe, W. B., & Milone, M. N., Jr. Modality. *Instructor*, January 1980, 44–47.

Bateson, G. *Steps to an ecology of mind.* New York: Ballantine Books, 1972.

Brodal, A. *Neurological anatomy* (3rd ed.). New York: Oxford University Press, 1981.

Day, M. E. An eye movement phenomenon relating to attention, thought and anxiety. *Perceptual and Motor Skills*, 1964, *19*, 443–446.

Denny, M. R., & Ratner, S. C. *Comparative psychology: Research in animal behavior* (Rev. ed.). Homewood, Ill.: The Dorsey Press, 1970.

Dilts, R. B., Grinder, J., Bandler, R., DeLozier, J., & Cameron-Bandler, L. *Neurolinguistic programming I.* Cupertino, Calif.: Meta Publications, 1979.

Dunn, R., & Dunn, K. *Teaching students through their individual learning styles: A practical approach.* Reston, Va.: Reston Publishing Co., 1978.

Entwistle, N. Strategies of learning and studying: Recent research findings. *British Journal of Educational Studies,* 1977, *25,* 225–238.

Ferguson, M. *The Aquarian conspiracy: Personal and social transformations in the 1980s.* Los Angeles: J. P. Tarcher, 1980.

Geschwind, N., & Levitsky, W. Human brain: Left-right asymmetries in temporal speech region. *Science,* 1968, *161,* 168–187.

Goldman, J. *A comparison of sensory modality preference of children and adults.* Unpublished doctoral dissertation, Yeshiva University, N.Y., 1967.

Goldstein, A. P., Sprafkin, R. P., & Gershaw, N. J. *Skill training for community living: Applying structured learning therapy.* New York: Pergamon Press, 1976.

Gordon, D. *Therapeutic metaphors: Helping others through the looking glass.* Cupertino, Calif.: Meta Publications, 1978.

Grinder, J., & Bandler, R. *The structure of magic II.* Palo Alto, Calif.: Science & Behavior Books, 1976.

Gur, R. E. Conjugate lateral eye movements as an index of hemispheric activation. *Journal of Personality and Social Psychology,* 1975, *31,* 751–757.

Haynie, N. A. *Systematic human relations training with neurolinguistic programming.* Unpublished doctoral dissertation. University of Georgia, 1981.

Kimura, D. Cerebral dominance and the perception of verbal stimuli. *Canadian Journal of Psychology,* 1961, *15,* 166–171.

Krashen, S. D. The left hemisphere. In M. C. Wittrock (Ed.). *The human brain.* Englewood Cliffs, N. J.: Prentice-Hall, Inc., 1977.

Korzybski, A. *Science and sanity* (4th ed.). New York: Science Press, 1958.

Laosa, L. Multicultural education: How psychology can contribute. *Journal of Teacher Education,* 1977, *28,* 26–30.

MacLean, P. D. New findings relevant to the evolution of psychosexual functions of the brain. *Journal of Nervous and Mental Disease,* 1962, *135,* 289–301.

MacLean, P. D. *A triune concept of the brain and behaviour.* Toronto: University of Toronto Press, 1973.

McCleary, R. A. Response-modulating functions of the limbic system: Initiation and suppression. In E. Steller & J.M. Sprague (Eds.), *Progress in physiological psychology.* New York: Academic Press, 1966.

Miller, G. A. The magical number seven, plus or minus two: Some limits on our capacity for processing information. *Psychological Review,* 1956, *63,* 81–97.

Mullally, L. Educational cognitive style: Implications for instruction. *Theory Into Practice,* 1977, *16,* 238–242.

Nebes, R. D. Man's so-called minor hemisphere. In M. C. Wittrock (Ed.). *The human brain.* Englewood Cliffs, N. J.: Prentice-Hall, Inc., 1977.

Raskin, L. M., & Baker, G. P. Tactual and visual integration in the learning processes: Research and implications. *Journal of Learning Disabilities,* 1975, *8*(2), 108–112.

Shaw, M. E., Corsini, R. J., Blake, R. R., & Mouton, J. S. *Role playing: A practical manual for group facilitators.* San Diego: University Associates, Inc., 1980.

Singer, J. L. *Daydreaming and fantasy.* London: George Allen & Unwin Ltd., 1976.

Snyder, M., & Monson, T. C. Control of social behavior. *Journal of Personality and Social Psychology,* 1975, *32,* 637–644.

Thomas, R. K. Unpublished classroom notes. University of Georgia, Department of Psychology, October 30–November 6, 1980.

Thomas, R. K. Personal communication, August 6, 1981.

Wada, J. A. Fundamental asymmetry of the infant brain. In S. J. Dimond & D. A. Blizard (Eds.), *Annals of the New York Academy of Sciences,* 1977, *299,* 370–379.

Watzlawick, P. J., Beavin, J., & Jackson, D. D. *Pragmatics of human communication.* New York: W. W. Norton & Company, Inc., 1967.

Witelson, S. F., & Pallie, W. Left hemisphere specialization for language in newborn: Neuroanatomical evidence of asymmetry. *Brain,* 1973, *96,* 641–646.

# Chapter 3

# Interpersonal Communication Skills in a Group Setting

Many years ago, during the infancy of group psychotherapy, L. C. Marsh conveyed his rationale for treating people in groups. To paraphrase, he said that by the crowd they have become broken; therefore by the crowd they shall be healed (Gazda, 1975). Moreno says that "people are born in groups, live in groups, work in groups, become ill in groups, and so why not treat them in groups" (Moreno & Elefthery, 1975). Gazda (1971) and others refer to psychotherapy groups as representing a microcosm of society and, as such, they constitute a very appropriate medium for "treating" individuals with personal difficulties. Carkhuff (1971) describes "systematic group training as the most potent form of therapeutic treatment known to man."

Since the purpose of this book is to teach or train individuals in better communication and interpersonal relationship skills rather than "treat" them for some behavior or personality disorder, Marsh, Moreno, and Gazda comments must be reinterpreted for, or adapted to, training.

What are the unique characteristics of small groups, then, that make them particularly amenable to treatment and/or training of individuals in communication and interpersonal relationship skills? From the observations of the group experts just cited, a common proposition is that interpersonal interactions can best be understood in situ, and the presence of several individuals provides the opportunity to observe how given persons interact with several different individuals—the ones they can interact with successfully and the ones with whom they need to improve interactions/communications. In other words, the small group offers an immediate situation for individuals to learn their strengths and deficits in interpersonal functioning—a chance to personally rate their interpersonal level of functioning as well as be rated by others.

After members have isolated their strengths and deficits in interpersonal functioning, the group provides the varied medium through which to practice unlearning and/or relearning interpersonal communication skills, viz., concentrating on the basic areas of listening and perceiving, and correctly responding.

While group members are modifying their deficits in interpersonal functioning through practice with others and feedback from them, they also are utilizing their strengths to model/help persons with deficits in their areas of strength. That is, they have an opportunity unique to the group setting to be able to give as well as receive help at the same time.

The small group, when conducted by a competent and responsible leader, also provides a relatively safe place for persons to practice or experiment with varied modes of responding. Repeated practice, with progressive improvement through positive reinforcement by several different group members and the leader, enables given individuals to achieve a level of mastery in interpersonal interactions that can be transferred to their day-to-day interactions.

In addition to the "process" variables that make the small group the preferred medium for training in sound interpersonal relationships, there is an economical factor that also supports the group method of training over the one-to-one method. It is, obviously, more economical to train several individuals simultaneously than one at a time.

## GROUP LEADERSHIP SKILLS

Carkhuff (1969) emphasizes that "the key throughout all group helping processes is the level of functioning of the leader." Since interpersonal communications skill training typically involves didactic instruction, modeling, and practice, the group skills required of anyone who assumes the instructor/trainer role include those of teacher/instructor as well as facilitator/therapist.

### The Instructor

As instructor, the trainer's first obligation is to determine the level(s) of group members' interpersonal communication skill deficits. Group members' self-reports of their deficits as obtained through interviews are, of course, one obvious means. A pretest using items from the *Nursing Index of Responding* (Appendix A) is perhaps the best indicator of their communication levels. It can be administered to individuals before and after training/study. The key may be used to compare their answers to the keyed ones and a global level of responding can be obtained by summing the scores and averaging them. If the evaluator is skilled in the use of the

Global Scale (discussed in Chapter 14), that rating method also can be used to score the answers.

The instructor's second obligation is to select materials appropriate to the learners' readiness level. Third, the instructor must organize the materials according to a schedule based on the length of study time and the frequency of practice sessions. This text provides the essential content for study; however, supplementing the text examples with trigger/stimulus statements, critical incidents, and the like on videotape is highly recommended.

## The Facilitator/Therapist

The facilitator/therapist role involves high levels of functioning on the core conditions outlined here. Individuals who cannot respond consistently with high levels will not be effective as instructors of interpersonal communication skills.

## Leader Modeling

Four processes in observational learning are identified by Bandura (1977) to explain the learning event: (1) attention, (2) retention, (3) motor reproduction, and (4) motivation. Characteristics such as interpersonal attractiveness, nurturance, warmth, perceived competence, perceived social power, sex, age similarity, and socioeconomic status of the model all can influence the observer's attending behavior. On the other hand, observer characteristics such as dependency, level of competence, race, sex, socioeconomic status, and previous social learning experiences also are related to learning.

The observed behavior must be coded symbolically (either imagined or verbal) to be retained. Once this coding has occurred, retention can be enhanced by rehearsal strategies (Holland & Kobasigawan, 1980).

Motor reproduction of the images and thoughts acquired through the observation is dependent upon the availability of the motor skills to the observer. In situations where several components are to be mastered for motor reproduction, the missing or deficient skills must be developed first by observation and practice.

External reinforcement influences the motivational process. Learned responses that are likely to result in some direct external positive consequences will be expressed overtly, whereas those that lead to neutral consequences or that are reinforced negatively may not be translated in behavior. Modeled behavior may be acquired or performed if the observed person is reinforced positively but if the individual is punished, the behavior may be suppressed (Holland & Kobasigawan, 1980). According to Bandura and Kupers (1964), observers also may manifest or inhibit an observed behavior based on evaluations of their own behavior compared to standards that have been assimilated through observation.

These modeling principles are used in the teaching/learning of interpersonal communication skills. In certain instances, the models are presented on videotape with prior orientation as to the rationale for the behavior to be modeled. Both positive and negative reinforcement are shown. When "live" modeling is done, a similar program is followed. Peers frequently are used as live models.

## Leader Use of Role Playing

Role plays should be based on relevant personal concerns of the players. Bradford (1945) stresses the importance of relevancy and concreteness of the role play to the participants. When the role play is relevant to the individuals' own concern and behavior, they are motivated to experiment with more efficient approaches that may be suggested by the leader's critiques and feedback.

In addition to the importance of the specific or concrete elements, others (Bohart, 1977; French, 1945; Moody, 1953) cite the value of the active involvement of the role player. Those authors contend that role playing breaks through the verbal barriers and generates insight and skill where other methods fail. Research by others (Huyck, 1975; O'Donnell, 1948; Planty, 1948) support their claims. According to Shaw, Corsini, Blake, and Mouton (1980), role playing provides the player the opportunity to participate actively in the subject matter being studied through exploring, experimenting, and actually trying out new solutions.

Moody (1953) shows that role playing can be used to expand social awareness, and others (Cohen, 1951; Speroff, 1953; Stahl, 1953) that it can increase personal respect for the feelings of others. These characteristics are, of course, related to the feedback dimensions of role playing. Feedback helps the role player to identify blind spots and to receive the kind of information that the person typically fails to see or hear. Players can compare and evaluate their perceptions against those of others. Alternative ways of responding that are explored under feedback conditions can be evaluated instantly. Having pretested various reactions, the learners can be more comfortable when practicing new responses (Shaw et al., 1980).

Role playing permits the players to practice more effective responses (Stahl, 1953). "The idea of skill practice is as appropriate in improving human relationships as it is in learning a new physical skill" (Shaw et al.,

1980, p. 22). Frequent use of role playing and behavioral rehearsal in interpersonal communications training thus permits participants to practice and perfect responses before applying them to their day-to-day interactions.

## Leader Use of Homework/Transfer of Training

A central concern in the teaching of interpersonal communication skills is their transfer to day-to-day relationships. To ensure this transfer, teaching/training typically is done in small groups of 10 or so. The small group encourages a degree of personal intimacy and cohesiveness that support and motivate the members. From the perspective of a transfer of learning, the small group represents a microcosm of society and therefore helps to ensure stimulus variability. In other words, the group provides a variety of individuals representative of the larger world and therefore the skills learned in this context are more likely to be transferable to the types of persons with whom the members later interact because of the variety of stimuli or cues present in the small group.

Homework assignments between training sessions are encouraged to facilitate learning transfers. These assignments vary from exercises in the text that are intended to increase cognitive understanding of the interpersonal communications model to those that involve practicing the skill on others. The use of personal journals also facilitates self-monitoring the responding that occurs between sessions. The scales for each of the dimensions and the Global Scale are taught so that participants can learn to monitor their responses against a proved standard.

Instruction of all members of a subsystem of society such as a work group, family, or educational unit, etc., is encouraged to enhance the external monitoring and mutual reinforcement of the learners. Group consciousness raising in communication is accomplished when all members are a part of the instructional unit.

Finally, inservice educational "booster shots" are recommended to maintain members' posttraining levels. Maintaining and improving upon interpersonal communication skills is a life-long endeavor. Like any other skill, failure to use effective communication skills will lead to their deterioration.

## STAGES OF GROUP DEVELOPMENT

Tuckman (1972) reviews the small-group literature by setting, including therapy groups, T-groups, natural groups, and laboratory-task groups. Based on a rather extensive review and intensive analysis of the literature, he concludes that although "the fit is not perfect," four stages of development can be defined. However, he acknowledges that some group experts describe fewer and some more than four stages. Those who cite four stages describe them somewhat differently, yet there is a greater commonality than difference. Tuckman labels these four stages, from beginning to end, as (1) forming, (2) storming, (3) norming, and (4) performing. He also observes that the four-stage developmental sequence holds up "under widely varied conditions of group composition, duration of group life, and specific group task. . . ."

Using the interpersonal communications training model described in this manual, the authors have observed that the small training groups (eight to 15 members) do in fact progress through basically the same four stages that Tuckman describes. It also has been observed that group composition, duration of group life, specific exercises employed, and level of functioning of the leader affect stage development with respect to when the stage occurs and its intensity and duration.

The characteristics that differentiate one stage from another are described next, along with methods for facilitating the development and resolution of each stage. Gazda (1971) describes the four stages of counseling groups as (1) exploratory, (2) transition, (3) action, and (4) termination. These stages are similar to Tuckman's; however, Tuckman does not include a termination stage as such. Gazda's stages also have been related to the Carkhuff (1969) model for helping (Gazda, 1971).

## The Exploratory Stage

Several features characterize the group at this stage. Especially relevant for leaders and group members alike is the role served by the leader's orientation. The ground rules for the group (or goals for the course) should be outlined and clarified to reduce ambiguity and to inform the members of their responsibilities. (The trainer should employ at least level 3.0 concreteness here.) If grades or credit are to be assigned to the members, they should be fully informed. It is recommended that interpersonal communications training be a required part of the health science curriculum and that each member's modal level of functioning be level 3.0, as measured by the Global Scale, before the individuals graduate or receive certification.

The exploratory stage also includes greater didactic emphasis by the leader than in later stages. The basic parameters of the model to be used (as outlined in Chapter 1) are described. The leader-centeredness of this phase tends to create member dependency; therefore, the leader must be prepared to involve the group members in discussion of and interaction with the information provided.

As Tuckman (1972) indicates, the group members will use their early contacts to test and thus identify the boundaries of both interpersonal and task behaviors, or as Gazda (1971) describes it, "the group members engage in a process of getting acquainted, learning the ground rules, and establishing their roles and functions in the group." In the process of exploring, group members may ask questions, take issue with the rationale of the model, or in other ways confront the leader. It is especially important in these early encounters that the leader model facilitative behavior. The leader must not become defensive or in any way put members down but should communicate high levels of empathy, respect, and warmth. This type of leader behavior is especially necessary when the members seriously question whether they can improve their level of functioning.

To reduce defensive behavior to a minimum at this early phase of group development, the leader should use only self-ratings by members or anonymous ratings by the group when engaged in any training function. Similarly, field exercises or homework should be scored by the member and part of the training period should be used to clarify concepts and to correct misunderstandings.

During the exploratory stage, the leader should use role-played stimuli rather than personally relevant interactions for practice in perceiving and responding to situations. An indication that the base is developing can be discerned when the members begin to volunteer personally relevant data for group reaction. At this point the leader may begin to use self-disclosure and genuineness at level 3.0.

## The Transition Stage

This is aptly characterized by Tuckman (1972) as the "storming" stage, "characterized by conflict and polarization around interpersonal issues, with concomitant emotional responding in the task sphere. These behaviors serve as resistance to group influence and task requirements. . . ."

When group members begin to realize the difficulty of consistently perceiving and responding at minimally helpful levels on the various core dimensions, their defenses are activated and they start to find fault with the model, the training exercises, and sometimes even the leader. The group norm becomes one of resistance to further involvement in training. By now, the members also have learned to rate themselves rather accurately, and realize they are not functioning at a very high level (usually around 2.0). Furthermore, they begin to realize that many of their interpersonal contacts in the past were not dealt with very effectively when they measure themselves against the model. Because it is difficult for individuals to look at their past and label their level of functioning as mediocre to harmful, considerable resistance to accepting the scales and the model may accrue. Because of this condition, the resistance often is greater with older persons (inservice trainees) rather than with preservice trainees.

Appropriate leader intervention is a critical factor in the group's progress at this point. A trainer who reacts defensively and punitively will invalidate the leadership role and seriously impede the ability of the group to resolve this stage of development. Rather, the leader must model at level 4.0 the dimensions of empathy, respect, and warmth; at level 3.0 or better the dimensions of concreteness, genuineness, and self-disclosure; and levels 2.5 to 3.0 on confrontation and immediacy.

During this resistive stage, leaders may need to buy time with the group. There are several ways of doing this. They can return to the rationale and the research support for the model and build a strong case for its overall proved effectiveness and the need for such a system in the health sciences. They can use tapes and films that illustrate the positive effects on the recipients of high-level responses and the negative effects of low-level responses. They can use the exhibits in the text that illustrate effective versus ineffective interactions. They can assume the helper role in an extended helper-helpee interaction, allowing group members to criticize their performance. And perhaps best of all, they can convey their steadfast belief in the model by responding facilitatively to the fears of the members.

## The Action Stage

Gazda's (1971) action stage subsumes the "norming" and "performing" stages offered by Tuckman (1972). Essentially this is the work stage of the group. Resistance is overcome, and trust and cohesiveness are developed. The new norm for the group is task centered. The group's energies and commitment are directed toward mastery of the model and maximum skills acquisition. Group members begin to self-disclose at deeper and more intimate levels as they enter into the personally relevant stage of group practice and interaction.

The structured helpee-helper training sessions are gradually discarded following practice in the effective use of confrontation and immediacy. Group members spontaneously volunteer to self-disclose to the total group, and other members spontaneously respond. Because spontaneity now is prevalent in the group, higher levels (level 4.0) of genuineness and self-disclosure are appropriate. Also, level 4.0 confrontation and immediacy is used along with continued high levels of the other dimensions.

During the action stage, most volunteers report on the successful use of the model in situations outside the group. Others seek help with problem situations with which they must contend. Expressions of how difficult it is to "live" the model are made frequently. Yet in spite of these references, the members show a renewed dedication to self-improvement and mastery of the skills inherent in the model. They express the need to continue to develop and to improve their levels of functioning through their lives. Confidence replaces insecurity and defensiveness.

The action stage at its most intensive level often resembles a counseling group. Here there is opportunity to employ high levels of concreteness as members consider plans for problem resolution or skill development (see Chapter 12 for a more detailed discussion of problem solving). As the leader and member consider various actions the latter may take, that would be conducive to skill mastery, the leader may confront the member with discrepancies in behavior that may preclude constructive action. The leader also may interpret how the member is experienced (immediacy), especially when the behavior is not growth-oriented. Finally, the leader shows the highest level of respect coupled with genuineness when not accepting the member as accomplishing anything less than the individual's potential.

During this stage of group development, the leader models high levels on all the dimensions; however, the group usually requires approximately 100 hours of training before its members approach mastery or high-level functioning on all dimensions. At this point, high-functioning members may become leaders.

## The Termination Stage

The termination stage usually is of short duration. It is apparent in its true form only if the group reaches a high-level action stage. The termination stage is characterized by decreased trainee self-disclosures, as they all seek to tie up their own package. At times, some regress near termination and others frantically seek just one more degree of skill mastery.

## COPING WITH PROBLEM GROUP MEMBERS

In dealing with group members who may be causing problems, the leader's first action to take is a self-inventory. The individual should ask the following kinds of self-questions:

1. How do I feel?
2. Why do I feel this way?
3. Is the problem member:
   - Challenging me?
   - Distracting the group?

- Seeking attention?
- Resisting involvement?

4. What payoff is the problem member receiving?
   - Punishment?
   - Reward?
   - Attention?
   - Safety?

5. Do other group members appear to feel the same as I do toward the problem member?

6. What behavior do they exhibit to confirm my feelings?

7. Does the problem member require an intervention? If so, from whom:
   - Me?
   - Another group member?
   - Self?

Following this self-analysis, the leader uses the responses in developing strategies for handling specific types of conduct or behavior by the problem member (Exhibit 3–1).

**Exhibit 3–1** Leader Strategies For Handling Problem Members

| Problem Member | Coping Strategies |
|---|---|
| Aggressive | Avoid negative confrontation.<br>Encourage member to be concrete about personal feelings.<br>Ask for a private conference and share feelings and ask for cooperation, point out harmful effects on others, or ask members to leave the group.<br>Assign aggressor the helpee role on a "personally relevant" topic. (Look for clues to the aggression from the person's self-disclosure.)<br>Arrange a dyadic practice session and assume helper role with aggressive members. |
| Silent/Withdrawn | Avoid negative confrontation.<br>Invite responses.<br>Pair with self or a higher level facilitator to build trust and confidence.<br>Assign nonthreatening roles that require responding but do not demand self-disclosure in the whole group. |
| Shy to Fragile | Avoid negative confrontation.<br>Reduce risk-level by supervising one-on-one interactions and avoid group exposure.<br>Arrange to be the helper in a role play but not in front of group.<br>Place member with high level facilitators for one-on-one practice.<br>Arrange a private conference to investigate reasons for member behavior. |

## Exhibit 3–1 continued

| | |
|---|---|
| Domineering/Talkative | Avoid negative confrontation.<br>Avoid eye contact.<br>Pair with similar person who will demand equal time.<br>Reward only very significant contributions.<br>Ask for a private conference and assess person's sensitivity/awareness of the problem, ask for cooperation.<br>Arrange for a presentation to the group that requires appropriate, extended verbalizing.<br>Assign a role of shy helpee and give feedback. |
| Clown/Attention Getter | Avoid negative confrontation.<br>Respond to insecure feelings if present.<br>Assign serious roles to play as a helpee.<br>Ask for a private conference and assess reasons for the behavior.<br>Assist members by using the Global Scale to rate inappropriate humor. |
| Bored | Avoid negative confrontation.<br>Assign responsible roles.<br>Provide options for creative involvement.<br>Pair with a friend.<br>Vary exercises.<br>Support involvement.<br>Ask for a private meeting and seek suggestions for improving the training procedures. |

## REFERENCES

Bandura, A. *Social learning theory*. Englewood Cliffs, N. J.: Prentice-Hall, Inc., 1977.

Bandura, A., & Kupers, C. J. Transmission of patterns of self-reinforcement through modeling. *Journal of Abnormal and Social Psychology*, 1964, *69*, 1–9.

Bohart, A. C. Role playing and interpersonal-conflict reduction. *Journal of Counseling Psychology*, 1977, *24*, 15–24.

Bradford, L. P. Supervisory training as a diagnostic instrument. *Personnel administration*, 1945, *8*, 1–9.

Carkhuff, R. R. *Helping and human relations: A primer for lay and professional helpers*, (Vol. 2), *Practice and research*. New York: Holt, Rinehart & Winston, 1969.

Carkhuff, R. R. Training as a preferred mode of group treatment. In G. M. Gazda (Ed.), *Group counseling: A developmental approach*. Boston: Allyn & Bacon, Inc., 1971.

Cohen, J. The techniques of role-reversal: A preliminary note. *Occupational Psychology*, 1951, *25*, 64–66.

French, J. R. P. Role playing as a method of training foremen. *Sociometry*, 1945, *8*, 410–422.

Gazda, G. M. (Ed.). *Basic approaches to group psychotherapy and group counseling* (2nd ed.). Springfield, Ill.: Charles C Thomas, 1975.

Gazda, G. M. *Group counseling: A developmental approach*. Boston: Allyn & Bacon, Inc., 1971.

Holland, C. J., & Kobasigawan, A. Observational learning. In G. M. Gazda & R. J. Corsini (Eds.), *Theories of learning*. Itasca, Ill.: F. E. Peacock, 1980.

Huyck, E. T. Teaching of behavioral change. *Humanist Educator*, 1975, *14*, 12–20.

Moody, K. A. Role playing as a training technique. *Journal of Industrial Training*, 1953, *7*, 3–5.

Moreno, J. L., & Elefthery, D. G. An introduction to group psychodrama. In G. M. Gazda (Ed.), *Basic approaches to group psychotherapy and group counseling* (2nd ed.). Springfield, Ill.: Charles C Thomas, 1975.

O'Donnell, W. G. Training employees and managers. In E. G. Planty, W. S. McCord, & C. A. Efferson (Eds.), *Training employees and managers for production teamwork*. New York: Ronald Press, 1948.

Planty, E. G. Training employees and managers. In E. G. Planty, W. S. McCord, & C. A. Efferson (Eds.), *Training employees and managers for production and teamwork*. New York: Ronald Press, 1948.

Shaw, M. E., Corsini, R. J., Blake, R. R., & Mouton, J. S. *Role playing*. San Diego: University Associates, Inc., 1980.

Speroff, D. J. The group's role in role playing. *Journal of Industrial Training*, 1953, *7*, 17–20.

Stahl, G. R. Training directors evaluate role playing. *Journal of Industrial Training*, 1953, *7*, 21–29.

Tuckman, B. W. Developmental sequences in small groups. In R. C. Diedrich & H. A. Dye (Eds.), *Group procedures: Purposes, processes, and outcomes—Selected readings for the counselor*. Boston: Houghton Mifflin Company, 1972.

# Chapter 4

# Helpee Statement Types

As soon as one person speaks to another, the latter begins to assess the former's situation. People do this quickly and without being aware of it, seeking answers to such questions as, "What does this person need? What might he or she want from me? What can I do?" The answers to those questions determine the way in which the individual responds to the helpee.

Helpee statements can be classified into five categories: (1) a request for physical help, (2) a request for information, (3) inappropriate interaction, (4) a request for understanding/involvement, and (5) permission to express anger. For each type there is a helper response style that is most likely to be effective, as shown in Figure 4–1. While the helper's response differs for each kind of statement, there are components of communication that are common to all, shown as "facilitative dimensions used in all communication."

Training in this manual covers responses to each type of helpee statement, with emphasis on the "request for understanding/involvement." As the diagram indicates, the first task is for the helper to classify the helpee's statement into one of the five types, which are discussed next.

## REQUEST FOR PHYSICAL HELP

The helpee may ask the helper to do something. For example, a hospitalized, bedfast patient might say, "Could you pull the drapes for me? The sun is in my eyes." This request is simple and straightforward; its meaning is obvious. An appropriate helper response would be to immediately pull the drapes, saying at the same time, "I'd be glad to," or something similar. The helper also would look around the room to see if any other conditions needed attention; for example, it now might be desirable to turn on the room light.

**Figure 4–1** Categories of Helpee Statements and Helper Responses

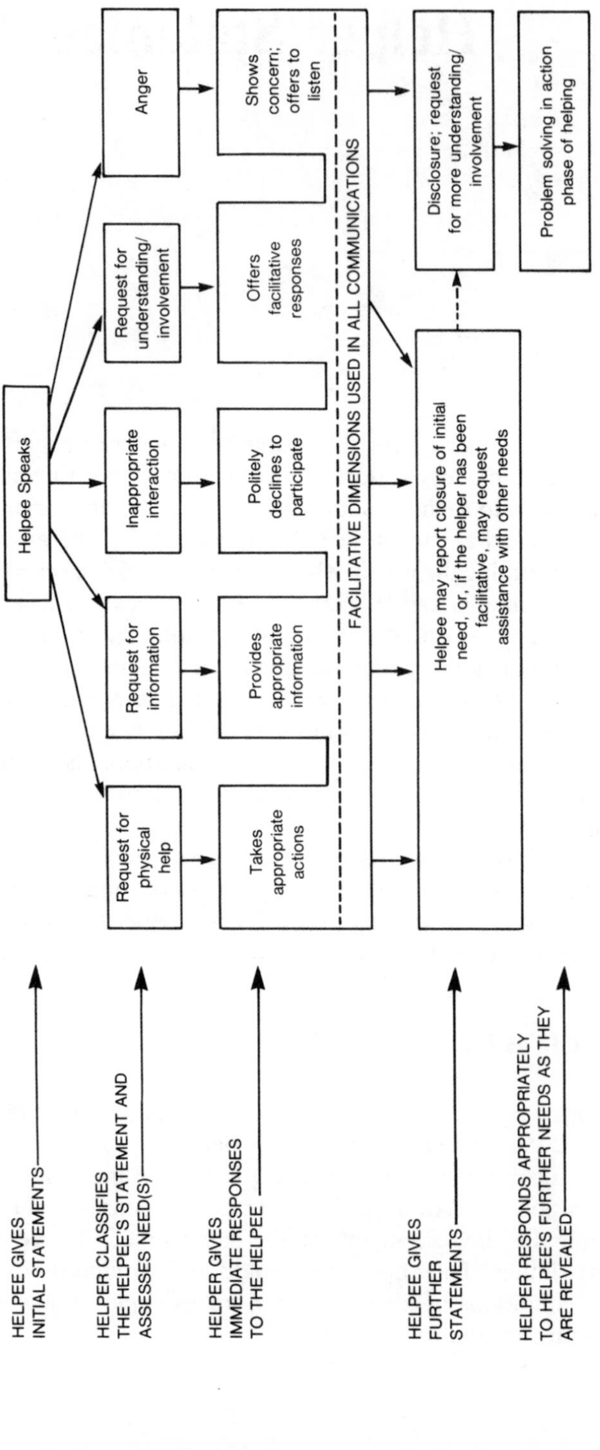

Requests for action may be as explicit as this example but often they are only implied. The statement, "I don't have a ride home," may mean, "Would you please give me a ride?" In the latter case, the helpee may be thinking, "I have a favor to ask you, but I'm a little afraid you might not say 'yes.' I wish didn't have to ask. Maybe if I tell you my need, you will offer to help. That would be a lot easier than asking." The helper must be aware of what is not said, and its significance, as well as what has been put into words.

Other requests, while simple to fulfill, require knowledge of the patient's condition before they can be met. For example, a hospitalized patient says, "I'd like to sit up. Would you help me out of bed?" or, "My cigarettes are in that drawer over there. Would you hand them to me?" These requests would be easy to perform, but the helper must know whether that patient is or is not allowed to sit up, or to smoke. The helper must know whether or not fulfilling the requested action is in the best interests of the helpee. Helping sometimes means doing, and sometimes means not doing, the things requested. Caregivers should use their professional training to decide what is appropriate under the circumstances. Chapter 16 describes how to respond to requests for action.

## REQUEST FOR INFORMATION

This type is similar in dynamics to the request for action because the helpee is asking the helper for something. For example, a patient might ask, "Can this prescription be filled at any pharmacy?" Some appropriate helper responses are "Yes," or "Yes, your usual pharmacy will have it," or "This is quite new; let me phone and make sure it is available at your pharmacy."

Again, the request may be explicit or implied. A hospitalized patient might ask, "Are visiting hours the same on weekends?" The same request, without a question mark, would be, "I'm not sure about weekend visiting hours." The helper can assume that the interaction is terminated unless it is continued by the helpee. Responding to the special conditions of requests for information is covered in Chapter 15.

## REQUEST FOR UNDERSTANDING/INVOLVEMENT

This category represents conversations in which the helpee's feelings are of major importance. It is called "request for understanding/involvement" because the helpee generally is seeking a relationship with another person rather than directive answers, at least at first.

A request for understanding/involvement may be explicit, such as, "There's something that is really bothering me. I wonder if I could talk with you about it." Or it may be implied, such as, "I have started dreaming about death and sometimes I can picture my best friends dying. It is really scary." This patient has verbalized a real concern and the most appropriate response is to listen fully and to respond to that concern with understanding and caring.

The major part of the book (Chapters 4 through 20) deals with communicating with persons about matters as intimate as this. In the process of learning to deal with such highly personal situations, helpers will acquire skills that will be useful in all other kinds of interactions and relationships with other persons.


## INAPPROPRIATE COMMUNICATION

There are several kinds of conversations that are potentially damaging to the persons talking, to persons not present, or to the organization. Such interaction is inappropriate because it can become destructive and disruptive. This category includes (1) gossip and rumor, (2) inordinate or chronic griping, (3) excessive dependency, (4) invitations to be involved in hurtful activities, and (5) hostile humor.

For example, a hospitalized patient might say, "I'm always glad to see your shift come on duty. Those old-timers on the first shift don't have a nice word for anyone." Engaging in this conversation could lead either to talking negatively about a person or persons not present or to defending others, perhaps without first-hand knowledge. Either way of responding would be ineffective. To disparage coworkers is to decrease patients' confidence in the organization or to encourage them to perseverate about things they do not like. Attempting to defend those referred to in the inappropriate interaction is to deny prematurely the patients' perception of the situation.

Generally, then, the best response to an inappropriate helpee statement is to politely decline to take part in it. This response must be made in a way that does not offend the other person, because if it does the caregiver may lose the opportunity to be a friend and helper. This is much more easily proposed than practiced.

When a helpee's comment is inappropriate, the individual usually knows it, and when another person does anything but go along, the helpee is likely to feel some degree of embarrassment. Still, there is no basis for a helper to encourage inappropriate behavior, even by passivity. Even the act of listening without comment to inappropriate communication positively reinforces the speaker's behavior, and the person may infer that the helper agrees. If caregivers encourage inappropriate behaviors, even by silence, they may lose their opportunity to be helpers.

An example of a response to a person who is trying to involve a caregiver in office gossip is as follows:

Helpee: "I'm sure glad to see that Gloria is getting 'chewed out' for being late again. Did you know that she is slipping out to lunch with Dr. X and he is a married man with five children. . . . et cetera." Helper: "I can see that you have been irritated with Gloria for being late and for meeting with Dr. X, but I prefer not to get into a discussion about her. I must admit that it sounds kind of 'juicy,' but I've found that I feel badly after I have indulged in this kind of talk." A detailed discussion and training exercise in the skills for responding to inappropriate communication appears in Chapter 17.

## SEEKING TO EXPRESS ANGER

Anger is a symptom of other problems that caregivers may need to learn about in order to help the person. It usually is not easy to be around angry persons because their enraged behavior is unpredictable and sometimes dangerous. So the first response to anger is different from the first response to either of the four other categories.

The best approach is for helpers to communicate their own respect and concern for the other person and to offer to listen. The verbal and nonverbal styles, genuine and low key, are explained further in Chapter 18.

## IT MAKES A DIFFERENCE

Helpers must learn to recognize these five types so they can look beyond the obvious. What may appear to be a simple request for physical help or for information may be the helpee's device for steering the conversation toward a substantive concern that the person is not able to express directly. Most individuals have occasions when they want to talk with others about matters that are important to them. It is not uncommon for helpees to approach sensitive topics gradually, to avoid the possible painful experience of being ignored or rebuffed.

For example, a patient might ask, "How much are they charging me for these boxes of tissue?" Taken at face value, this is a request for information that can be answered with a word or two, but there may be much more on the helpee's mind than just that cost. The patient may be wanting to say, "I'm worried about paying my hospital bill" or "I'm afraid the cost of this illness is going to use up all my savings and if I'm sick again, what will become of me?"

Displays of anger often are cries for help, signals of intense frustration or hurt that no longer can be endured. Again, caregivers must not assume that the issue mentioned first is the only one, or even the most important one. It probably is not.

Helpers must try to always be alert for needs that are not verbalized. To be fully effective, health care specialists must be able to examine every helpee statement to ascertain whether it might be masking needs that go beyond the literal message.

# Chapter 5

# Verbal Villains: Popular Styles of Ineffective Communication

There are many ways of responding to any situation but some are more effective than others. People often do not choose the best way even though they would like to.

This chapter shows some of the ways of responding that generally are not helpful and may even be harmful. It explains why, and shows alternatives.

The Verbal Villains (Walters, 1981) are mistakes that intelligent and well-meaning persons such as caregivers often make. They are not the harsh, blatant, or cruel communication styles such as slander, insult, dishonesty, or personal condemnation—not the worst things people might say—but they are damaging nevertheless.

The common feature that makes these ineffective is that they do not respond to speakers' emotional needs and they impose on, rather than show acceptance of, those who voice them. The results are resistance, indifference, and discouragement on the part of the helpee.

Each Verbal Villain has good features when used under the proper conditions. (If they were completely bad, people would never use them.) But used early in a conversation with persons not known well, and in any emotionally important conversation, they are almost certain to be destructive or at best ineffective.

Everything individuals say has an effect upon listeners, and the effect can be for better or for worse. Sometimes speakers know what the effect of their communication is but often they do not. Persons often are too polite, timid, or disinterested to provide the feedback that may be needed about ineffective communication. When there is no negative feedback or obvious resistance, speakers are likely to assume that their communication has been good. That usually is not an accurate assumption.

The following conversations show the Verbal Villains in action, describe what the listener might say and might be thinking, and explain why the

Verbal Villain style is ineffective. Everyone has two or three likely Verbal Villain blunders, so in reading these examples, caregivers should not think just of other persons who use Verbal Villains but should try to notice the ones they themselves are likely to use.

## SITUATION 1

A nurse to a coworker: "That head nurse! She keeps making me do all those unimportant things. It's getting ridiculous, and I'm fed up with it!"

| Coworker Verbal Villain Responses | Nurse | Discussion |
|---|---|---|
| SWAMI: "You better make her think you do what she tells you to do or you'll be in trouble and it will end up on your employment record." | SAYS: "Yeah, I guess you're right." THINKS: "I don't need one more person on my back. It seems like everyone is ganging up on me." | The SWAMI pretends to know the future. When the SWAMI declares a forecast and then sits back to let it come true, it's actually a way of staying uninvolved. |
| HANGMAN: "Well, if you had taken on more responsibility and not run from the hard work, you wouldn't be stuck with the routine things now." | SAYS: "That's not the way it was." THINKS: "I know I'm to blame, so you don't need to rub it in. What do I do about it now?" | The HANGMAN likes to punish, or at least to point an accusing finger. This may be accurate but is rarely helpful if given before the helpee is ready to accept and use it. |
| SIGN PAINTER: "You're just a complainer. You don't seem to like anything that happens." | SAYS: "You don't understand what's happening." THINKS: "Call me names, huh?" | The SIGN PAINTER thinks that a problem can be solved by giving it a name. It's easy to paste a label on a problem, but it doesn't change anything. |
| DICTATOR: "You need to tell her how you feel. Stick up for yourself. Next time, have it out with her. Refuse to do any unnecessary work." | SAYS: "Thanks for the ideas." THINKS: "Maybe you could do that, but I couldn't. What can I do that fits my personality and abilities?" | The DICTATOR gives orders and expects them to be obeyed with no need to give explanations, listen to the helpee, or consider whether the suggestions are realistic for the person involved. |
| ANALYST: "This is a classic case of an aggressive, ego-starved histrionic making ataxic extrapolations of her perceptions, treating you as a surrogate archetype." | SAYS: "Yeah." THINKS: "What was that all about?" | The ANALYST pretends to explain why things are as they are. It's more fun to keep things theoretical, but probably not very helpful. |

*AN EFFECTIVE RESPONSE:*

| | | |
|---|---|---|
| HELPER: "You feel you've been treated as less qualified than you are, and it makes you angry." | SAYS: "Exactly. Because . . ." THINKS: "At last I've found someone who will listen." | This is helpful because it shows acceptance and understanding. It gives permission to the other person to feel what already is felt. |

## SITUATION 2

A patient to a nurse: "They wouldn't let me go to the dayroom. I had to stay in bed all day. The doctor told me I could get up, but they wouldn't let me."

*Nurse*
*Verbal Villain*

| Responses | Patient | Discussion |
|---|---|---|
| DETECTIVE: "Who said? A doctor or nurse? An intern? A dark-haired female intern, or who? Someone you've seen before? And when did you get that message?" | SAYS: "I'm not sure who it was." THINKS: "Why are you giving me the third degree and what are you going to pry into next?" | The DETECTIVE, eager to track down the facts of the case, grills the helpee for details of what happened. This is more likely to produce mistrust than to be helpful. |
| MAGICIAN: "Well, don't worry about it. Everything is going to be okay." | SAYS: "Well, I hope so." THINKS: "Oh, come on. Don't you think I have already tried to quit worrying? Don't insult me." | The MAGICIAN pretends to make problems vanish, but fools no one else. How many times have you been told to not worry and that proved to be all the help you needed? Probably never. |
| ZEALOT: "I'll take care of that. Let's get . . . uh, no, that wouldn't work, so we'll . . . er, uh . . . Hey! You could go . . . oops, well . . . I don't know. Maybe you got a point there. | SAYS: "Thanks for trying." THINKS: "Thanks for nothing and don't hurry back." | The ZEALOT rushes in where the more sensitive fear to tread. Don't promise what you can't produce. |

*AN EFFECTIVE RESPONSE:*

| | | |
|---|---|---|
| HELPER: "It sounds as if you think you were treated unfairly since the doctor had already given you permission to get up." | SAYS: "You got it. And it really surprised me, since . . ." THINKS: "Looks like we'll get this straightened out." | This is helpful as an opening response because it recognizes the patient's feelings, and shows that the listener has accurately heard the complaint. |

## SITUATION 3

Patient to nurse: "You've *got* to give me something for this pain; it's just about to kill me!" (For the past three days, the patient has been

62 INTERPERSONAL COMMUNICATION

receiving medication for postoperative pain. Yesterday, after frequent complaints, the dosage was increased 50 percent. The patient has continued to complain.)

*Nurse*
*Verbal Villain*
*Responses*

FLORIST: "A great big strong man like you? I'll bet you're just teasing me. I'll bet you can tolerate almost anything. Say, didn't you get the nicest cards today."

GURU: "Well, grin and bear it. Pain is part of getting well. Into each life some rain must fall, but remember—every cloud has a silver lining. Keep your chin up."

FOREMAN: "You need to get your mind off it. Here, I'll switch on the TV for you, and when I come back I'll bring a magazine."

HISTORIAN: "You know, I've gone through this operation myself. It was about nine years ago, maybe 10, and during that time I was . . ."

*EFFECTIVE RESPONSE 1:*

HELPER: The nurse thinks the pain may be genuine, so says, "I'll check the chart right now and then we'll know more about what we can do for you."

*Patient*

SAYS: "I'm not kidding— *please* get me something." THINKS: "If you could just feel this, and I wish you could, you wouldn't make fun of my pain."

SAYS: "I *can't* bear it. You've *got* to get me something." THINKS: "Talk is cheap. you just don't care how much this hurts.

SAYS: "Please get me some medicine. That's what I need." THINKS: "I don't want to do what you want to do, I want you to do what I need.

SAYS: The patient doesn't get a chance to speak. THINKS: "Maybe this will bore me to sleep."

SAYS: "Thank you. Please don't forget about me." THINKS: "Here's somebody who really cares about me."

*Discussion*

The FLORIST is uncomfortable talking about anything unpleasant, so gushes flowery phrases to keep the helpee's problem at a safe distance. The florist mistakenly thinks that the way to be helpful is to hide the problem under bouquets of compliments and optimism.

The GURU dispenses proverbs and cliches on every occasion as though the sole possessor of the accumulated wisdom of the ages. Unfortunately, the words are too impersonal and general to apply to any individual's situation with force or accuracy, and often are too trite to be noticed at all.

The FOREMAN believes that if a person can be kept too busy to think about a problem there will be no problem, so gets the person busy doing something—anything. It doesn't work.

The HISTORIAN grabs the spotlight for a trip down memory lane. If you want to bore people, talk about yourself; if you want to help people, let them talk.

This is effective because it clearly states what will be done. The responsiveness itself shows a lot of respect for the patient.

*EFFECTIVE RESPONSE 2:*

HELPER: The nurse thinks the patient's report of pain is exaggerated, so says, "The pain is so bad you just don't know how you're going to make it."

SAYS: "It seems like I've been in pain forever." THINKS: "At last, here's somebody who listens to me without arguing about it. Maybe now I can say some other things I've wanted to talk about."

This is effective because it shows that what the patient has said so far has been accurately heard. This encourages the patient to say more, giving the nurse a chance to learn the patient's true condition.

## SITUATION 4

A supervisor to the supervisor of another department; "They expect us to do more work on this shift than the other two shifts but they don't give me any more help. It just isn't fair. We do more work on this shift than the other two shifts put together."

Helper Responses That Are Not Helpful:

DETECTIVE: "How can you prove that? Do you have your facts together? How do you know you're not exaggerating. Do you really know?"

FLORIST: "We're just so fortunate to have someone like you who can work so well under these conditions. You're an inspiration to everyone!"

HANGMAN: "Well, it could be your own fault. You know if you ever once let them get used to your doing more than your share, you will always have to do more than your share. You are probably reaping the consequences of your past mistakes."

SIGN PAINTER: "You're a born pessimist."

DICTATOR: "Here's how you take care of that: leave some work for the next shift to do, then they will help you pressure the administration into giving you more staff."

GURU: "Things always look the worst before they get better."

SWAMI: "If you don't get things straightened out pretty soon, you never will. Then your staff will want to get off your shift and get on an easy shift. Then you'll look bad as a supervisor."

FOREMAN: "Well, this is the last day you work this week. Have a good time, do some fun things, and forget about the hospital."

MAGICIAN: "I think you're just imagining things. The work you do always seems harder than the work other people do. That's just the way it is. Those other shifts probably feel the same way."

HISTORIAN: "I went through that once. It was rough. We had a boss who wouldn't put up with any guff, but it got so I couldn't take it. I went to the boss and . . ."

ZEALOT: "Let's get up a petition. Scare the pants off 'em. Look, I'll type up a form and you bring your people down here one by one and let them sign it. Let's get going—what are you waiting for?"

ANALYST: "I can tell you exactly what is happening. You're second shift, right? So, number one, you have patients at their most tired time of day. Two, you have more visitors on your shift. The list could go on and on. The upshot of it is, it only seems to be busier on your shift. Actually, if you look at statistics on . . ."

*Effective response*:

HELPER: "You're angry because you can't get the extra help you need to do your job right. Without help, you're always struggling to keep up with the work."

## SITUATION 5

Supervisor to administrator: "Somehow I've got to get more money. If food prices keep going up I won't even be able to feed my family."

SIGN PAINTER: "You're overreacting. You must be a worry-wart."

DETECTIVE: "Are you overspending? Driving too much? Frittering money away on luxuries? Giving too much to your kids? Abusing credit cards?"

MAGICIAN: "The government will get inflation under control. Don't worry about it."

DICTATOR: "Budget your money. First, keep track of your spending for a month. Then, see where you can improve your habits. Stick to a careful plan of how you spend your money and you'll come out okay."

FLORIST: "You have things pretty good. I know your house payment is low and your car is paid for. And you do have an interesting job. Plus, the benefits are good. You're really quite well off."

GURU: "Easy come, easy go, as they say. Everybody's in the same boat. Besides, we all eat too much anyway. A little belt-tightening would be good for us. Work hard and grow strong."

ANALYST: "Some of the economic signs are a little grim, I grant you. Only history will tell if the Keynesians or the supply siders prove to be right, but there were some penetrating insights on this in the *Wall Street Journal* yesterday. Did you see the article?

SWAMI: "If you don't take care of the problems right now, you'll soon regret it."

ZEALOT: "I can't do anything about it officially, but as private citizens we could do some things. Let's start a committee and get together tonight at my house to plan our course of attack. We could . . ."

HANGMAN: "If you don't have a bunch of money saved up, you're in real trouble and you're going to have a lot of regrets about the money you wasted."

HISTORIAN: "I've seen things get bad before. I went through the Depression, you know. Let me tell you, things were bad then. Why . . ."

FOREMAN: "So why fight it? Get a good hobby that you can plunge into when you get off work. That will keep your mind off your troubles."

Effective response:

HELPER: "It sounds like your situation is pretty difficult, in that you think that you can't make ends meet. I'm not sure there's anything I can do, directly, but if you want to talk about it—go over the options you've thought of—I'd be willing to listen. I can't talk about it right now, but we could check my appointment book and find a time. Want to?"

---

## REFERENCE

Walters, R. P. *How to be a friend people want to be a friend with.* Ventura, Calif.: Royal Books, 1981. This is a humorous description of Verbal Villains. A sound filmstrip on Verbal Villains is available from C.H.I., 5500 Waterbury Place, S.E., Kentwood, Michigan 49508.

# Chapter 6

# Perceiving Helpee Feelings

The first step in perceiving helpee problems or attitudes is identifying the person's feelings. The examples of "not helpful" communication in Chapter 5 were characterized by the helpers' ignoring or denying the helpee's feelings—they seemed unaware of how these individuals felt.

Strebe (1971) examined the need for listening and communication skills for supervisory nurses. She postulates that the employment of more nursing aides and assistants will increase the need for effective human relations and people management skills on the part of all nurses, but especially of supervisors. These nurses will either enhance or detract from the quality of care given to patients, depending on the ward atmosphere they create. According to Strebe, "If nurses can learn to understand each other better by improving their listening skills, interpersonal problems, and conflicts (nurse-nurse and nurse-patient) may seem less formidable, easier to solve."

In this communication model, caregivers learn to respond to the helpees' feelings as well as to the content of their situation. Before helpers can respond, they must perceive, that is bring into awareness what helpees are saying about what is happening to them and how they feel about it.

Perceiving means tuning in to the helpee's words and behavior. Perceiving involves caregivers' using their senses at their sharpest level to receive the helpee's message with understanding. Helpers must detect the tone of voice and consider what that might mean, must watch for nonverbal behaviors that modify the words, and must note things left unspoken that may point to important paths of helping. Perceiving at this level is difficult—it demands full attention—but it is essential if caregivers are to help.

## EXERCISE IN PERCEIVING FEELINGS

This exercise concerns one of the most important components of effective interpersonal functioning—the ability to communicate feelings from one person to another accurately. So many times in interactions, opportunities to be really helpful with another person are lost. In observing interactions between people, it is clear that in the majority of cases helpful communication is intended. That is, the person on the listening end of the conversation intends to be helpful but frequently, through a deficit of skill training, the end result is that the would-be helper is ineffective or hurtful.

The purpose of this exercise is to provide practice in listening closely for feeling words, to differentiate levels of feeling, and to increase the repertoire of feeling words.

Some of the feelings persons experience are obvious from the words they use and/or from the way in which they are spoken. Those feelings are clearly related to the situations being described. These are called surface feelings. If a listener is sure of a feeling based only on what the person has just said, it probably is a surface feeling. Sometimes the other person will use a feeling word, as in a nurse's saying, "Their sloppy charting really makes me mad." In this case, the listener's perception of the feeling word is easy: the person is mad. The helper thus would be accurate in responding to "mad" or its synonyms in communicating understanding to the nurse.

It is possible to go beyond the surface feeling words and infer the presence of other feelings. This can be done by interpreting the way in which portions of the conversation are put together, by reading between the lines, by observing the person's nonverbal communication, or through previous knowledge of the individual or the situation. Inferred or interpreted feelings that may be present in the preceding example are resentment of the persons responsible for the situation, hostility toward the system that allows them to get away with sloppy work, or discouragement in personal life that is being expressed toward others. The range of underlying feelings obviously is endless, limited only by the ability to think of various contingencies.

When caregivers first begin responding to a patient it usually is advisable to refer only to the surface feelings but it is important to be aware of the underlying ones and to keep them in mind for possible use later. Caregivers form tentative ideas about these underlying feelings and about the real nature of the patient's situation but regard them as hunches and keep them in reserve, or in the back of the mind. They watch for further evidence from the patient to see whether or not these hunches are validated.

The nurse in this example may indeed feel hostility or resentment but is not likely to accept talking about it this early in the conversation. Underlying feelings are connected to other events about which listeners may know nothing. They must learn a lot more before they will understand the other person at the level of underlying feelings. They must allow the other person to relate these things when ready, i.e., when the individual feels comfortable talking to the listener about them.

Many health care professionals' conversations will not involve discussing underlying feelings with the patient. Still, caregivers must be aware of these underlying feelings to give the best possible answer and to guard against responding to something superficial and ignoring other deeper, more significant needs.

In Exhibit 6–1, the surface and underlying feeling words in the five cases should be studied. Caregivers should challenge themselves to think of a broad range of words that they might use in similar cases.

**REFERENCE**

Strebe, R. "Just what do you hear?" *Supervisor Nurse* 2, 1971, 28–35.

**Exhibit 6–1** Case Studies of Surface and Underlying Feelings

---

*Case 1*

HCP to coworker: "I'm so mad at myself. I was upset and tired and I blew up at one of my patients for no reason at all. I know she felt hurt."

| Surface Feelings | Possible Underlying Feelings |
| --- | --- |
| mad | enraged |
| upset | revengeful |
| angry | discouraged |
| uncomfortable | |
| concerned | |

*Case 2*

Nurse to nurse: "Why do we have to take an inservice course in human relations? That has nothing at all to do with our work."

| Surface Feelings | Possible Underlying Feelings |
| --- | --- |
| frustrated | mad |
| confused | resentful |
| concerned | discouraged |
| annoyed | |
| upset | |

**Exhibit 6–1** continued

*Case 3*

HCP to coworker: "Our job would be a lot easier if the administration would give us some support in enforcing visiting hours. I have to spend half my time stepping over people's legs in those small rooms."

| Surface Feelings | Possible Underlying Feelings |
|---|---|
| concerned | exasperated |
| irritated | abused |
| ignored | belittled |
| trapped | |
| frustrated | |

*Case 4*

HCP to coworker: "Mr. Jackson in 509 asked me if he could call me when he gets home because he gets so lonely. I really like him but I just didn't know what to say."

| Surface Feelings | Possible Underlying Feelings |
|---|---|
| baffled | insecure |
| uncertain | anxious |
| concerned | scared |
| apprehensive | |
| confused | |

*Case 5*

Patient to HCP: "I think part of my problem is my family. They have had me so upset lately that I have been beside myself. You see, they want me to take over the family business but I want to go to graduate school next year."

| Surface Feelings | Possible Underlying Feelings |
|---|---|
| discouraged | depressed |
| frustrated | resentful |
| upset | insecure |
| torn | |
| anxious | |

# Chapter 7

# Perceiving and Communicating Empathy

Empathy is the attempt by a helper to tune in to the feelings of a helpee. It is described in the expressions "seeing things through another's eyes" and "putting yourself in someone else's shoes."

Bowers (1960) interviewed 200 patients about their likes and dislikes concerning doctors. Fifty percent ranked kindness, understanding, interest, and encouragement as their first expectation. The study indicates that patients want not only their physical needs but also their interpersonal, emotional, and psychological needs to be met. They want health care delivery to be warm and personal, rather than cold and aloof. They want to feel a closeness with the health care professionals who they see as having control over their lives, and they want to be able to communicate with them.

Peplau (1952) notes that the major professional concerns of nurses are those involving the communication of understanding and skill in establishing and maintaining effective interpersonal relations with patients. She feels that "experiences that have to do with how people feel about themselves and how they feel about what is happening to them . . . require counseling roles on the part of nurses." To help persons with these experiences, nurses should be skilled in communicating caring for persons and their feelings, as well as be able to meet their physical needs.

The patients' feelings must be understood, and this understanding must be put into words—the patient is the judge. There are three phases to the formulation of the empathic response: (1) careful listening, (2) deciding upon accurate feeling words, and (3) communicating the understanding to the patient verbally. The first two have been discussed; this chapter concerns the third: accurately communicating understanding. This process is not easy. To succeed, the caregiver must listen while the helpee is talking and not spend that time thinking about what to say in response.

Empathy and sympathy are different. Sympathy means that the helper experiences the same emotions as the helpee. If the helpee is sad, the helper feels sad; if the helpee is afraid, the helper also experiences fear and perhaps also the physical sensations that may accompany it (such as trembling, sweaty palms, and upset stomach). Fortunately, it is not necessary to experience the helpee's feelings to be helpful. Health care professionals can help if they can understand how the other person feels. That is what is meant by empathy.

All persons at one time or another have experienced the same emotions, even though it may have been under different circumstances. For example:

I have been afraid and you have been afraid. The thing that made me afraid may not cause you to be afraid but, if I talk about fear and if I describe how I feel when I am afraid, you can understand that because you can remember how it felt when you were afraid.

Feelings are universal—they are the same among all peoples throughout the world—even though the things that cause individuals to experience a particular emotion may be quite different from one culture to another.

When communicating with empathy, helpers prove to the other person that they understand, as best they can, what the individual is saying about personal feelings. Some persons try to take a shortcut and say, "I know what you mean " or "I understand." Probably something like that has been said to caregivers, and when it was, they may have realized that the person who claimed to understand had no idea what they were talking about. Those phrases are overused and as a result they lose their meaning.

What is the effect on the helpee when helpers communicate with empathy? The helpee will realize that the caregivers are listening with full attention and that they really understand what the individual wishes to have understood. Giving full attention to another person is the greatest compliment helpers can give because it shows that the caregivers think that individual is important and worth their time. This is a compliment that is made all the more meaningful because there is no way that giving time and attention can be faked.

The helpfulness of empathic communication is not limited to severe problems. It can be a part of everyday life that will help bring about more meaningful relationships. If caregivers show by their communication that they are seeking to understand the other person's point of view, that individual will be attracted to the helpers and will seek to understand their needs, interests, and feelings. Helpful communication begets helpful interaction.

## EXAMPLES IN PERCEIVING EMPATHY

The examples in Exhibit 7–2 are evaluated according to the accompanying empathy scale (Exhibit 7–1). Caregivers should study the scale first so that they become familiar with the levels. A number of responses are given that illustrate the levels. Caregivers may perceive both surface and underlying feelings but at this stage of helping will respond only to surface feelings. It is possible for caregivers to include in their response none of the helpee's surface feelings (level 1), some of them (level 2), or all of them (level 3). Accurately going beyond surface feelings to underlying feelings (level 4) is an advanced skill and not recommended for use in the relationship-development phase of helping. The recommended starting point on the empathy scale is level 3. The objective of this section is to determine to what extent and with what accuracy caregivers are communicating the helpee's feelings.

### Example of Levels of Empathy

*Case 1*

Health care professional (HCP) to coworker: "I haven't been feeling myself lately. I guess you can tell that my work is falling off. With three teenagers to take care of, I feel like I have two full-time jobs."

---

**Exhibit 7–1** The Empathy Scale

| *Levels* | |
|---|---|
| 1.0 | Helper response is irrelevant or hurtful, or does not respond at all to the surface feelings of the helpee. |
| 2.0 | Helper response communicates a partial awareness of surface feelings. |
| 3.0 | Helper response communicates directly that surface feelings are understood by accurately reflecting their essence to the helpee. |
| 4.0 | Helper response communicates an understanding of the helpee beyond the level of immediate awareness or beyond the person's willingness to self-disclose by accurately responding to the helpee's underlying feelings. |

*Levels*    *Helper Responses*

1.0    Responses that include none of the helpee's surface feelings:

1. "You think all that extra work is making you sick?

*Discussion:* This responds to what is happening but not how it feels when that happens. The helper's response includes none of the helpee's feelings."

2. "I didn't realize that you had three children. Exactly what are their ages? Do you have both boys and girls? Tell me more about them."

*Discussion:* The first thing helpers want to do is to show the helpee that they hear the individual and are seeking to understand what is happening to the person and how the helpee feels about it. This response makes no attempt to do that.

3. "You must get a lot of satisfaction from being able to help your family. Your children are turning out so well, you must be very proud of them."

*Discussion:* This response includes feelings that the helpee probably has, but they are not the feelings being talked about at this moment. The helper should allow the helpee to talk about what that person wants to discuss.

2.0    Responses that include some of the helpee's surface feelings.

4. "You're feeling pretty run down?"

*Discussion:* The helpee's feelings go beyond just feeling run down. The helper's response picks up only part of the feelings expressed. What the helper said is correct but it is incomplete. The helper should try to label the feeling as accurately as the helpee has.

5. "Having three children that age is frustrating at times."

*Discussion:* Again, the response falls short of expressing everything the helpee has said. Also, the word "frustrating" is one that is used so frequently in everyday conversation that it may not have as much impact on the helpee as another word.

3.0    Responses that include all of the helpee's surface feelings.

6. "I guess it is pretty exhausting to work here all day and then tend to your family at night. You never get caught up with all you have to do."

*Discussion:* This response includes the surface feeling "exhausting." This word was chosen to summarize the helpee's feelings, rephrasing what the helper has heard the person say about feelings and the situation. The helper has listened carefully and now is telling the helpee what the helper has heard the person say. Doing this proves to the helpee that the helper is listening with full attention.

7. "You must really be dragged out. With so much to do at home, it's beginning to affect your work here."

*Discussion:* This response, like number 6, tells the helpee what the helper has heard about how the person is feeling. It could be said that this response "reflects" the helpee's message—in other words, the helper is giving back an impression of what the helpee is feeling, based on that message. The term "reflective response" is used to stand for a reply in which the helper describes the helpee's feelings. This tells the helpee that the helper heard what the person said about the situation and is attempting to understand how the helpee feels about it.

It should be remembered that the objective is not to solve the problem for the helpee—the helper probably could not do that. The first objective should be to show that the helper is trying to understand the situation as well as possible and accepts the helpee as the person that individual really is. This allows the helpee to be comfortable discussing the problem and to continue the conversation. Very likely, then, the helpee will go on to describe and probe deeper feelings and attitudes, the process called self-exploration. Providing an atmosphere of acceptance and caring is the first phase of building a base or establishing a good relationship.

For each of the next two helpee situations, several caregiver responses are given. Each response is evaluated according to the amount of empathy that is communicated. Level 1.0, 2.0, or 3.0 appears next to each response. In these examples, the preferred response would be the level 3.0.

## Further Examples of Levels of Empathy

*Case 2*

HCP 1 to HCP 2: "Rhonda invited me to an inservice workshop she is doing after our shift on Friday. I don't know what to do. I don't want to go—I know it will be dull—but maybe I ought to. You see, several of the other women on our floor told her they would come but I know they won't be there. If no one shows up, she'll really feel bad."

*Levels    Helper Responses*

1.0    1. "I wonder why all the other people said they would go if they never intended to go in the first place?"

1.0    2. "You try to look out for everybody's feelings at the expense of your own."

2.0    3. "I don't think that has to be your problem. Besides, you'll be embarrassed when nobody else shows up."

3.0    4. "You've been caught in a bind. You don't want to go to Rhonda's inservice but since no one else from the hospital is going, you feel an obligation to be there."

3.0    5. "You really don't look forward to being bored Friday afternoon but you will go to the inservice to spare Rhonda from being too hurt."

## Case 3

HCP to Coworker: "When I came in this morning the treatment room was filthy again. The last thing I do every day is clean it, and this morning it even had water standing in it. It would be different if this was the first time this has happened but it is getting to be too frequent to ignore."

*Levels    Helper Responses*

1.0    6. "When was the last time this happened?"

1.0    7. "Well, there's a clear-cut policy about that. When you find out who did it, they are going to be in real trouble!"

2.0    8. "I hope you didn't need to use it before you could get it cleaned up again. If you weren't ready to give a treatment when it was needed, you'd get all the blame, and that would be pretty embarrassing."

3.0    9. "That must be pretty upsetting. You're doing your part, but for some reason things are out of your control. That must leave you feeling kind of helpless."

## Case 4

Mother of child in Pediatrics Unit to nurse: "Bobby has been crying for an hour—ever since that nurse who worked last night gave him his medicine. I think he would be better off being left alone than to upset him with the medicine."

*Levels* *Helper Responses*

1.0    10. "I wish you would work here just one day and try to keep all the children from crying. This job is enough to drive a person crazy."

1.0    11. "I'm glad you came to discuss Bobby. He really has become a problem on the ward."

2.0    12. "It sounds like you are unhappy about the way we do things here."

3.0    13. "You are concerned about Bobby because he seems so uncomfortable.'

## COMMUNICATING EMPATHY

Chapter 6 and the preceding section have led up to communicating empathy through discussion and practice in the areas of perceiving feelings accurately and recognizing the extent to which empathy is communicated in caregiver responses. The next logical step in the process is to formulate and deliver effective empathic responses. The following guidelines should be helpful:

• Empathy involves a perception on the part of the other person that the helpers understand. Caregivers always must be aware of the verbal and nonverbal behavior of the person with whom they are talking to determine, in part, how effective they are being.

• The other person also will be checking out the caregivers as they talk. Any verbal or nonverbal distractions will take away from their ability to be helpful.

• Caregivers with a high energy level will be perceived more positively than those with a low energy level.

• The most effective type of response early in the caregiver/helpee relationship is one that includes both components of the empathic response—accurate surface feelings and the essence of the content that is being communicated.

- Equaling the intensity of the helpee's statements will enable the care-givers to develop rapport more rapidly.

- Caregivers' speaking in language that is similar to the helpee's will put the person at ease and facilitate relationship development.

- Caregivers need not have knowledge of the helpee's subject. By def-inition, empathic responses neither add to nor subtract from what the helpee is saying. Consequently, helpers can have an interaction with most anyone on almost any subject without a lot of knowledge of that category.

- The exploratory process that is launched as a result of empathic re-sponding will give the caregivers additional information to use in help-ing. The more they know about the helpee and the situation, the easier it will be to help the other person make the right decisions.

### Feelings and Content: The Formula Response

The empathy responding mode, as has been mentioned, involves com-municating an accurate surface feeling word along with the essence of the content. Other terms for this include facilitative response, listening re-sponse, active listening response, interchangeable response, or mirror re-sponse. When the empathic response is made in a natural way, the helpee will feel listened to and in most cases will perceive the caregivers in a positive way.

Critics of the empathic response argue that it turns the other person off because it does nothing more than restate what the helpee said. That is true but that is by design. The caregiver uses the additional information obtained through empathic responding to assist the helpee in making the best decisions possible. One of the biggest mistakes caregivers make in helping others with decision making is giving advice before the facts from the helpee's point of view are out in the open. Many times, this leads to helpee frustration because the premature advice is related more to what the caregivers would do in a similar situation than what is possible for the helpee.

### Empathic Responding Exercises

The cases in Exhibit 7–2 are representative of formula responses. They can be used as models in guiding caregivers as to how they would put the formula into a response that would be natural for them. Even though the

**Exhibit 7–2** Six Examples of Formula Responses

---

*Case 1*

Nursing attendant to HCP: "All I ever do is make beds and bathe patients. I know how to do more important things if they would let me."

*Formula Response:*
"You feel ____upset____ because you think your talents are not being used well in your present job."

*Formula Adapted to Helper's Style:*
"It's pretty upsetting to feel that you are doing less than you could be doing."

*Discussion:* A helpee would tire very quickly at hearing the formula type response over and over. Of course, the purpose of using the formula is to accustom the caregiver to including surface feeling words and the essence of the content into a response. As illustrated, it is possible to give an empathic response that does not sound like it is parroting the other person. With practice, the empathic response becomes more and more natural sounding and makes the other person glad to have talked with the caregiver.

*Case 2*

Patient to HCP: "Sometimes I get the feeling that nobody wants to talk with me about this illness."

*Formula Response:*
"You feel ____concerned____ because ____you seem to be getting the silent treatment."

*Formula Adapted to Helper's Style:*

_____

_____

_____

*Case 3*

HCP to HCP: "I think I can learn a lot from my supervisor about dealing with patients. One of the hardest things for me to do in nursing is to explain procedures to patients and their families."

*Formula Response:*
"You feel ____encouraged____ because ____you found what you think will be a good role model."

*Formula Adapted to Helper's Style:*

_____

_____

_____

**Exhibit 7–2** continued

Case 4

HCP to HCP: "The thing I like best about nursing is talking with my patients. Now with the short staff situation, there is not much time for that."

*Formula Response:*
"You feel _____ frustrated _____ because you don't have as much time as you would like to talk with your patients."

*Formula Adapted to Helper's Style:*

_____

_____

_____


Case 5

Patient to HCP: "The person who took the blood kept talking about WBC's and some kind of gas she was doing. It's all so confusing. I've never been in a hospital before."

*Formula Response:*
"You feel _____ anxious _____ because _____ all of these things are happening to you that you don't understand."

*Formula Adapted to Helper's Style:*

_____

_____

_____


Case 6

HCP to HCP: "When my husband graduates from law school, he says he does not want me to work. I think he is trying to repay me for working while he is in school. What I can't get him to understand is that I want to work."

*Formula Response:*
"You feel _____ trapped _____ because _____ even though your husband thinks he is doing something for you, it is not what you want for yourself."

*Formula Adapted to Helper's Style:*

_____

_____

_____

formula response is not intended as one that a caregiver would deliver as is, it is important to maintain the essential elements (feelings and content). That is, HCPs should adapt the formula so that it sounds natural for them. Space is provided for readers who may want to write their natural responses in the handbook. Exhibit 7–3 involves a case of communicating empathy.

Helpers are the best authorities on their own experiences. For example, the helper could put it this way:

> I can never know as much about you as you know. I can never know exactly what is happening to you or how you feel about it, but it is possible for me to discuss with you what I have heard you tell me. When I respond, I will emphasize talking about you, but under the condition that my perception of you, like all perceptions, may be inaccurate.

Therefore, when responding to a helpee, caregivers should focus on the helpee and make it clear that they are talking about the individual's feelings as they perceive them.

## PHRASES THAT ADD VARIETY TO RESPONSES

There are many ways caregivers can communicate the same message. The following lists suggest different ways to begin a sentence in response

**Exhibit 7–3** Protocol: Communicating Empathy

| SITUATION: A parent in the emergency room waiting area walks up to the E.R. clerk and says: | | |
|---|---|---|
| *Helpee* | *Helper* | *Comments* |
| "My daughter has been back there almost half an hour. Is there any word yet on how she is doing?" | "I know you are anxious about her. I'll see if the nurse can talk with you." | The helper communicates the surface feeling of anxiety to the parent. This is level 3.0 empathy. |
| "Thank you. I feel so helpless out here." | "It is nerve-racking to want to do something but not know what to do." | Again, the clerk communicates level 3.0 empathy. This kind of interaction, though not action, tends to make others feel more at ease. |
| "I'm glad you said you would try to get the nurse out here to talk with me." | "I'll be right back." | A good combination of empathy and action that makes the clerk an integral part of the helping team. |

to what the helpee has told them. Increasing their repertoire will allow helpers to add variety to their style that will make it more interesting for the listener. These lists can be used as bases for ideas about additional ways to add variety to communication patterns.

A. Phrases that are useful when the caregiver trusts that the perceptions are accurate and that the helpee is receptive to these communications:

*Visual*
From your point of view . . .
From where you stand . . .
As you see it . . .
It looks to you . . .

*Kinesthetic*
You feel . . .
It seems to you . . .
You're . . . (identify the perceived feeling)
So, what's happening to you is . . .
When (specify) happened, it made you feel . . .
That caused you to feel . . .
You figure . . . (or, mean, think, believe)
I'm picking up that you . . .
Where you're coming from . . .
In your experience . . .

*Auditory*
What I hear you saying . . .
I really hear you saying that . . .
It sounds like you . . .
You're telling me that . . .
From what you're saying, then . . .

B. Phrases that are useful when the caregiver is having some difficulty perceiving clearly, or it seems that the helpee might not be receptive to the helper's communications:

*Visual*
From where I stand . . .
It looks to me as though . . .
Your point of view on it seems to be . . .
Apparently, from my perspective at least, you see that . . .
You appear to be feeling . . .

*Kinesthetic*
I wonder if . . .
What I'm picking up is . . .
Is there any chance you . . .
This is just a hunch, but . . .
I guess when that happened, you felt . . .
I can't help thinking that maybe . . .
This may be off base, but . . .
I get the impression that . . .

*Auditory*
What I guess I'm hearing is . . .
Does it sound reasonable that you . . .
This is what I think I hear you saying . . .
As I hear it, you . . .

C. Phrases that are useful to determine whether the caregiver is perceiving accurately what the helpee is saying, state the helper's perception and ask for clarification or correction, should that be needed:

*Visual*
Do I understand that, as you see it . . .
It looks to you that . . . Am I seeing it right?
Do I see it the way you see it?
Is that the way it looks to you?

*Kinesthetic*
I'm not certain I understand. Do you mean . . .
I'm not sure this is right; you felt . . .
I keep wondering if . . . Could that be?
Is that what you mean?
Is that how it is?
Do you feel a little . . .

*Auditory*
Are you saying that . . .
Am I hearing you right?
Is that what you're saying?
So, it sounds to you that . . . Did I hear you right?

**REFERENCES**

Bowers, W.F. *Interpersonal relationships in the hospital.* Springfield, Il.: Charles C Thomas, 1960.
Peplau, H.E. *Interpersonal relations in nursing.* New York: G.P. Putman's Sons, 1952.

# Chapter 8

# Perceiving and Communicating Respect

The next dimension of helpful communication discussed is respect. Respect, as used here, means belief in the value and potential of a person. This means that helpers must have, and communicate, confidence in helpees' ability to help themselves. Caregivers must put their attention on the helpees' interests and needs, not on their own. They must defer what is best for themselves so they can do what is best for the helpees. They assist the helpees in meeting their needs, without seeking to control, dominate, or otherwise limit their freedom to help themselves and to pursue their own values.

Hepner, Boyer, and Westerhaus (1969) examined the need for effective human relations skills in the administration of hospital staff members and in their contacts with patients. According to those authors, rapid scientific and medical changes have led to the impersonalization of health care. They feel that a loss of concerned and respectful responding toward patients occurs as health care becomes more complex. They contend that as the number of services increases, there is a danger of losing sight of the dignity of the patient as a person and instead the individual is perceived as a consumer.

Apparently people's mouths, stomachs, legs, and arms are treated while their emotional states, feelings, and inner pains often are ignored. As a result, patients frequently do not follow the advice of their doctors, nurses, and therapists because they do not feel "cared for" as persons and thus they do not get well.

King (1973), in a survey of undergraduates using the services of a university health center, finds that a patient's satisfaction is higher when the person believes the physicians are competent. Competence is defined as taking an interest in the patient as a person, treating the person with zeal and concern, and not showing disrespect by suggesting that a complaint is minor or unfounded. King concludes that "effectiveness in the delivery of medical care depends in part on positive attitudes by the patient population toward the organization rendering that care."

Respect is communicated as much through things that caregivers do not do as it is through what they do or say. Some of the factors that communicate lack of respect are arguing about the facts of a matter as the helpee sees them, making fun of the individual's feelings, saying that those feelings are wrong, and HCPs giving their own opinions freely.

Much of what is considered to be helpful is often disrespectful. Caregivers should think for a moment about the last time someone gave them advice, and answer these questions: (1) Was the advice something the caregivers hadn't already thought of? (2) Did they use that advice? (3) Would they have been just as well off if they hadn't been given that advice?

It may be suspected that many times caregivers have felt insulted by inappropriate, worthless advice, even when it was given with good intentions. Most people have given thoughtless advice without realizing that when they do so they are saying to the helpee, "Any simple thing that I think of off the top of my head is better than what you have thought of, even though you have been thinking about this matter for a long time."

The positive side of communicating respect involves affirming the worth of the helpee as an individual. If helpers can value and believe in the helpee and can communicate this, the individual also begins to develop self-value, to gain confidence in the ability to overcome particular deficits, and thus to risk involvement with the helpers and the process of helping and problem solving. All normally functioning humans have tremendous potential for achievement and for solving their own problems and improving their circumstances in life. Helping is frequently more a matter of providing emotional support and encouragement, and generating conditions in which helpees can think through and make decisions on their own, than it is a matter of educating those persons in the basic facts of life. Helpers can assist helpees in this process but should not, and in fact cannot, do it for them.

Effective helpers must be able to communicate at an early stage in the relationship willingness to become involved. Sometimes the task is clear-cut and brief but more often the caregivers must share the concerns of the helpee over a long period. Effective helping demands much from the helpers and should not be entered into lightly. Respectful HCPs enter the helping relationship cautiously, recognizing that it may mean the investment of considerable time and effort on their part, and that it potentially can bring them hurt and disappointment.

Helping requires an investment of the helper's self in the helpee, an investment that may later be rejected or ignored. Investment of the self means spending time with the helpee and expending the physical, cognitive, and emotional energy required. If this investment is made with genuineness and caring, as it must be in order to be effective, there is a risk to the helper of feeling some pain if the helpee is not responsive. It is minimally helpful in the early stages to communicate to the helpee that the caregiver is open to the possibility of helping.

Helping carries the risk of being harmful to the helpee; therefore, potential helpers must carefully consider whether or not they can be helpful. They must not jump into a helping relationship half-heartedly or carelessly, or enter a situation in which they cannot be effective. If they cannot help, or do not want to help, they must not pretend that they can or will. Caregivers must not try to help another person with a problem that they have been unable to resolve in their own lives and not try to help an individual with a serious personality disturbance or other major problem for which they have not been trained. Such efforts are doomed, at best, to being not helpful, and are more likely to harm the helpee.

Respect is rarely communicated by itself. It frequently is included in responses that contain empathy, warmth, and genuineness.

Exhibit 8–1 presents the Respect Scale. Each example in this chapter is evaluated on this scale. The examples should be studied as they relate to the scale so the concept of respect can be understood better.

## EXAMPLES OF LEVELS OF RESPECT

*Case 1*

HCP to team leader: "I sure hate to say anything about this but I think I have to. The way things are now they are beginning to interfere with

**Exhibit 8–1** The Respect Scale

| *Levels* |
|---|
| 1.0   Helper response focuses on what the helper thinks about the helpee's statement, thereby ignoring the rights of the helpee to an opinion. |
| 2.0   Helper response communicates, either overtly or implicitly, an unwillingness to become involved with the helpee or with the situation. |
| 3.0   Helper response communicates an openness to involvement and suspends acting on the caregiver's judgment of the helpee or the person's situation. |
| 4.0   Helper makes a personal commitment to working with the helpee, thereby making sacrifices for that individual. |

giving good patient care. I try to do a good job but lately it's been difficult because other members of our team aren't doing their share. I've got all my work to do and then they ask me to do things for them. Every time I pass the lounge I see them goofing off and laughing but I haven't been able to take a break all week. You know I don't mind working, but I just wish the others would do what they are supposed to do instead of leaving it to me. If I didn't work as hard as I do, a lot of things wouldn't get done. It shouldn't be that way. I don't know how much longer I can keep it up. I feel like I'm carrying the entire team on my back.

*Levels    Helper Responses*

1.0    Responses that give the helpee no respect.

1. "You let people push you around and you shouldn't. If you are not willing to stand up for yourself, people are going to take advantage of you."

*Discussion:* This is disrespectful because it devaluates the worth of the helpee as a person. It is as though the caregiver said, "You are inferior—something is wrong with you. If that causes you to be unhappy, it is your own fault." To attack a person's intrinsic worth is the most extreme form of disrespect. Nothing is more painful to receive than an attack on one's personal characteristics.

2. "Everyone is here for the same amount of time—eight hours. I expect everyone to do a fair share. I don't expect you to stay late and clean up after the others."

*Discussion:* This response is disrespectful because the caregiver did not hear accurately what the helpee said. It is easy to imagine how disappointed the helpee must be after saying all that, only to find out that the team leader wasn't really listening.

3. "That's all very interesting, but there are two sides to every story. I believe that if you knew what I know about the team members and the job we have to do, you would revise your attitude."

*Discussion:* This is disrespectful because it challenges the helpee's opinion. It is as though the leader had said, "You don't know what you're talking about." All persons have the right to their own opinions—even opinions the caregiver may think are wrong. The helper may wish to change some of those opinions but will not influence another individual to that view by beginning with an insult or other remark that belittles the person. The process of influencing others begins by accepting their right to see things as they see them.

2.0 Responses that give the helpee some respect.

    4. "You do work hard, and I think you know I appreciate it. But all teams are made up of people with different levels of ambition and energy. There probably isn't anything we can do to change human nature."

    *Discussion:* This response offers some respect by replying to what the helpee has said. The caregiver wants to maintain a good relationship with the helpee and thus pays a compliment by suggesting a reason why things are as they are, but withholds further involvement on that subject. This response probably will close the conversation. The helpee will continue to be frustrated with conditions since the attempt to get some help from the team leader has failed.

    5. "I know we've been very busy lately. Believe me, I've noticed how hard you have been working. That's why, when I was developing the work schedules for next month, I arranged for you to get three days off in a row. What do you think you will do with that time?"

    *Discussion:* This response gives the helpee some respect but the helper gets only partly involved by withholding association with the basic issue. When the caregiver sidesteps the emotions and seeks to shift the conversation to something else, it is the same as saying, "I'll talk with you but only if it is about something pleasant. I don't want to get involved with anything that might be difficult, even though it is important to you."

3.0 Response that gives the helpee complete respect.

    6. "It makes you mad to have to do all that extra work, especially when the others seem to be wasting time. That situation is important to you, so let's talk about what we might be able to do."

    *Discussion:* This response is respectful because it communicates the fact that the caregiver regards the helpee as significant and is open to doing what can be done to assist. For example, as a result of this interaction the team leader might decide to discuss the situation with the rest of the staff in an effort to correct the problem.

## Exercise in Perceiving Respect

In the following five cases, several responses are given, representing levels 1.0, 2.0, and 3.0 respect. Caregivers should study the responses so as to be able to differentiate between levels of respect. They also should think about alternate responses they might make using level 3.0 respect.

*Case 2*

HCP 1 to HCP 2: "I asked Dr. Robinson how to convert cc's to milliliters and he said, 'You mean you don't know how to do that? Why that's the first thing you learn in pharmacology!' "

*Levels    Helper Responses*

1.0    1. "Well, that is pretty basic conversion."

1.0    2. "Being new here means that you have to put up with things that you wouldn't ordinarily encounter later on. Sometimes you have to grin and bear it."

1.0    3. "After you've been here for a while you find out that most nurses don't even bother to work it out. They just consider them the same volume."

2.0    4. "That makes me furious. Why does he have to say things like that? He knew that was going to hurt your feelings."

3.0    5. "It must have made you angry to be ridiculed like that. He acted as though you never had known the answer; you had learned it but you just couldn't remember it then."

3.0    6. "It embarrassed you to be corrected like that, especially since you made such a simple request."

3.0    7. "I know it must have made you feel awfully stupid when he responded in such a gruff way."

*Case 3*

HCP 3 to HCP 4: "A lot of times I have been ready to give up—just quit. But if I quit, I might regret it later, maybe even the next day. There are times I can't stand coming here, but there are times I love it. If I thought we would ever get fully staffed, I wouldn't mind staying."

*Levels    Helper Responses*

1.0    8. "Hang in there, you'll make it.

2.0    9. "What are the things you don't like?"

3.0    10. "You feel pulled two ways—one part of you wants to quit, and one part wants to stay. That's a pretty uncomfortable feeling."

3.0    11. "You're having both good and bad feelings about your job. Sometimes you're up, sometimes you're down. You think that if you only had a long-range goal and if you were sure about how things would come out, that would help stabilize your feelings."

*Case 4*

HCP 5 to HCP 6: "If I had done what I thought was best instead of asking the supervisor, the mess wouldn't have happened and the other team member wouldn't be mad at me now."

*Levels  Helper Responses*

1.0    12. "I'll bet you won't make that mistake again."

1.0    13. "You think you have problems on your floor. Let me tell you what my supervisor got me into."

1.0    14. "I've got to run down for a soft drink. Tell me the rest of it when I get back."

3.0    15. "You're mad at yourself for depending on someone else's opinion instead of acting on your own."

*Case 5*

HCP 7 to HCP 8: "You just don't realize what it's like to be laughed at behind your back. I can't help it if I'm so clumsy."

*Levels  Helper Responses*

1.0    16. "I can't believe anyone here would do that."

1.0    17. "We all have that feeling at one time or another during our lifetimes. It's nothing to worry about."

2.0    18. "It hurts to be made fun of."

2.0    19. "It's hard for you to understand how people can be so cruel."

3.0    20. "I realize that it is not an easy thing for you to talk about, but if you want to share some of this, I'll listen and do whatever I can."

## COMMUNICATING WITH EMPATHY AND RESPECT

Five guidelines for responding with respect are summarized from Carkhuff (1969).

1. Initially, helpers are most effective in responding with respect when they can be nonevaluative with the helpee. In addition, they should encourage full expression by the helpee.
2. Initially, helpers should respond in a modulated tone of voice until a basis is built for warm expression. With some helpees, initial expressions of warmth would be inappropriate.
3. Respect is perhaps best communicated when helpers give the helpee undivided attention and demonstrate  commitment to understanding the person.
4. Helpers should provide conditions that will allow the helpee to self-reveal so the caregivers can develop positive regard for the person. Since there is no initial basis on which the helpers can like the helpee, they must create conditions so that respect can develop.
5. With the development of a facilitative base, helpers can respond with respect when they are genuine and spontaneous. They demonstrate helpee respect when they share their full range of feelings with the individual.

In each case in Exhibit 8–2, caregivers should write a response that would communicate level 3.0 respect to another person (space is provided). It should be remembered that giving high levels of respect differs sharply from agreeing with others. A health care professional might agree or might disagree. The point is that the most efficient way of developing a relationship is to listen with respect. It would be most inappropriate to disagree before hearing the other person out.

In case of a disagreement, caregivers are more likely to get their point across and be influential in the other person's life by first listening with respect to develop the relationship before communicating any disagreement with what the helpee has said. Respect implies an openness to involvement and not a commitment to the other person. Caregivers make that decision based on their values, beliefs, or commitment to others and their cause.

**Exhibit 8–2**  Exercise in Level 3.0 Responses

1. A female coworker says: "Things have been pretty rough at home. The cost of living keeps going up, the kids have been sick off and on for a month, my back has been giving me fits, and my husband doesn't lift a finger to help me out."

   *Response:* _____

   _____

   _____

   _____

2. A patient says: "I heard my doctor talking about me and he was using a lot of awful-sounding long words. I guess that means I'm in pretty bad shape."

   *Response:* _____

   _____

   _____

   _____

3. A coworker says: "They said that special training was open to everyone but when I went to sign up, they told me they couldn't accommodate any more persons. I wonder if that was really it?"

   *Response:* _____

   _____

   _____

   _____

4. A patient says: "You're the nicest person in the hospital. In fact, you're the only one who really seems to care about me."

   *Response:* _____

   _____

   _____

   _____

5. A coworker says: "My supervisor just doesn't have any confidence in me. She is always checking up on what I have done. If she doesn't trust me to do my job, I might as well quit."

   *Response:* _____

   _____

   _____

**Exhibit 8–2** continued

6. A patient says: "My doctor brought another doctor with him when he came to see me today. I wonder what that means?"

Response: _____

_____

_____

_____

7. A coworker says: "My husband wants me to quit working after the baby is born, but I'm not sure—we'll need the money and I enjoy my work here—but still, maybe it's better that I quit."

Response: _____

_____

_____

_____

**Exhibit 8–3** Protocol: Communicating Respect

SITUATION: The head nurse is making rounds in the morning. A patient says:

| Helpee | Helper | Comments |
|---|---|---|
| "I have been here almost a week and still feel as bad as I did the night they brought me in." | "You really seem discouraged." | The nurse tunes in to the patient's feelings and does not try to "reassure" the person. This is level 3.0 respect because there is an implied openness to involvement. |
| "I am discouraged. I hope something happens fast." | "I know you must be anxious to get over this thing after being sick so long." | Again the helper is open to involvement. This also is level 3.0 respect. |
| "This is not the first time this has happened. I was here about this time last year." | "I really am interested in talking with you some more. As soon as I finish making rounds I'll stop by. I'm interested in what happened when you were here last year." | This response moves to level 4.0 respect because of the commitment to involvement by the helper. Involvement to this extent is not always realistic in a health care institution. |

Exhibit 8–3 deals with specifics on communicating respect, rising to level 4.0.

**REFERENCES**

Carkhuff, R. R. *Helping and human relations: A primer for lay and professional helpers*, (Vol. 1) *Selection and training.* New York: Holt, Rinehart, & Winston, Inc., 1969, pp. 205–206.

Hepner, J. O., Boyer, J. M., & Westerhaus, C. L. *Personnel administration and labor relations in health care facilities.* St. Louis: The C. V. Mosby Company, 1969.

King, S. H. How students view the health services. *Journal of the American College of Health,* 1973, *21*, 351–352.

# Chapter 9

# Perceiving and Communicating Warmth

The dimension of warmth is the third of the facilitative conditions that are essential for establishing a helping relationship. This chapter describes warmth and explains how it is communicated. Because the condition of warmth is so dependent upon nonverbal behaviors, this chapter includes the discussion of nonverbal communication for all the core conditions.

Warmth is the degree to which caregivers communicate their caring about helpees. It seldom is communicated by itself but most often is included in communications of empathy and respect. Alone, warmth is insufficient for building relationships, for the development of mutual respect, or for problem solving but appropriate communication of warmth accelerates these processes.

Health care professionals can help some people they do not care about. However, they can assist more individuals—and they will receive that aid more quickly—if the helpers care. The facilitative condition of warmth is communicating that caring.

Warmth is communicated primarily through a wide variety of behaviors such as gestures, posture, tone of voice, touch, or facial expressions. These behaviors do not use words so they are referred to as "nonverbal communication." These nonverbal messages are received by others and given meaning, just as words are, and their impact can be just as strong as that of verbal messages.

For example, there are the common expressions about the use of the eyes: "an icy look; a piercing stare; a look that kills." Or, the rage that can be expressed by a shaking fist. These examples only suggest the powerful impact nonverbal behaviors can have.

The nonverbal messages conveyed by nursing and hospital staff members have been analyzed by This (1971). She points out that a nurse who hides a temperature from a patient, who comes into a hospital room whispering, who allows the individual to fully express fears about being in a strange, all-white building, conveys a message. Nonverbal, as well as verbal, messages can be helpful or detrimental to a patient. If nursing personnel attended more fully to the feelings and thoughts of patients, those individuals' fears might be reduced, their sense of security enhanced, and their feelings of satisfaction increased.

Gottesman (1973), writing from his own experience as a physician awaiting the outcome of his father's surgery, stresses the necessity for good doctor-patient-family relationships. He discusses the anxiety and frustration he and his family members experienced while awaiting word from the surgeon—feelings of desperation that mounted with the passage of time. Gottesman believes that physicians need to show more human kindness and that if they are unsure how to communicate kindness and caring they should learn how to do so. One way is to become more aware of nonverbal messages so that they can become more appropriate to the situation.

It is chiefly through nonverbal messages that helpers communicate their caring for helpees. However, warmth also can be expressed in words, such as "If this is important to you, it's important to me. Let's talk about it some more." Or, "You are my friend, and I'd like to help you."

Compliments, too, express warmth. They are a valuable communication method when used honestly. Unfortunately, there are some phony types of communication, as identified by Walters (1980):

- Bait: Given by persons fishing for a compliment in return.

- Motivation: Given to urge the person to work harder.

- Foot in the door: Used as an introduction to criticism—first the good news, then the bad news.

- Bandaid: Used to cover up the hurt inflicted on another.

- Setup: Used in the form of cheap flattery to soften up an individual.

A few people are overly reluctant to receive compliments. There are several possible reasons:

- They think the compliment might be phony.

- They feel a compliment gives them a standard of performance to live up to in the future.

- They habitually deny compliments, perhaps having been taught this style of self-negation as a reaction to being proud.

- They can't believe it and feel they don't deserve it, which probably is a sign of low self-esteem.

If people tend to be leery about trusting compliments, is it safe to give them? Will people think one compliment giver phony simply because five out of the last six compliments they received from others seemed false to them? They might. There is some risk, but it's a risk worth taking because if the caution is overdone someone is deprived of affirmation that is deserved and probably needed. Risk is minimal when the following conditions (Walters, 1980) are met:

1. The compliment is deserved.
2. The person knows the giver has been in a position to know whether or not it is deserved.
3. The individual wants to give the compliment. It doesn't mean the giver has to like the person. The giver may even be struggling with envy. These circumstances may even enhance the value of the compliment to the receiver. But, most of all: if people want to give it, they should; if not, they should not.
4. Givers should say it in their own style and keep it short and simple.
5. Givers, to the best of their ability, are doing it for the recipient's benefit, not their own.

Caregivers can be rated on the level of warmth they communicate just as they are in regard to empathy and respect. Exhibit 9–1 presents the Warmth Scale and Exhibit 9–2 gives examples of behaviors associated with the various levels.

The communication of warmth has been shown to have a powerful effect in counseling situations. Since many health care situations have the same

---

**Exhibit 9–1** The Warmth Scale

| *Levels* | |
|---|---|
| 1.0 | The helpers' responses communicate nonverbally that they are either disinterested or disapproving of the helpees or their situation. |
| 2.0 | The helper's nonverbal response is neutral so that no clear message is communicated. |
| 3.0 | The helper's nonverbal response clearly shows attention and interest. |
| 4.0 | The helper's nonverbal response is intense, resulting in the helpee's feeling complete acceptance and significance in the interaction. Physical contact may occur. |

**Exhibit 9–2** Examples of Helper Behaviors on the Warmth Scale

*Level 1.0*

- Does not respond when approached or spoken to.
- Laughs when helpee is sad or frightened.
- Uses ineffective attending skills (described later in this chapter).
- Mumbles or does not speak loudly enough to be heard.
- Appears impatient for helpee to go away, as communicated by fidgeting, frequently looking at watch, drumming fingers on desk, etc.
- Uses "baby talk" or patronizing tone of voice.
- Is ingratiating or overly familiar.
- Makes physical contact to which helpee responds negatively.
- Uses compliments that are phony or manipulative.

*Level 2.0*

- Is apathetic in level of energy.
- Faces helpee, but slouches.
- Does not change behavior with changes in helpee's affect, e.g., does not laugh out loud.
- Uses effective attending skills only occasionally.
- Uses compliments that are mechanical or based on incomplete information.

*Level 3.0*

- Uses most effective attending skills consistently.

*Level 4.0*

- Has high level of alertness.
- Uses all attending behaviors effectively.
- Makes physical contact in a way acceptable to helpee.
- Uses facial expressions congruent with helpee's affect.
- Uses compliments that are deserved and deeply felt by both giver and receiver.

dynamics—in this case, explicitly involving deeply emotional conditions—a brief review of the counseling literature is appropriate. LaCrosse (1975) finds that counselors communicating with an affiliative manner are rated as more attractive and persuasive than counselors in an unaffiliative manner. Wright (1975) associates warmth with favorable outcomes in counseling and Rogers (1957) describes it as unconditional positive regard and includes it as one of his necessary and sufficient conditions for therapeutic personality changes. Studies by Mehrabian (1969) and Reece and Whitman (1962) show that greater warmth produces more words from their subjects. Gibb (1972) states that warmth is "significant, necessary, therapeutic, and enhancing for personal learning. The expression of warmth is self-fulfilling. Warmth feeds on itself and breeds new warmth" (p. 471).

In a study of the behavioral cues of interpersonal warmth, Bayes (1972) points out that the cues are elusive and varied but that enough studies have been done to offer a consensual behavioral description of the components of nonverbal warmth. Exhibit 9–3 summarizes the findings of nine research studies that examined the behavioral correlates of client perceptions of counselor warmth. The nine studies were by Bayes (1972), D'Augelli (1974), Duncan, Rice, and Butler (1968), Kelly (1972), LaCrosse (1975), Mansfield (1973), Mehrabian (1969), Shapiro (1972), and Strong, Taylor, Bratton, and Loper (1971).

A high rating on nonverbal warmth does not automatically follow high levels of empathy or respect. A helper may have and attempt to communicate high levels of empathy and respect but, because of quiet, unexpressive nonverbal behaviors, may be perceived by the helpee as uncaring. This caregiver may find that it takes more time to build a base than it takes

---

**Exhibit 9–3** Major Nonverbal Cues of Helper Warmth

- Smiling
- General positive affect, especially as communicated through facial expression
- Verbal fluency and absence of filled pauses (e.g., "um" or "ah")
- Movement, with greater movement being interpreted as alertness
- Posture, in which helper's trunk is leaning forward
- Voice tones that are normal to soft in loudness, open, and normal to low in pitch; vocal quality is relaxed, serious, and concerned
- Attentive listening
- Maintenance of eye contact
- Absence of fidgeting
- Face-to-face orientation
- Closer proximity (39″ vs. 55″ or 80″)

a person whose nonverbal behaviors are more clearly warm. Such a helper must demonstrate caring through words and deeds, and take care that nonverbal behaviors are not harmful to the development of the relationship.

On the other hand, high-level warmth may occur with low-level empathy or respect, as in a caregiver who presents interested, responsive nonverbal communication but who gives low-level empathy or respect. In this case the warmth is not genuine, the helper is likely to be considered phony, and there will be no opportunity to establish a helping relationship.

Warmth that is not genuine usually can be detected by the helpee. Even if a caregiver is able to manipulate some nonverbal behaviors, for example, put on a forced smile, other behaviors will reveal the helper's true attitudes. When verbal and nonverbal messages do not agree, the helpee usually believes the nonverbal message, even though not consciously aware of having received it. For example, if a helper claims to be interested in talking but frequently glances at a watch, the helpee probably will conclude that the caregiver doesn't mean what that person says.

The way warmth is expressed varies. When a helper with low-level warmth talks with a helpee who has been accustomed to high-level warmth, the base-building process probably will be lengthened. On the other hand, warmth and intimacy cannot be forced. The caregiver should allow the helpee to exercise the right to maintain distance in the relationship if this is preferred. High levels of warmth during the early stages of a relationship can harm the base-building process with helpees who have received little or no warmth in the past or who have been taken advantage of.

The helper should avoid effusive and chatty, buddy-buddy behavior. The salesperson's smile, handshake, and strained attempts to be friendly are the opposites of warmth. Patients, for example, should not be called on a first-name basis until they have offered that familiarity in words or through some other means. Caregivers must remember that when they are helpers, they are entering the helpee's world, and to be effective they must respond in a manner that is acceptable, understandable and useable to the patient.

## ATTENDING SKILLS

Attending is probably the most powerful single communication skill (Walters, 1980). Caregivers probably can enhance the quality of their communication more by improving their attending skills than any other one thing they might do.

That is so because caregivers send, as well as receive, messages while they listen. They never fail to communicate; there is no way to not communicate something, 24 hours a day.

People communicate continuously through nonverbal modes—behaviors such as posture, eye contact, facial expression, and energy level—and these behaviors are interpreted by the receiver and influence the person's attitude and behaviors toward the giver. The group of nonverbal behaviors used while listening is called attending skills.

Attending skills have a powerful effect on the talker. The talker observes the caregiver's attending skills and from that observation forms a first impression of whether or not the helper is listening and interested in the conversation and of how the health care professional feels about the helpee as a person. This first impression may or may not be accurate, but nevertheless it is formed. A caregiver can listen but give the impression of not listening. It is too bad if that happens because it probably turns off the talker—shuts down the conversation—because most people do not like to talk when they think they are not being listened to.

The better the caregiver's attending skills, the more comfortable the talker will feel, which usually leads to the helpee's telling things the helper needs to know to understand the individual as a unique and special person. Is that what caregivers want to have happen? If so, they must give attention to the attending skills they are using.

Health care professionals use attending skills now, of course. Any time they are listening to another person talk, their bodies are there and they are doing something with them. What do they communicate with their eyes, gestures, or posture? Do they communicate interest and acceptance, or indifference and rejection?

Effective attending skills: (1) are comfortable to use; (2) help caregivers listen and remember; (3) show their interest in the talker; (4) do not work if used in a false and manipulative way because true feelings will leak out and be noticed; (5) look attractive from the talker's perspective; (6) increase the talker's feelings of trust and self-worth; (7) are a mark of respect for others; and (8) have more impact on the talker than any other single communication skill.

The chart of attending skills gives general guidelines (Exhibit 9–4). These are not absolute, specific rules and there is room for considerable individual variation within them. They are worthy of careful study. If it takes some effort to acquire good attending skills, it is well worth that effort.

Caregivers can discover the impact of attending skills by observing other persons while listening to them and regulating the quality of the attending skills. During a conversation, helpers use effective attending skills, then gradually reduce the level of effectiveness, carefully watching the behavior of the other person. As their effectiveness decreases, they probably will see an increase in one or more of these behaviors in the talker: restlessness;

**Exhibit 9–4** Guidelines for Helpers in Using Attending Skills

| ATTENDING SKILLS | | |
|---|---|---|
| *Ineffective Use (Any of these behaviors probably will close off or slow down the conversation )* | *Nonverbal Modes of Communication* | *Effective Use (These behaviors encourage talk because they show helper's acceptance and respect for the other person )* |
| spread among activities | Attention | given fully to talker |
| distant; very close | Space | approximate arm's length |
| away | Movement | toward |
| slouching; rigid; seated leaning away | Posture | relaxed, but attentive; seated leaning slightly toward |
| absent; defiant; jittery | Eye contact | regular |
| slow to notice talker; in a hurry | Time | responds at first opportunity; time shared with talker |
| used to keep distance from the talker | Feet and legs (in sitting) | unobtrusive |
| used as a barrier | Furniture | used to draw persons together |
| does not match feelings; scowl; blank look | Facial expression | matches own or other's feelings; smile |
| compete for attention with helper's words | Gestures | highlight helper's words; unobtrusive; smooth |
| obvious; distracting | Mannerisms | none, or unobtrusive |
| very loud or very soft | Voice: volume | clearly audible |

**Exhibit 9–4** continued

| impatient or staccato; very slow or hesitant | Voice: rate | average, or a bit slower |
| apathetic; sleepy; jumpy; pushy | Energy level | alert; stays alert throughout a long conversation |
| sloppy; garish; provocative | Dress, grooming | tasteful |

Source: Reprinted by permission from *Amity: Friendship in Action*. R. P. Walters. Kentwood, Michigan: Christian Helpers, Inc. 1980, p. 31.

pauses; talking louder, faster or slower; changing the subject; moving closer or moving away; or stopping talking.

These are signs that the talker has noticed, though probably not consciously aware of it, that the helpers seem to be less interested. The talker then adjusts, perhaps trying to finish the story before attention is lost completely, perhaps trying to brighten up the delivery, perhaps deciding it isn't worth it after all and just stopping, or perhaps being puzzled by the change and wondering why the caregiver seems to be losing attentiveness. The last-named condition gives the talker two things to think about—the story and analyzing the response—and accounts for the pauses and uneven flow of words.

A word of caution: attending skills have such a powerful influence that caregivers should be careful not to be rude in trying such an experiment. They will not need to do much to see a distinct change in the other person, which is additional proof of the potency of attending skills. Helpers always should give other persons plenty of their best relational skills.

## THE ROLE OF TOUCHING

Touching others, and being touched by them, is important. The many studies that have shown the detrimental effects of tactile deprivation on infants should have put debate about the need for touch to rest long ago. However, touching between adults is risky for there are wide variations in levels of comfort among them about being touched.

The personal preference here is to encourage nonsexual touching that the other person will be comfortable with. Especially during illness or times of other emotional stress, most persons not only welcome, but need, the stronger bond that touch can communicate so much more completely than can words.

There can be few suggestions about touching outside of context because there are so many variables: the other person's attitudes and practices, the relationship between the persons, their past and present level of other communication, and the physical setting. The two most important aspects that regulate the use of touch are: (1) the level of trust between the two persons and (2) whether or not the touching is perceived (it is perception, not intent, that determines this) as sexual.

To help caregivers evaluate this for themselves, these questions might be helpful:

1. How does the other person perceive this? Is it seen as genuine or as a superficial technique?
2. Is the other person uncomfortable? If the other person draws back from being touched, the helper must adjust the behavior accordingly.
3. Are the caregivers interested in the person, or in touching the person? Who is the touching for: the caregiver, the other person, or to impress those who observe?

The reassurance of physical touch can be very meaningful to everyone, especially to the ill. When used appropriately it is soothing, comforting, and emotionally healing because it is a tangible link with life and health and is a demonstration of caring. It should be used well and often.

This handbook has referred throughout to the importance of perceiving the feelings of other persons. There are several ways of learning about the feelings of others: (1) they may say so in words, (2) someone else tells the caregivers, (3) the helpers have had previous, similar experiences with them, (4) the caregivers interpret from observed changes in their behavior, or (5) they think about how they would feel in a similar circumstances and assume they may feel somewhat the same. These all are quite useful but even under the best conditions are incomplete without also considering the other person's (6) facial expression, (7) tone of voice, and (8) other nonverbal cues.

Nonverbal communication channels are the primary means of expressing emotion. Without observing the nonverbal signals, health care professionals' understanding of the feelings of another person will be incomplete— enough so that their effectiveness will be sharply reduced. Studies support this statement. For example, Haase and Tepper (1972) conclude that "to rely solely on the verbal content of the message reduces the accuracy of the judgment by 66 percent." A study by Mehrabian and Ferris (1967) concludes that the words carried only 7 percent of the emotional message while vocal components carried 38 percent and facial expression 55 percent. The study used just those three factors; there are other nonverbal modes that can carry emotion. The message is clear: if caregivers miss the nonverbal messages, they will not understand the other person as well as they might.

Yet there are some hazards in interpreting nonverbal communication. Helpers can minimize those risks if they understand how nonverbal communication differs from verbal communication.

## NONVERBAL COMMUNICATION CHARACTERISTICS

Nonverbal communication has some characteristics that make it distinctly different from verbal communication. Caregivers first must consider those characteristics so they can go on to learn how to improve their own nonverbal communication and to understand that of other persons.

### Sending and Receiving Channels

Nonverbal communication uses many channels for sending and receiving. People receive through each of the senses: hearing, sight, touch, smell, and (rarely) taste. Messages may be sent in many ways, as Exhibit 9–5 shows.

This list presents a few specific nonverbal communication behaviors from among the thousands that may be observed in human interactions. It can only suggest the wide range of behaviors that exist.

The purpose of the list is to help caregivers become more aware of the variety and complexity of nonverbal communication. It is believed that with greater awareness they will develop greater understanding of the ways in which the nonverbal signals they send out are interpreted by others. Also, by improving their skills in reading the nonverbal responses others make to their communication, they will learn about the ways in which others perceive their verbal and nonverbal communication.

The nonverbal behaviors are categorized to assist the process of observation and awareness. Because meaning is so highly individual and dependent on context, only minimal information on possible interpretations is included. Again, helpers are cautioned against making snap interpretations of the meaning of a helpee's nonverbal message.

### The Basic Purposes

Nonverbal communication has several purposes. The following categories are adapted from Ekman and Friesen (1969a):

**Exhibit 9–5** Examples of Types of Nonverbal Communication

## I. Nonverbal Communication Behaviors Using Time

*Recognition*

Promptness or delay in recognizing the presence of another, or in responding to that person's communication

*Priorities*

Amount of time another is willing to spend communicating with a person
Relative amounts of time spent on various topics

## II. Nonverbal Communication Behaviors Using the Body

*Eye Contact* (Important in regulating the relationship)

Looking at a specific object
Looking down
Looking steadily at helper
Looking defiantly at helper ("hard" eyes); glaring
Shifting eyes from object to object
Looking at helper but looking away when looked at
Covering eyes with hand(s)
Looking frequently or infrequently at another

*Eyes*

Sparkling
Tears
Wide-eyed
Position of eyelids

*Skin*

Pallor
Perspiration
Blushing
Goose bumps

*Posture* (Often indicative of physical alertness or tiredness)

Eager, as if ready for activity
Slouching, slovenly, tired looking, slumping
Crossing arms in front as if to protect self
Crossing legs

**Exhibit 9–5** continued

*Posture* (continued)

Facing the other person when sitting, rather than sideways or away from

Hangs head, looks at floor, head down

Positioning body to exclude others from joining a group or dyad

*Facial Expression* (Primary site for display of affects, subject to involuntary responses)

No change

Wrinkled forehead (lines of worry), frown

Wrinkled nose

Smiling, laughing

"Sad" mouth

Biting lip

*Hand and Arm Gestures*

Symbolic hand and arm gestures

Literal hand and arm gestures to indicate size or shape

Demonstration of how something happened or how to do something

*Self-Inflicting Behaviors*

Biting nails

Scratching

Cracking knuckles

Tugging at hair

Rubbing or stroking

*Repetitive Behaviors* (Often interpreted as signs of nervousness or restlessness but may be organic in origin)

Tapping foot, drumming or thumping with fingers

Fidgeting, squirming

Trembling

Playing with button, hair, or clothing

*Signals or Commands*

Snapping fingers

Holding finger to lips for silence

Pointing

Staring directly to indicate disapproval

Shrugging shoulders

Waving

**Exhibit 9–5** continued

*Signals or Commands* (continued)

Nodding in recognition
Winking
Nodding in agreement; shaking head in disagreement

*Touching*

Getting attention, such as tapping on shoulder
Showing affection, tenderness
Approaching with sexual intent
Challenging, such as poking finger into chest
Showing other symbols of camaraderie, such as slapping on back
Belittling, such as a pat on top of head

## III. Nonverbal Communication Behaviors Using Vocal Media

*Tone of Voice*

Flat, monotone, absence of feeling
Bright, vivid changes of inflection
Strong, confident, firm
Weak, hesitant, shaky
Broken, faltering

*Rate of Speech*

Fast
Medium
Slow

*Loudness of Voice*

Loud
Medium
Soft

*Diction*

Precise versus careless
Regional (colloquial) differences
Consistency of diction

**Exhibit 9–5** continued

## IV. Nonverbal Communication Behaviors Using the Environment

*Distance*

Moves away when the other moves toward
Moves toward when the other moves away
Takes initiative in moving toward or away from
Widens distance gradually
Narrows distance gradually

*Arrangement of the Physical Setting*

Neat, well-ordered, organized
Untidy, haphazard, careless
Casual versus formal
Warm versus cold colors
Soft versus hard materials
Slick versus varied textures
Cheerful and lively versus dull and drab
Discriminating taste versus tawdry
Expensive or luxurious versus shabby or spartan

*Clothing* (Often used to tell others what people want them to believe about them)

Bold versus unobtrusive
Stylish versus nondescript

*Position in the Room*

Helpee protects or fortifies position by getting objects such as a desk or table between self and helper
Helpee takes an open or vulnerable position such as in the center of the room, or side-by-side on a sofa, or in simple chairs with nothing between self and helper
Helpee takes an attacking or dominating position, perhaps blocking the exit from the area or maneuvering helper into a boxed-in position
Helper moves about the room
Helper moves in and out of the other person's territory
Helpee stands when helper sits or gets position higher than the helper

**Exhibit 9–5** continued

---

**Exercises:**

The first step in effective use of nonverbal signals is awareness. This exhibit can be used as a checklist to guide observations. Once a day it should be reviewed quickly to identify examples of each behavior. Caregivers also should:

1. Observe nonverbal communication used by others, noting examples of specific behaviors they particularly like or dislike. Nonverbal behaviors that seem to interfere with and/or terminate conversations between two persons should be listed. Other nonverbal behaviors that seem to cause a conversation to move ahead, and that might indicate that the helpee is accepting the helper as a person and accepting what is being said, should be identified.

2. Observe their own nonverbal communication behaviors. They should list nonverbal behaviors that they wish to modify as well as any that they think might be misinterpreted by others.

---

1. Those that make complete statements, e.g., a policeman directing traffic, a wave of the arm as a greeting, or curling the index finger to beckon. These nonverbal behaviors are the most precise in meaning.
2. Those that change the meaning of the words. They may give added emphasis, alter the meaning, or even contradict the words. An example would be a person whose teeth are clenched while denying being angry, or whose voice wavers while they claim to feel confident or relaxed.
3. Those that illustrate the words. It is much easier to show a person how to hold a tennis racket than to put that action into words.
4. Those that regulate the interaction, e.g., to look frequently at a watch as a way of saying, "I'm in a hurry" or "I would like to leave;" to point to a chair in the room as a way of saying, "Please sit down and stay a while."
5. Those that display emotions, e.g., the wrinkled brow of worry, the teary eyes of fear or sorrow, the clenched fist of suppressed anger.

To improve perception of nonverbal signals, caregivers should keep a list of examples of behaviors that fit each of these categories. They also should observe themselves as well as others.

Vocal emphasis can change the meaning of the words of a sentence. Thelen (1960) points out that the tiny muscles of the vocal chords are extremely sensitive to the various states of tension in the body and reflect these changes in audible ways. An example is the following sentence and the variations on it:

"I WANT YOU TO TAKE CARE OF YOUR PATIENTS."

By simply changing the emphasis on one of the principal words, as though the speaker were "pointing" to that word, the message of the sentence can be altered. There also is likely to be a change in the listener's perception of the speaker's attitude, as shown by the possible, though somewhat tongue-in-cheek, statements of attitude.

"*I* want you to take care of your patients."
    Message: "It doesn't matter what others want you to do, this is what *I* want."
    Attitude: "This is *me* talking, your *boss*, and you'd better remember that *I'm your boss!*"
"I want *you* to take care of your patients."
    Message: "They are *your* responsibility."
    Attitude: "Don't pass the buck."
"I want you to *take care* of your patients."
    Message: "Do it right."
    Attitude: "Instead of goofing off like you usually do."
"I want you to take care of *your* patients."
    Message: "Put your effort where it belongs."
    Attitude: "Quit butting in on other people's jobs."
"I want you to take care of your *patients*."
    Message: "The patients must come first."
    Attitude: "Your magazine can wait. It really makes me angry when you goof off instead of being fully professional."

The dramatic difference a small emphasis here or there can make is obvious. Caregivers should listen for more examples during the week.

## Lack of Self-Awareness

People usually are not aware of their own nonverbal signals, and probably perceive only a fraction of those of others—signals that, if perceived, would help everyone understand them much better. Health care professionals have not had much, if any, formal training in nonverbal communication. Their ability to help others will increase greatly as they increase their skills in this field.

## Habituated Patterns

Nonverbal behaviors are habits. If this sounds unlikely, caregivers can try this: They can place their hands in front of them, palms together, and clasp hands with fingers intertwined. They should note how natural it feels. They then should notice which thumb is on top, place the other thumb on top, and reposition the fingers so they are intertwined again. This probably will feel quite awkward. The way it was done the first time is the way each individual always does it. People have a habit of clasping their hands together in a certain way. If they did it with equal frequency the two ways, they would feel equally natural. Caregivers may wish to repeat this experiment by folding their arms over their chest, then reversing the position.

Changing habituated nonverbal patterns is a long and difficult process. Even so, if they find themselves using nonverbal behaviors that reduce their ability to be helpful to others, it may be worth the effort required to change them.

## The Visibility of Deception

Deception leaks out through nonverbal signals. That's because they are habits—not nearly as easy to regulate as words. Freud pointed this out when he wrote: "He that has eyes to see and ears to hear may convince himself that no mortal can keep a secret. If his lips are silent, he chatters with his fingertips; betrayal oozes out of him at every pore" (1905/1963).

Studies by Mehrabian (1971) and Ekman and Friesen (1969b, 1972) have shown experimentally that persons cannot mask all signs of feeling from view. This certainly is a practical argument, in addition to other stronger ones, in favor of congruence between the inner self and the self presented to others.

## Priority in Validity

Nonverbal communication is given greater validity than verbal communication. When there is a contradiction between the two, it usually is the nonverbal that is believed. Observers may not be aware of why they do not believe the words but will make adjustments in their minds anyway. For example, the patient who says, "I'm not worried about the operation," but whose muscles are rigid and who clenches the sheet in each hand probably is denying expression of true feelings.

## The Cultural Variances

Nonverbal behaviors vary culturally. They may even have opposite meanings from one culture to another. For example, in today's society a simple up-and-down head nod means "yes" and a side-to-side shake means "no," but in Bulgaria and among some Eskimos these signals mean the opposite. Expressions of fear and the smile come close to being universally true but helpers should be aware of the rich variety of signals used and of the nonverbal language used by the persons with whom they interact.

## The Variances Within Individuals

Nonverbal behaviors vary within individuals. For example, the behavior of arms folded across the chest often is interpreted as a sign of defensiveness or rigidity. Indeed, some popular (but irresponsibly written) books state that that behavior represents an underlying attitude of defensiveness. That is true part of the time, but the crossed arm behavior also may occur because (a) it is comfortable, (b) the person is cold, (c) the person is covertly scratching, (d) the person is hiding a blemish or tattoo on the arm, (e) the person is hiding dirty hands, or (f) any of a number of other reasons. Similarly, tears may come from joy, relief, anguish, guilt, or self-pity. Silence may be generated out of spite, embarrassment, confusion, feeling of being at an impasse, or overwhelming gratitude. Making and acting on snap interpretations is likely to get people into trouble, so caregivers always should set nonverbal behavior in context.

## The Variances Between Individuals

Nonverbal behaviors vary from person to person. A given act or gesture may have opposite meanings for two persons. For example, a frown might mean concentration when displayed by one person, annoyance by another. Scheflen (1964) points out that variations may relate to differences in personality, gender, age, status, position, and health.

## Anticipation of the Verbal

Nonverbal actions anticipate the words. Strong emotions can be observed in behavior before they are expressed verbally. Sometimes the behavior is symbolic: e.g., a patient may tighten the jaw muscles when asked how things are at home. Later the patient mentions not having enough insurance.

The nonverbal behavior may be symbolic. For example, a patient reads a get-well card, then drops it on the floor, or pulls the sheet over the head, or rolls over to the side away from the door when family members arrive for a visit. What might any of these mean? Health care professionals cannot know for sure but they should observe these behaviors and remember them as clues to possibly important inner conflict or attitudes that may need to be understood.

## The Relationship Feedback

Nonverbal communication offers feedback about the relationship. Persons may not put into words all that caregivers need to know about their relationship with them. Health care professionals should watch these nonverbal signals. What attending skills do these patients use? Since they are habits, perhaps they use ineffective attending skills much of the time, so caregivers should watch for changes in their level of attending.

## Simultaneous Contradictions

Simultaneous nonverbal behaviors may contradict one another. Who has not been told by a person with red face and bulging veins, "No! I'm not angry!"? Even facial expression can be in conflict as in the person whose forehead is wrinkled in apparent concern but smiles, saying, "Oh, everything is going to be all right." Part of the face shows optimism, part of it shows pessimism. This is not necessarily an effort to deceive but is likely to be the actual state of the person—the familiar mixed emotions. The caregivers' best response might be to listen so that both they and the other person come to understand more completely the complex situation.

## THE HELPER'S NONVERBAL BEHAVIOR

Even though individuals do not consciously control many of their nonverbal behaviors, they can become consciously aware of them and control some of them. Exhibit 9–6 summarizes some of the behaviors that frequently are associated with high or low levels of the core conditions. (Core conditions are several clusters of behavior identified by a common stereotype rather than by a long behavioral description.) Only those that are of unique importance to a particular condition are listed. These behaviors,

**Exhibit 9–6** Nonverbal Communication of the Core Conditions

| | Helper Nonverbal Behaviors Likely to Be Associated With Low Levels | Helper Nonverbal Behaviors Likely to Be Associated With High Levels |
| --- | --- | --- |
| Empathy | Frowning resulting from lack of understanding | Positive head nods; facial expression congruent with content of conversation |
| Respect | Mumbling; patronizing tone of voice; engages in doodling or autistic behavior to the point that helper appears more involved in that than with the helpee | Spending time with helpee; fully attentive |
| Warmth | Showing apathy; delay in responding to approach of helpee; insincere effusiveness; fidgeting; signs of wanting to leave | Smiling; physical contact; close proximity |
| Genuineness | Making low or evasive eye contact; lack of congruence between verbal and nonverbal; less frequent movement; excessive smiling | Congruence between verbal and nonverbal behavior |
| Concreteness | Shrugging of shoulders when helpee is vague instead of asking for clarification; vague gestures used as a substitute for gestures or words that carry specific meaning | Drawing diagram to clarify an abstract point; clear enunciation |
| Self-disclosure | Bragging gestures; points to self; covers eyes or mouth while talking | Making gestures that keep references to self low-key, e.g., a shrug accompanying the words, "It was no big deal" when talking about a personal incident |
| Immediacy | Turning away or moving back when immediacy enters the conversation | Showing enthusiasm |
| Confrontation | Pointing finger or shaking fist at helpee; tone of voice that communicates blame or condemnation; loudness of voice may intimidate some helpees so that opportunity to aid is lost; wavering quality of voice; unsure of self | Using natural tone of voice; confident |

*Source:* Reprinted with permission from *Human Relations Development: A Manual For Educators* (2nd ed.) by G. M. Gazda, F. R. Asbury, F. J. Balzer, W. C. Childers, and R. P. Walters; Allyn & Bacon, Inc., © 1977.

along with good eye contact and the other behaviors described as attending skills, usually must be present to attain high levels of a given condition.

As noted, the dimension of warmth depends on nonverbal media more than any other core condition. Concreteness uses nonverbal media the least.

Adjustment of nonverbal behavior so the other person knows the caregiver more accurately can raise the level of genuineness of communication. Removal of ineffective patterns that intrude or distract can increase the level of respect that caregivers show. All HCPs should do everything they can to communicate helpfully, both verbally and nonverbally.

## USING ANOTHER'S NONVERBAL SIGNALS

Health care professionals obviously observe the helpee's nonverbal behavior. These observations can assist them in understanding the helpee—they add to perceptions of the person and the situation. If caregivers always respond at the minimally helpful or higher levels of empathy and respect, and formulate interpretations in a tentative frame, perceptions of helpee nonverbal communication can be constructive to both sides.

Nonverbal communication is highly idiosyncratic, or personalized; an act or gesture may have opposite meanings for two persons or for the same person on two different occasions. For example, a frown might mean concentration in one instance, annoyance in another. Nonverbal behaviors always must be judged in context and their meaning considered tentative. Perceptions of the helpee's nonverbal behavior should be used as clues to possible underlying feelings or motives rather than as proof that such exist.

The best way to think of observations of the nonverbal behavior of another person is as a hunch or as a hypothesis to be proved or discarded. Caregivers should give the other person a chance to help them learn more. A simple remark, delivered with warmth, may bring more information. For example, "You have been pretty quiet today," or "You seem unusually restless." If a helper is making an interpretation, it should be phrased tentatively; for example, "You've been staring out the window the last several times I've seen you. It makes me wonder if you might be worried about something. If so, and you'd like to talk about it, I'd sure be glad to listen."

Beginning gently in this way is less threatening to the other person, who then can deny the significance of the nonverbal behavior if the individual so chooses. It is better to allow for this denial, especially when the interpretation is tentative, than to be pushy. Premature or overly harsh actions on the basis of the interpretations of nonverbal behavior run the risk of hurting the relationship and possibly of losing the opportunity to help.

**Exhibit 9-7** Helpee Nonverbal Behaviors Frequently Associated With Attitude Toward Helper

| | Relationship of Mutual Acceptance | Dependent Quasi Courtship | Cautious, Considering, Evaluating | Rejecting, Hostile |
|---|---|---|---|---|
| Head | affirmative nods | | | shakes head |
| Mouth | smile | mirroring | tightness | sneer; tightness |
| Level of arousal | alertness | passive | alertness | disinterest |
| Position | faces helper; moves toward | places self in subordinate position | stationary; uses physical barriers | disinterest; moves or turns away; attacking moves or simulated attack |
| Eye contact | equal to helper's | much; seductive | little; looks down | avoids; defiant |
| Hands | palm open or up | reaching | fidgeting; rubbing face | clenched fists; gripping |
| General | spends time around helper; touches | "puppy dog" behaviors; mirroring of helper's mannerisms | locking up of emotions; uses great care over what is communicated; afraid to be fully open | unresponsive; passive-aggressive behavior; overt disruption of activity; noisy |
| Posture | open | courtship; seductive; helpless | protective | defensive |
| Proximity | normal | very close | | distant |

*How to Use This Table:* Each column lists behaviors that might be seen under certain conditions. If the helper-helpee relationship is characterized by the helpee attitude described in the column heading, at least several of the behaviors are likely to be listed. But the attitude should not be assumed from the behaviors. The behaviors may be used as clues to the quality of the relationship and explored as appropriate.

*Source:* Reprinted with permission from *Human Relations Development: A Manual For Educators* (2nd ed.) by G. M. Gazda, F. R. Asbury, F. J. Balzer, W. C. Childers, and R. P. Walters; Allyn & Bacon, Inc., Publisher; © 1977.

**Exhibit 9–8** Nonverbal Behaviors Frequently Associated With Various Group Member States

| | Despair/ Depression | Excitement/ Euphoria | Fear/ Anxiety | (Hostility/Rejection of Another Person) | | Dependency/ Attraction Toward Another | Resistance to Learning |
| | | | | Active/ Overt | Passive/ Covert | | |
| --- | --- | --- | --- | --- | --- | --- | --- |
| Head | down | mobile movement | stiff movement; chin down | head, and often chin, thrust forward and/or tilted upward | | head slightly down while making eye contact ("Poor me") | |
| Face | sad frown (eyebrows down at outer ends) | mobility of expression | flushing | angry frown (eyebrows down at center) | squinting | mirrors expression of other | rigidity of expression |
| Mouth | tightness | smiling; laughing | tightness; clenching teeth | lips tensed and pushed forward slightly | | frequent smiling | tightness |
| Eye contact | little or none; may cover eyes with hand | tries to capture and hold eye contact of all other persons ("Look at me") | darting glances to others; wants to keep watch on others but not meet their gazes ("I'll watch you") | defiant | aversion; blank staring | frequent | avoidance |
| Hands | autistic behaviors; body-focused self-stimulating movements | sweeping, expansive movements | tightness; gripping; sweaty palms (clenched and drenched) | clenching; fist; thumping (symbolic hitting) | body-focused movements; self-inflicting behaviors | reaching motions | clenched; looking at watch; body-focused movements |

| | | | | | | | |
|---|---|---|---|---|---|---|---|
| Posture | approaches fetal position | frequent change; seductive | frequent movement; crouching; hunching shoulders | poised on edge of chair | infrequent change | quasi courtship | held in; stiffness of limbs |
| Position | withdrawing movements; moves away from others | movements toward others | angled away; protective | face to face | angled or sideways (cold shoulder) | beside and angled toward | turns away from stimulus |
| Proximity | distant | close; pushes into personal space of others | moderately distant | moves boldly into personal space of others | may gradually and unobtrusively encroach on personal space of others | close | increases distance; moves back |
| Level of arousal | apathy; indifference | hyperactivity | watchful alertness | high | high, but effort to disguise it; real or feigned sleep | | real or feigned fatigue |
| General | avoidance of others | grandiose, exaggerated nonverbal behaviors | jerking movements, tics, mannerisms; fear-related physiological changes; carefully guards a small territory | acting out, such as slamming door or shifting chair noisily | efforts to control movement and disguise affect; sneezing, coughing, wheezing | mirroring of behavior | silences; absences from or lateness to sessions; behaviors that break the group's social norms; sudden onset of physical symptoms |

*Source:* Reprinted from *Group Counseling: A Developmental Approach* by G. M. Gazda by permission of Allyn & Bacon, Inc., © 1978.

Because of the variability of meaning associated with nonverbal cues from one person to another and by one person from one time to another (as well as the other characteristics of nonverbal communication mentioned earlier), it is risky to present any "definitions" of nonverbal cues. At the same time, there are patterns that are generally consistent and therefore likely to be somewhat accurate. These qualifications should be kept in mind in using Exhibits 9–7 and 9–8. These may help caregivers formulate hunches about possible affects and attitudes on the part of other persons. The presentation of this information may be overly cautious but there have been so many oversimplified statements about interpreting nonverbal signals in the popular literature in recent years that this extra care is necessary.

## RECOMMENDED READING

The following books contain interesting and reliable general analyses of nonverbal communication:

Davis, F. *Inside intuition: What we know about nonverbal communication.* New York: Signet Books, 1971.

Harper, R. G., Wiens, A. N., & Matarazzo, J. D. *Nonverbal communication: The state of the art.* New York: John Wiley & Sons, Inc., 1977.

Harrison, R. P. *Beyond words: An introduction to nonverbal communication.* Englewood Cliffs, N. J.: Prentice-Hall, Inc., 1974.

Knapp, M. L. *Nonverbal communication in human interaction.* New York: Holt, Rinehart & Winston, 1972.

Ruesch, J., & Kees, W. *Nonverbal communication: Notes on the visual perception of human relations.* Berkeley, Calif.: University of California Press, 1966.

For application to counseling, see:

Walters, R. P. Nonverbal communication in group counseling. In G. M. Gazda, *Group counseling: A developmental approach* (2nd ed.). Boston: Allyn & Bacon, Inc., 1978.

## REFERENCES

Bayes, M. A. Behavioral cues of interpersonal warmth. *Journal of Consulting and Clinical Psychology,* 1972, *39,* 333–339.

D'Augelli, A. R. Nonverbal behavior of helpers in initial helping interactions. *Journal of Counseling Psychology,* 1974, *16,* 647–655.

Duncan, S. D., Jr., Rice, L. N., & Butler, J. M. Therapists' paralanguage in peak and poor psychotherapy hours. *Journal of Abnormal Psychology,* 1968, *73,* 566–570.

Ekman, P., & Friesen, W. V. The repertoire of nonverbal behavior: Categories, origins, usage, and coding. *Semiotica,* 1969, *1,* 49–98. (a)

Ekman, P., & Friesen, W. V. Nonverbal leakage and clues to deception. *Psychiatry,* 1969, *32,* 88–105. (b)

Ekman, P., & Friesen, W. V. Hand movement. *The Journal of Communication*, 1972, *22*, 353–374.

Freud, S. Fragment of an analysis of a case of hysteria (1905). In Dora: *An analysis of a case of hysteria*. New York: Collier Books, 1963.

Gibb, J. R. TORI theory: Nonverbal behavior and the experience of community. *Comparative Group Studies*, 1972, *3*, 461–472.

Gottesman, D. M. Prognosis: Patient—good, family—guarded. *The New Physician*, 1973, *20*, 20–23.

Haase, R. F., & Tepper, D. T. Nonverbal components of empathic communication. *Journal of Counseling Psychology*, 1972, *19*, 417–424.

Kelly, F. D. Communicational significance of therapist proxemic cues. *Journal of Consulting and Clinical Psychology*, 1972, *39*, 345.

LaCrosse, M. B. Nonverbal behavior and perceived counselor attractiveness and persuasiveness. *Journal of Counseling Psychology*, 1975, *22*, 563–566.

Mansfield, E. Empathy: Concept and identified psychiatric nursing behavior. *Nursing Research*, 1973, *22*, 525–530.

Mehrabian, A. Significance of posture and position in the communication of attitude and status relationships. *Psychological Bulletin*, 1969, *71*, 359–372.

Mehrabian, A. Nonverbal betrayal of feeling. *Journal of Experimental Research in Personality*, 1971, *5*, 64–73.

Mehrabian, A., & Ferris, S. R. Inference of attitude from nonverbal communication in two channels. *Journal of Consulting Psychology*, 1967, *6*, 109–114.

Reece, M. M., & Whitman, R. N. Expressive movements, warmth, and verbal reinforcement. *Journal of Abnormal and Social Psychology*, 1962, *64*, 234–236.

Rogers, C. The necessary and sufficient conditions of therapeutic personality change. *Journal of Consulting Psychology*, 1957, *21*, 95–103.

Scheflen, A. E. The significance of posture in communication systems. *Psychiatry*, 1964, *27*, 316–331.

Shapiro, J. G. Variability and usefulness of facial and body cues. *Comparative Group Studies*, 1972, *3*, 437–442.

Strong, S. R., Taylor, R. G., Bratton, J. C., & Loper, R. G. Nonverbal behavior and perceived counselor characteristics. *Journal of Counseling Psychology*, 1971, *18*, 554–561.

Thelen, H. A. *Education and the human quest*. New York: Harper & Row, 1960.

This, L. E. Why don't they? *Supervisor Nurse*, 1971, *2*, 66–71.

Walters, R. P. *Amity: Friendship in action*. Kentwood, Mich.: C.H.I., Author, 1980.

Wright, W. Counselor dogmatism, willingness to disclose, and clients' empathy ratings. *Journal of Counseling Psychology*, 1975, *22*, 390–395.

# Chapter 10

# The Transition Dimensions

Caregivers have studied the dimensions of empathy, respect, and warmth and have learned that when they use them to communicate all that a helpee has said (facilitative response) they assist the person in self-exploration. They also learned that by emphasizing the dimensions of empathy, respect, and warmth they are operating out of the helpee's framework, or view of self and everyday world. In other words, in the early stages of a helping relationship caregivers are nonjudgmental.

The dimensions of concreteness, genuineness, and self-disclosure contain elements of facilitation and action phases. Aspects that promote helpee self-exploration are facilitative, whereas those that generate better understanding of self or of a problem are similar to the action dimensions. Whenever helpers use, for example, a level of concreteness higher than that used by the helpee, they are initiating from within their own understanding and experiencing of the helpee. If the concreteness communicated goes beyond that expressed by the helpee, they are adding greater understanding to that of the helpee. In other words, they assist the helpee to discover underlying feelings and meaning by responding with additive (level 4) concreteness.

With helper-initiated meanings given to helpee responses come a greater amount of evaluation and hence a greater risk that the response will hinder the relationship. Nevertheless, unless the risk is taken, the helpee will frequently remain with a surface or superficial level of understanding of the problem and will be in no position to resolve it.

This chapter defines each of the transition dimensions, gives guidelines for training in responding with each dimension, offers examples in each level of each dimension, provides exercises in perceiving and responding with each dimension, and illustrates ineffective and effective applications of these dimensions.

## CONCRETENESS

Concreteness means being specific. It often is complementary to empathy because helpers need to be specific to show understanding. Concreteness is especially important in the early and late phases of helping. It is important in the early phases because it complements empathy and facilitates thorough problem exploration. It is especially necessary in late phases when the helpee begins to formulate specific plans to solve problems. (See Concreteness Scale, Exhibit 10–1).

Four guidelines developed by Carkhuff (1969) for responding with concreteness are summarized:

1. The helper encourages helpee concreteness when the former is concrete. The helper should respond with concreteness to vague and abstract responses and should otherwise solicit helpee specificity.
2. The helper should focus on the personal relevance of helpee communications and must avoid rewarding evasive and irrelevant ones.
3. The helper, on limited occasions, may need to ask for specific details to permit moving into and following through in areas where the helpee

**Exhibit 10–1** The Concreteness Scale

| Levels | |
| --- | --- |
| 1.0 | Helper response is specific and/or premature so that it is hurtful or punishing. |
| 2.0 | Helper's response is not as specific as helpee's but communicates a very general understanding and/or asks a question for greater clarity/specificity without first having attempted to communicate understanding of what helpee already has communicated. |
| 3.0 | Helper responds to same level of specificity as helpee; if latter's level is abstract, helper attempts a nonthreatening level of specificity. |
| 4.0 | Helper responds to the helpee's underlying content and feelings in specific and concrete terms and actively solicits clarification of vague or abstract statements. During the later stages this may entail assisting the helpee to enumerate clear and concrete alternatives that derive from the interaction, summarizing the person's newly acquired self-understanding or outlining future action. |

is unable to initiate exploration. Questions lead to helper dominance and helpee dependency and therefore should be used with extreme caution. This is especially true in the early phases when the helpee is easily conditioned to accept the passive role.

4. The helper must be guided by experience in determining the level of concreteness.

## Examples of Levels of Concreteness

*Case 1*

Student nurse to student nurse: "I wish the instructors in this department could agree on something. One tells me my work is OK and five minutes later another one tells me, 'This won't do, redo it.' How do they expect me to ever learn what is right? I'm getting sick and tired of their different standards."

*Levels*   *Helper Responses*

1.0   1. "Have you heard that all the instructors are now required to enroll in teaching method courses?"

*Discussion:* This response shows no concreteness or specificity for the helpee's concern—namely, anger, frustration, and possible fear of inadequacy or failure. Rather, the response is only tangential to the helpee's expression.

1.0   2. "You seem to be projecting the blame for your failure onto your instructors."

*Discussion:* This shows no "helpful" concreteness. Although the response may be true, there is nothing in it to indicate that the helpee is soliciting and/or is prepared to accept this degree of concreteness. It is likely that this degree is harmful because it is premature and possibly inaccurate, too.

2.0   3. "It is difficult to know what is right and wrong around here."

*Discussion:* This shows some concreteness. It does not go right to the heart of the helpee's expressions, especially of anger and exasperation, but it does convey understanding of the person's lack of certainty in the evaluations of the day's work.

3.0    4. "You sound furious over the inconsistent evaluations by the instructors. If they can't agree on what is satisfactory work, how can you know when you've reached a satisfactory level of performance?"

*Discussion:* This shows complete concreteness. It conveys the anger and uncertainty that the helpee has expressed, including all the basic feelings and concerns that are on the surface.

4.0    5. "You really are angry over the inconsistency of evaluations by our instructors. It is difficult to evaluate yourself when the experts can't agree, isn't it? Could it be, however, that you are unable to judge the level of your performance, are uncertain about it, and therefore you become quite threatened and anxious over criticism from the instructors?"

*Discussion:* This response goes beyond the helpee's level of concreteness (additive). It includes everything that the helpee communicated directly and goes beyond that to what may have been communicated indirectly. Since the caregiver does not know at this point whether or not the helpee felt uncertain over the job performance and was easily threatened by criticism, it can only be speculated that this response could be additive and helpful if the health care professional had a good base with the helpee and was prepared to look at these feelings of inadequacy.

### Exercises in Perceiving Concreteness

For the helpee situation in Case 2, several helper responses and rating levels are given.

*Case 2*

Patient to doctor: "The pain is going to return just as soon as I get back on my feet. There is no sense in kidding ourselves. I knew I shouldn't have undergone this operation. Things like this always happen to me. I knew I shouldn't have listened to you. My back will never be the same again."

*Levels    Helper Responses*

1.0    1. "It is easier to blame me for your decision than to accept responsibility for it."

1.0    2. "What is the name of the doctor who referred you to me?"

2.0    3. "It is scary to think that you have endured so much pain, and there is a possibility that your problem will be unchanged—that the pain will still be there. Important decisions are difficult for you to make. You don't seem to trust your judgment and therefore it is necessary for you to transfer the blame to me if the operation is unsuccessful."

2.0    4. "It is difficult for you to make important decisions, especially when they may bring immediate pain to you."

2.0    5. "We won't know the results for sure until you are able to walk around."

3.0    6. "Now that the operation is completed you're afraid that it won't work, that the pain will still be there, and that in some way or other you've been victimized."

4.0    7. "Pain is really difficult for you to endure."

4.0    8. "You were reluctant to agree to the operation and now that it is time to test the results, all your uncertainties have been aroused. The possibility of continued pain is very difficult to accept but it makes it a little easier if you don't have to share all the blame."

Another detailed analysis of communicating concreteness—a conversation between a cancer patient facing surgery and a nurse—is presented in Exhibit 10–2.

## GENUINENESS

"Man's search in helping and in life is a search for authenticity, both intrapersonal and interpersonal" (Carkhuff, 1969). Genuineness refers to being real, honest, or authentic (See the Genuineness Scale, Exhibit 10–3). In training to respond with genuineness, health care professionals can be assisted through attention to Carkhuff's guidelines, summarized as follows:

1. The caregiver should minimize playing roles with the helpee, especially the facade of a professional helper. The helper must model authenticity if the helpee is to be authentic. The helper chooses to be silent rather than give an inauthentic response.
2. The helper must be able to inquire into the difficulties being experienced with a helpee. That is, the caregiver must honestly seek to

**Exhibit 10–2** Protocol: Communicating Concreteness

SITUATION: A man with cancer of the bladder is talking to a nurse regarding proposed surgery.

| Helpee | Helper | Comments |
|---|---|---|
| "The only man I knew who had this type of surgery died about six months after he had it." | "You're afraid that you might not live very long if you have this surgery." | The helper is slightly more concrete than the helpee. The helper labels the unspoken fear of dying. The response would be about 3.0 level. |
| "Yes, and that is major surgery only to die anyway." | "It's a very big decision for you to make—probably one of the most difficult that you have ever had to make." | Again the helper becomes more concrete than the helpee regarding the importance of the decision—again level 3.0. |
| "It sure is, and there is no guarantee. But I guess I'd die anyway without it. Could you explain more about the surgery?" | "Surely, and I can give you some literature to read, too." | The helpee appears to use the helper's concreteness to begin moving toward action, gathering more data on which to make the decision. |
| "Good, I'm going home this weekend, so my wife and I can discuss it and make the decision together." | The nurse describes the surgery and provides the man with literature. | Together with previous response, this one is level 4.0 since the nurse is initiating out of professional expertise. |

learn the source of the difficulty, whether it originates with self, the helpee, or is the result of the interaction of both.

3. The helper's genuineness will be communicated when the caregiver can respond based on personal experiences rather than those of the helpee. Therefore, the helper must be tuned in to self as well as to the helpee.

## Examples of Levels of Genuineness

*Case 1*

Patient (Mr. Smith) to HCP: "I'm telling you, I've about had it with this place. Nobody around here listens to me. You people that work here act like a bunch of jerks. I wonder why you even bother to come here at all. And that doctor of mine—well, he about takes the cake. Somebody better do something before I explode!"

**Exhibit 10–3** The Genuineness Scale

| *Levels* |  |
|---|---|
| 1.0 | Helper uses genuineness to punish/hurt the helpee. |
| 2.0 | Helper hides behind a role, e.g., doctor, nurse, teacher, or parent, and responds according to the role but not in accord with personal or professional beliefs and/or feelings when responding genuinely would facilitate the helping process. |
| 3.0 | Helper's feelings are expressed in a controlled/monitored fashion but they facilitate the development of the relationship with the helpee. The caregiver refrains from expressing feelings that could impede the development of the relationship. |
| 4.0 | Helper's verbal and nonverbal messages, both positive and negative, are congruent with how the caregiver feels. These feelings are communicated in a way that greatly strengthens the relationship. |

*Levels*   *Helper Responses*

1.0    1. "Now, now, I know that you don't mean what you're saying."

*Discussion:* This response shows no   genuineness. It denies the irritation that the HCP must feel over this attack. Therefore, it would appear to be phony or belittling to the helpee.

1.0    2. "You are such an ungrateful loudmouth it is no wonder everyone avoids you."

*Discussion:* This response shows no "helpful" genuineness. The helper takes out anger on the helpee by using the patient's problem against him. This type of leveling is quite likely to be very harmful because the helpee has no reason to believe that the caregiver intended to be helpful, if, in fact, that is true.

2.0    3. "Mr. Smith, you must have had a difficult day. We are all busy, but we want to see you get well."

*Discussion:* This is a response that shows some genuineness.

3.0    4. "It is upsetting to me to hear how angry you are about your treatment here."

*Discussion:* This response shows complete genuineness.

4.0    5. "Your attacking me makes me hurt and angry. I feel that you are taking out your frustration and hurt on me. You must feel badly about yourself. Perhaps you're afraid and no one is giving you any reassurance. I'm ready to listen and do what I can if you are willing to tell me what is troubling you."

   *Discussion:* This response goes beyond the helpee's level of genuineness (additive).

## Exercise in Perceiving Genuineness

For the helpee situation in case 2, caregivers are given several helper responses. Rating levels also are included.

*Case 2*

Psychiatric nurse to supervisor: "I just don't know what to do. I want to quit my job here but don't have another job yet. I'm so fed up with this place. I'm getting out of the field of psychiatric nursing. It is full of mixed-up people."

*Levels  Helper Responses*

1.0    1. "It sounds like you're the one who is frustrated and mixed up."

1.0    2. "One's job is what one makes of it."

2.0    3. "I'm sorry that you feel so unhappy with your work. If there is anything that I can do, please let me know."

2.0    4. "You're really disgusted with your job and don't know if you should stay with it or not. I'm sorry you feel that way."

2.0    5. "You know that you are welcome to stay here as long as you want."

3.0    6. "It bothers me to know that you feel so dissatisfied working here. I feel some personal responsibility to see this through with you—both to try to help you and also to satisfy myself that I have done my best."

4.0     7. "It sounds like you are very unhappy here and that your job is not meeting your needs. You seem to be telling me that I have not helped you enough. This upsets me. On the other hand, you also have indicated that you are confused about your goals—about knowing what it is that you really want for yourself. Can I be of help?"

4.0     8. "You sound very upset with this place and I guess you are telling me that I'm part of your reason for being so dissatisfied. This is not easy for me to accept, since my work has been my life and I don't feel that my colleagues are all mixed up. Your vocation has not been what you hoped it would be and your response is to put it down and look for something else. Another alternative might be to look at what you might do to get more from your work. I'd like to try to help you if you still feel something can be changed."

## Exercise in Responding with Genuineness

The caregiver should write responses to the helpee statements that follow. The response should be directed to the feelings and content of the helpee, matching predicates when possible, and making sure that it also is genuine.

1. Nurse to supervisor: "You have it in for me. You always make a fool of me in front of the entire shift. You ask me the most difficult questions just to make me look stupid. It isn't fair."

*Response:* _____

_____

_____

2. HCP to a former peer who is now the superior: "I've had this uncomfortable feeling lately that things aren't the same between us now that you are my boss. Am I just imagining this or is the job changing you?"

*Response:* _____

_____

_____

3. Member of patient's family to HCP: "I hate to sound this way, but when we brought Billy in for emergency treatment everyone seemed

more concerned over whether we could pay for it rather than for our feelings. Even though Billy was in severe pain, no one would help him until your business office approved it."

*Response:* _____

_____

_____

_____

4. Wife of seriously ill patient to ICU nurse: "Nurse, you seem real worried since you checked my husband. Can I go in to see him now?"

*Response:* _____

_____

_____

_____

5. Patient with a terminal diagnosis requests the truth from the head nurse: "Nurse, I'm real scared that I won't ever get well. I don't know if I can handle the truth, but it is even more painful fearing the worst and not being able to come to grips with it. Will I ever get better?"

*Response:* _____

_____

_____

_____

6. Doctor on the phone to x-ray technician: "I've got to have those films for Mrs. Washington right away. Can you have them ready in about an hour?"

*Response:* _____

_____

_____

_____

7. Patient to ICU nurse: "Nurse, you saved my life and I will be forever grateful to you. If there is anything that I can ever do for you, let me know. I can never really repay you though!"

*Response:* _____

_____

_____

_____

## SELF-DISCLOSURE

Helper self-disclosure is related closely to helper genuineness. Self-disclosure means revealing to the helpee the caregiver's experiencing of similar problems or conditions. The key to self-disclosure is its appropriateness. The value of this dimension is that it communicates a similarity and closeness and a deeper understanding between the helper and the helpee. By modeling self-disclosure the helper shows the appropriateness of revealing personal information in the relationship, which encourages the helpee to self-explore more thoroughly and more deeply. (See Exhibits 10–4 and 10–5.)

Guidelines for responding with self-disclosure are as follows:

1. The helper should initially avoid self-disclosure to concentrate the focus on the helpee.
2. The helper should only self-disclose when that is relevant to the helpee's concern. Helping is for the helpee.

---

**Exhibit 10–4** The Self-Disclosure Scale

| *Levels* |  |
|---|---|
| 1.0 | The helper's self-disclosure is so incriminating that the helpee is overwhelmed and loses faith in the caregiver's ability to assist. |
| 2.0 | The helper does not volunteer personal information. The caregiver may answer direct questions but in a guarded, sometimes somewhat vague fashion. |
| 3.0 | The helper relates personal ideas, attitudes, and experiences to the helpee's concerns and reveals feelings at a surface level. The helper's uniqueness as a person is not fully communicated. |
| 4.0 | The helper reveals uniqueness as a person by relating specific ideas, attitudes, experiences, and deep feelings to the helpee's interest and concerns in such a way that they can be utilized for in-depth problem solving. |

**Exhibit 10–5** Protocol—Communicating Genuineness and Self-Disclosure

SITUATION: The daughter of a terminally ill patient speaks to a nurse.

| Helpee | Helper | Comments |
|---|---|---|
| "You know, Daddy has accepted death. He is prepared to die, and I believe that we have accepted it, too. I just don't want anything else done to him, no tracheotomy, no IV's, nothing. Do you understand what I'm saying?" | "You're saying that you love your father very much and that you want him to die as easily as possible. And you don't want me to think that your decision is based on anything else such as giving up, being tired, or something like that. I can appreciate your feelings because my family and I had to make a similar decision when my mother was dying." | The helper communicates high level genuineness through being very concrete, nonjudgmental and self-disclosing; level 3.0. |
| "That's right. Because I know it seems kind of cold-hearted for me to be saying some of these things, especially to people who don't know us very well." | "I, too, wanted the people who helped my mother to know that my family and I could give up our mother because we loved her so much and didn't want her to suffer." | Again, the nurse self-discloses and reflects very specifically that the helpee is clearly understood and the caregiver is not judging the family, level 4.0. |

## Examples of Levels of Self-Disclosure

*Case 1*

Nurse to supervisor: "I did very well my first two years here but now that I am getting more difficult work, I'm not doing very well. It seems like I will never be able to do some procedures, no matter how hard I try. Maybe I should quit and go to law school."

*Levels  Helper Responses*

1.0  1. "Would you please come over here and give me a hand with this IV?"

Discussion: This response shows no helper self-disclosure. It totally ignores the helpee's feeling and focuses on the caregiver's own need for help with work.

1.0  2. "I wish I could help you with your troubles but I feel just like you and I have to teach nurses the very procedures that I cannot do myself. I agonize over every day, fearing the day that my boss will have to dismiss me."

*Discussion:* This response shows no "helpful" self-disclosure. The helper discloses a personal inadequacy and because it is so extensive, it would be likely to overwhelm the helpee. This totally shifts the focus to the caregiver. The "helper" becomes the helpee; therefore, there is no "helpful" self-disclosure in the response.

2.0   3. "Everyone feels uncertain about his or her performance from time to time. I doubt if you should quit and go to the law school just yet."

*Discussion:* This response does show some self-disclosure. The helper picks out some of the helpee's feelings of insecurity and answers an implied question but says nothing about any personal feelings of inadequacy.

3.0   4. "I used to question my clinic work, too, as a student and occasionally I still do. You will be likely to do less questioning and doubting with increased experience."

*Discussion:* This helper response shows complete self-disclosure. The caregiver discloses at surface level but does not offer anything that would set that individual apart as unique from other instructors.

4.0   5. "When, as a young nurse, I had to do procedures on my own without anyone's assistance, I used to become almost immobilized with fear that I couldn't do the task. I had never done anything skillfully with my hands before I went to nursing school and I got the scare of my life when I became solely responsible for procedures. Just the fear of failure caused me to do less well than I was capable of doing. I believe you are experiencing some of the kinds of fear in this area that I did. If you would like me to give you an assist when things aren't going right, I'd be glad to do it."

*Discussion:* This shows disclosure that goes beyond the helpee (additive). The helper risks considerable self-disclosure and shows high levels of empathy toward the helpee. The caregiver has been where the helpee is and is able to be genuinely supportive.

## Exercises in Perceiving Self-Disclosure

For the helpee situation that follows, caregivers are given several helper responses. Ratings are indicated for each response.

*Case 2*

Patient to nurse: "My roommate makes me so blasted mad! Every time I try to get some rest, she comes storming into the room, banging the door, pulling out drawers loudly, and stomping around. After all, she knows that I'm to get as much sleep as possible for my recovery, and yet she's so inconsiderate. This has happened at least six times, and I know I should say something to her, but I'm too scared. What do you think I should do?"

*Levels    Helper Responses*

1.0    1. "It seems like you are going to have to find some way to tell her how her activities are interfering with your recovery."

1.0    2. "I had a similar experience when I was hospitalized. I finally got so angry that I lost complete control. I yelled at my roommate and called her a few choice names. I told her I didn't care if she would get well and leave, or hurry up and die, just so she got out of my hair."

1.0    3. "This is something that you ought to take up with your doctor."

1.0    4. "Perhaps you are being overly sensitive because you're not feeling well."

1.0    5. "I think that you should tell her to keep the noise level down because it interferes with your rest and recuperation."

2.0    6. "Well, that kind of inconsiderate behavior would make me furious, too. I can see why you might want to say something to her about it. Yet, you are roommates and you are concerned about not making matters worse."

3.0    7. "You certainly are angry with your roommate and I would be, too. I guess I would have some of the same fears as you do about telling her if I couldn't predict how she would accept my response."

4.0    8. "I am pretty hard to live with when I'm ill and the last thing I need is for someone to fail to recognize it. I guess it is because when I'm very ill I feel so helpless and vulnerable. I resent being vulnerable and I resent those who may take advantage of my vulnerability. Perhaps you have similar feelings and are afraid to confront your roommate from such a weak and vulnerable position."

## Exercises in Responding with Self-Disclosure

The caregiver should write responses to the helpee statements that follow. The responses should be directed to the helpee's feelings and content while at the same time, matching predicates when possible, and adding to the helper's understanding with appropriate self-disclosure.

1. Patient to HCP: "I have been here for a week and only had one opportunity to talk to my doctor. I don't believe anyone here cares whether I get any help or not."

*Response:* _____

_____

_____

2. Patient to HCP: "I can't understand why my husband has so much hostility inside. Sometimes he gets me so infuriated that I would just like to throw all my wrath on him. His parents must have been awful."

*Response:* _____

_____

_____

3. Patient to physical therapist: "You must think that I'm gutless because I cry when I exercise my leg and the pain gets so intense."

*Response:* _____

_____

_____

4. Nurse to supervisor: "Look, Mrs. Jones, I know and the whole world knows that Mrs. Smithson is the wife of Dr. Smithson, but if she doesn't stop bossing the rest of us nurses around, there is going to be a lot of trouble!"

*Response:* _____

_____

_____

5. Security guard to HCP: "I know that you are running a bit late and that you are closer to your building parked behind those bushes, but the lighted lot is for employees working the night shift. Would you please park there where we can give you the best protection?"

*Response:* _____

_____
_____
_____

The protocol in Exhibit 10–5, which combines the communicating of genuineness and self-disclosure, is an excellent example of appropriate conduct.

**REFERENCE**

Carkhuff, R. R. *Helping and human relations: A primer for lay and professional helpers,* (Vol. 1), *Selection and training.* New York: Holt, Rinehart & Winston, 1969.

# Chapter 11

# The Action Dimensions

Chapter 10 introduced the transition dimensions of concreteness, genuineness, and self-disclosure. It explained that when health care professionals moved to additive levels (went beyond the helpee) on these dimensions they had to draw upon their own experiences. In doing this, they did not remain entirely nonevaluative or unconditional with the helpee. They can risk being evaluative (or, judgmental or conditional), however, only when they have built a strong relationship with the helpee through repeated use of the facilitative dimensions of empathy, respect, and warmth.

Now caregivers are going to incorporate into their repertoire of skills two additional dimensions that involve being evaluative: confrontation and immediacy. These are referred to as action dimensions because it is through their implementation that the helpee action toward problem resolution frequently is generated. Exhibit 1–1 in Chapter 1 illustrates this process.

This chapter defines each of the action dimensions and gives guidelines for training in responding with each one, examples of each level of each dimension, and exercises in perceiving and responding with each.

## CONFRONTATION

Chapter 1 defines confrontation as the helpers' pointing out discrepancies between things helpees have been saying about themselves and what they actually have been doing. The value of confrontation is that it provides helpees with another point of view to consider in the self-evaluation process. It is hoped that the helpers' confrontation and point of view are more accurate than the helpees'.

Facilitative confrontation presupposes high levels of the other dimensions discussed. Confrontation without a solid relationship created through the communication of empathy, respect, warmth, and genuineness rarely is helpful. The caregivers also must have an accurate understanding of the helpee. The existence of a strong relationship gives the helpers permission to confront. The understanding increases the probability that the confrontation will be accurate and helpful.

Confrontation is wasted unless the helpee can use what is said. Indeed, confrontation can be very damaging and often threatening to the helpee, but a certain amount of anxiety can increase the chances that it will be useful because anxiety indicates that the confrontation has aroused emotions in the helpee. Guidelines such as the following about the conditions that regulate the intensity of confrontation can make it less intense and less threatening. The caregivers should:

1. Establish a good relationship of mutual trust and caring.
2. Precede the confrontation with responses rated at level 3 on the dimensions of empathy, respect, warmth, and genuineness.
3. Generalize, talking about people in general instead of the helpee specifically. This gives the helpee a chance to make it personal. A caregiver might say to the helpee, for example, "A lot of people I have spoken with tell me that they feel better about themselves when they do things for other people."
4. Build in some loopholes for the helpee by using such words as: sometimes, maybe, once in a while, often, you think you'd like to. For example, "It sounds like now and then you almost get the urge to fudge a little on your work." This makes it easier for the helpee because the helpers' manner is not accusative.
5. Use humor. This probably will fit in better when the other person is absorbing information to improve self-understanding than it will when confrontation is used in a disciplinary or enforcing situation.
6. Consider the spirit in which confrontation is employed. There is no justification for being punitive, vengeful, or hurtful.
7. Improve the attractiveness of their own lives. If caregivers are living their own lives in a way that others would like to imitate, it is easier for them to accept help.

There also are factors that can make confrontation more intense and threatening. The caregivers should:

1. Personalize, making it clear that they are talking about the helpee.
2. Specify events because a high level of concreteness forces the helpee to either accept or reject the accuracy of what the helpers say.

3. Deal with issues close in time. There is more threat involved in dealing with recent behavior than with something that happened a long time ago.
4. Deal with actions rather than words. If caregivers are talking about something the other person said, it is easy for that individual to say, "That is not what I meant." It is more difficult to rationalize behavior than it is to explain away words.
5. Use what the helpee has said or done earlier to contradict what the person is saying or doing now.

The intensity of confrontation must be strong enough for it to have an effect but not so strong that it causes the helpee to feel inadequate or unable to act constructively. Regulating the intensity requires the helper's best judgment. It is desirable to begin with gentle confrontation and raise the intensity gradually, as indicated by the helpee's progressive reactions.

If confrontation is too strong, several undesirable outcomes are possible:

1. The helpee uses defense mechanisms to build a wall against the caregivers, thus reducing constructive communication.
2. The helpee is driven away.
3. The helpee is angry and goes on the attack, which is likely to ruin caregivers' chances of helping.
4. The helpee pretends to accept the confrontation but actually ignores it.
5. The helpee feels helpless and seeks to become inappropriately dependent on the helper.

If the confrontation is too weak, the outcome also can be quite undesirable:

1. The helpee loses respect for the caregivers. The person may assume that the helpers don't really believe in what they are talking about or that they do not have the courage to speak up on behalf of their beliefs.
2. There is no effect. The helpee does not notice the purpose of the confrontation or else it goes in one ear and out the other.
3. The confrontation is so feeble that it actually reinforces the discrepant behavior. The confrontation is interpreted as if a caregiver had said, "I think that this discrepancy is really okay but I was obligated to say something to you about it as a mere formality."

If any of the effects listed under "too strong" or "too weak" confrontation occur, the action probably has not been useful. Above all, the helpee must sense that the helpers are being real, not playing games or being phony in the confrontation. As a general rule, it is wise not to confront unless the health care professionals have established a solid relationship with a person and plan to stay involved. On the other hand, confrontation is an essential element in many treatment situations. In such cases, the establishment of a helping relationship may be secondary to other demands.

## THE TWO TYPES OF CONFRONTATION

### Experiential

An experiential confrontation points out discrepancies that HCPs have noticed in their own personal experiencing of the helpee: (1) the helpee may be contradicting something stated previously, (2) the helpee's behavior may contradict the verbal expression, or (3) the helpee's experiencing of self may be different from the caregivers' experiencing of the individual. An experiential confrontation may refer to limitations (confrontation of weakness) or to resources (confrontation of strength).

### Didactic

In didactic confrontation, the caregivers provide the helpee with additional information concerning problems. They may point out helpee behaviors that are socially undesirable or fill gaps in the person's information about social reality. Another type of didactic confrontation occurs when helpers enforce a regulation or exercise some kind of social control over the helpee.

Some didactic confrontations deal with inappropriate helpee behavior. An example of a confrontation about social reality would be to say to the helpee:

> Perhaps you are not aware of this but when you are in a small group you talk rather loud—louder than most other persons. I think this is having an adverse effect for you. Many persons will get somewhat annoyed by the loudness even though they are interested in what you have to say. (Gazda, Asbury, Balzer, Childers, & Walters, 1977, pp. 162–164)

The levels of this action are identified in the confrontation scale (Exhibit 11–1).

**Exhibit 11–1** The Confrontation Scale

| Levels |  |
|---|---|
| 1.0 | The helper response does not allow consideration of helpee discrepancies by either explicitly accepting them, contradicting the person's expressed conflict, or ignoring the discrepancies, thus closing off possible fruitful avenues of investigation. |
| 2.0 | The helper does not explicitly point out or accept helpee discrepancies. In either case, possible useful areas of inquiry are lost. |
| 3.0 | The helper indicates discrepancies without pointing out the specific directions in which they lead. The caregiver is tentative in comparing diverging communication of the helpee. |
| 4.0 | The helper points out discrepancies of which the helpee has limited or no awareness. The caregiver also points out the specific directions in which these discrepancies lead, i.e., the HCP becomes evaluative regarding where they are taking the helpee. |

## Examples of Levels of Confrontation

*Case 1*

Nurse to colleague: "I'm about ready to give it all up. I just can't see how I can make a success of it. I've tried as hard as I know how, yet I'm not doing as well as I'd like to in my work. It's not enough for me to get high ratings from my supervisor; I also want to feel that I'm really doing something useful."

*Levels  Helper Responses*

1.0  1. "I'm really happy that you are getting high ratings."

*Discussion:* The helpee's conflict of feelings is completely ignored in this response and the helper appears to accept the discrepancy.

1.0  2. "You're getting good ratings, so that means that you are already successful."

*Discussion:* This contradicts the discrepancies felt by the helpee. The helper tries to sell the helpee on viewing accomplishments as successful when the person is in fact dissatisfied to the extent of considering them a failure.

1.0    3. "You don't seem to know when you are well off. If you can't be happy with high ratings, then you ought to quit."

*Discussion:* This response picks up on the discrepancy but is premature as well as punitive in the advice given.

2.0    4. "You feel dissatisfied because you are not getting enough from your work even though your ratings indicate that you are doing a good job."

*Discussion:* This does not fully and accurately express the helpee's conflict or discrepancy. The helpee does not view the ratings as a good indicator of success but the helper chooses to use them in that way.

3.0    5. "While you are succeeding by someone else's standards, your own deepest feelings tell you that you are failing."

*Discussion:* This is a tentative statement of the discrepancies felt by the helpee but without an indication of directions in which to move.

3.0    6. "You want to do more than achieve high ratings, but I haven't heard you describe what you are doing to make your work more meaningful."

*Discussion:* This response leaves the helpee free to consider what can be done to improve the situation.

4.0    7. "You are defeating yourself right now. You are rejecting high supervisor ratings as a sign of success and yet you have not made it clear to yourself just what will make work more meaningful to you. It's up to you to define your goals for yourself now."

*Discussion:* The helper offers another view of the helpee's problem. In this confrontation the helper is giving direction by describing what action should be taken to move toward a resolution of the conflict. The helper is taking a calculated risk here and the helpee may reject this confrontation. However, the helper has acted on a best judgment basis, i.e., the helpee is prepared for the confrontation. The helper has heard the helpee's plea for an undistorted, external evaluation of the conflict and has answered that plea. The helper still places the responsibility for appropriate action on the helpee.

### Exercises in Perceiving Confrontation

In the following case, several helper responses are given, with ratings for each one. Caregivers should try to understand why each response is rated as it is.

*Case 2*

HCP to a peer HCP: "I've lived and worked in this community all of my life but I really don't know anybody. I can't seem to make friends even here at the hospital. I try to be nice to other employees but I feel very uncomfortable inside and things just don't go right. Then I tell myself I don't care, people aren't any good, they're out for themselves, I don't want any friends. Sometimes I think I really mean it."

*Levels*  *Helper Responses*

1.0   1. "That's okay. Many people learn to live secluded lives."

     2. "You can join this club I belong to. We have a small group and need members. You'll make lots of friends and have great fun."

2.0   3. "You say that you try but you excuse yourself when you don't succeed in making friends."

     4. "You want to make friends yet you question whether it is worth the price you are paying."

3.0   5. "You're in a real bind. You want to make friends but you wind up excusing yourself when you don't succeed as you'd like to."

     6. "You say you try but it doesn't work out, but just what are you doing, or trying?"

     7. "You tell yourself you don't care but you still wind up feeling miserable inside."

4.0   8. "You're excusing yourself when you find it is difficult to go out to others. You know that you need and want others in your life. As long as you make excuses and don't act positively on what you want and need, you will feel this emptiness."

### Exercises in Responding with Confrontation

Caregivers should write responses to the helpee statements that follow. The answers should respond to the helpee's feelings and content. Predicates should be matched when possible; at the same time the response should be elevated to a level 3.0 confrontation.

1. Obese patient to HCP: "I really want to get out of this hospital so that I can get back to work. My bills are just piling up. My doctor is starving me in here and I don't see how I'll ever get my energy back this way."

*Response:* _____

_____

_____

_____

2. HCP to supervisor: "You don't treat me fair. I've only missed five days of work this month yet my rating by you was that I was not dependable. You know that I've improved a lot since I've started work here."

*Response:* _____

_____

_____

_____

3. Physician to nurse: "I ordered a change in Mrs. Riley's medication yesterday. She just told me that she is taking the same pills that we had been giving her. Let me see her chart!"

*Response:* _____

_____

_____

_____

4. Head nurse to administrator: "I know that this unit dose system for dispensing drugs is an improvement over our old system, but when you are as understaffed in nursing service as we are on this unit, we will just have to keep a supply of the more basic drugs in the nursing station so that we don't have to run down to the pharmacy for everything that we need."

*Response:* _____

_____

_____

_____

5. Head nurse in street clothes to nurse in street clothes: "Look, Mr. Smith, I'm aware that uniforms are now optional, but that doesn't mean you should never wear them. What did you do with yours, sell them?"

*Response:* _____

_____

_____

_____

6. Male nurse to male HCP: "It is really neat being the only male among all those good-looking nurses. I've had a date every weekend with a different one since I began working here. They treat me like something special. My work is really taxing, though; the female nurses always ask me to help when there is any heavy lifting or difficult work to be done."

*Response:* _____

_____

_____

_____

An example of communicating confrontation, in which a staff nurse complains to the head nurse about disorganized conditions on a ward, is presented in Exhibit 11–2.

**Exhibit 11–2** Protocol: Communicating Confrontation

SITUATION: A staff nurse approaches the head nurse with a complaint.

| *Helpee* | *Helper* | *Comments* |
|---|---|---|
| "This ward is so disorganized that no one can do a decent job. If I make a mistake it isn't going to be my fault." | "You're pretty upset with the organization of this ward. On the one hand you state your mistake won't be your fault, and on the other hand, you seem so upset that you will not be able to carry out your duties very well." | The helper first communicates a level 3.0 empathy response and follows with a level 3.0 confrontation of the helpee's discrepancy. |
| "When I work while I'm upset it is just a matter of time before I know I will make a mistake." | "You're worried that working under this kind of emotional state will lead to a mistake and you're fearful of the consequences." | The helper's previous confrontation appears to be accepted by the helpee, who moves toward greater acceptance of responsibility for making a mistake. The helper then gives a high level (4.0) response and refocuses on the helpee's feelings of fear. |

## IMMEDIACY

In Chapter 1 immediacy was described as what occurs between the helper and helpee. Its value or use in helping, especially in responding, is in the answer to the question posed by Carkhuff (1969): "What is the helpee really trying to tell me that he cannot tell me directly?" To answer that question and to respond more accurately with immediacy, the guidelines formulated by Carkhuff should be helpful as presented in summary form:

1. Helpers must be able to tune in to their own experiences in the helpee-helper interaction. They must then employ their interpretations to resist helpee distortions of the situation.
2. Helpers often must disregard the content of the helpee's communication and focus on the underlying message. The helpee may be having difficulty with self-expression because of not being able to understand the relationship with the helper.
3. Helpers should be able to step outside of interactions that appear to be directionless. They must be able to determine whether the helpee is taking an emotional or psychological rest or deliberately confounding the relationship to block the helpers' efforts.
4. Helpers should periodically evaluate what is going on in the relationship, whether it be positive or negative. They should be guided by the extent to which they are themselves modeling facilitative and initiating behavior.

The Immediacy of Relationship Scale (Exhibit 11–3) categorizes the ratings involving this subject.

### Examples of Levels of Immediacy

*Case 1*

Child patient to female HCP: "Mrs. Lincoln, you've been so good to me! You're just like my mom. I love you!"

*Levels   Helper Responses*

1.0   1. "Johnny, it's time for your medicine now. That's a good boy!"

*Discussion:* This response shows no attention to the immediacy dimension. The HCP ignores the child's attempt to communicate his caring. It is as though the response fell on deaf ears.

**Exhibit 11–3** The Immediacy of Relationship Scale

| *Levels* | |
|---|---|
| 1.0 | The helper actively discourages helpee attempts to deal with their interpersonal relationship. |
| 2.0 | The helper purposefully gives token recognition to helpee-initiated statements about their interpersonal relationship but postpones discussing it or dismisses it after having commented on it superficially. |
| 3.0 | The helper initiates discussion and/or responds to helpee-initiated discussion of their relationship. The helper's responses deal only with surface feelings about the relationship. |
| 4.0 | The helper and helpee initiate explicit discussions of their interpersonal relationship as it exists at the moment. |

2.0     2. "That's nice, Johnny. You are a nice little boy."

*Discussion:* Although the helpee's response is acknowledged, it is done somewhat superficially and with little personal involvement.

3.0     3. "Johnny, I'm pleased that you compare me to your mother, who is a very special person to you."

*Discussion:* The helper acknowledges the pleasure of being compared to the child's mother and thus in a general way deals with their interpersonal relationship. However, the helper immediately returns the focus to the child's mother rather than specifically focusing on their own relationship.

4.0     4. "Johnny, I'm pleased that I have been able to help you feel safe and loved here. It can be a frightening experience for someone as young as you are to be separated from his family and be in a strange place like a hospital. I want you to know that I love you, too, and that I will look after you when I'm here and that I'll ask Miss Jones and Miss Brown to look after you when I cannot be here."

*Discussion:* This response is rated as going beyond the helpee's feelings because this case hypothesizes that the child is grateful for the security and kindness shown by Mrs. Lincoln. She communicates her love for the child and in addition interprets some of the possible reasons for it. She also offers continued love and protection even though the child did not solicit it directly.

## Exercises in Perceiving Immediacy

In the following case, several helper responses are given, with ratings for each one. Caregivers should try to understand why each response is rated as it is.

*Case 2*

Patient to HCP: "Sure, you're always nice to me but you have to be; you're paid for it. It is part of your job."

*Levels*   *Helper Responses*

1.0   1. "Mr. Adams, it is time to take your medicine."

      2. "Mr. Adams, I don't have time to discuss our relationship just now."

2.0   3. "You feel that I'm not really being myself—sort of phony."

      4. "It's hard to accept kindness from others, isn't it?"

3.0   5. "I really do care about you. Sometimes I have a hard time communicating this. Perhaps that is why you question my sincerity."

3.0   6. "It is really important for you to be sure of my feelings toward you. It is kind of difficult for you to believe that I care about you just because you are you, apart from the fact that taking care of you is part of my job."

3.0    7. "You find it hard to believe someone could like you when they are paid to care for you. I could work elsewhere, but people who are ill need special care. I enjoy trying to give it and I benefit from their appreciation. I hope that you will discover that I am not phony."

4.0    8. "It sounds like you may have been hurt by showing your true feelings to someone. Now you have difficulty accepting kindness for fear of the price it may cost you. If I remind you of someone who has taken advantage of you or if I appear phony, I can only regret this state of affairs. Maybe I have tried harder to be nice to you because I've sensed your fear of me. I do genuinely care about you and I hope we can continue to be honest about our relationship."

## Exercises in Responding with Immediacy

Caregivers should write responses to the feelings and content of the helpee statements that follow. They should match predicates when possible and at the same time add to the response a level 3.0 of immediacy.

1. Patient to physican: "I don't want to appear rude, doctor, but it upsets me when you ask me all those questions at the same time that you're taking my temperature. You know I can't respond. All I can do is grunt, and that makes me feel like an idiot."

*Response:* ⎯⎯⎯⎯⎯⎯⎯⎯⎯⎯⎯⎯⎯⎯⎯⎯⎯⎯⎯⎯⎯⎯
⎯⎯⎯⎯⎯⎯⎯⎯⎯⎯⎯⎯⎯⎯⎯⎯⎯⎯⎯⎯⎯⎯⎯⎯⎯⎯
⎯⎯⎯⎯⎯⎯⎯⎯⎯⎯⎯⎯⎯⎯⎯⎯⎯⎯⎯⎯⎯⎯⎯⎯⎯⎯
⎯⎯⎯⎯⎯⎯⎯⎯⎯⎯⎯⎯⎯⎯⎯⎯⎯⎯⎯⎯⎯⎯⎯⎯⎯⎯

2. HCP to supervisor: "Look, Mr. Jefferson, you've been calling me 'boy,' 'hey you,' and everthing but 'nigger.' I can't demand that you like me but I can demand that you respect me as a human being."

*Response:* ⎯⎯⎯⎯⎯⎯⎯⎯⎯⎯⎯⎯⎯⎯⎯⎯⎯⎯⎯⎯⎯⎯
⎯⎯⎯⎯⎯⎯⎯⎯⎯⎯⎯⎯⎯⎯⎯⎯⎯⎯⎯⎯⎯⎯⎯⎯⎯⎯
⎯⎯⎯⎯⎯⎯⎯⎯⎯⎯⎯⎯⎯⎯⎯⎯⎯⎯⎯⎯⎯⎯⎯⎯⎯⎯
⎯⎯⎯⎯⎯⎯⎯⎯⎯⎯⎯⎯⎯⎯⎯⎯⎯⎯⎯⎯⎯⎯⎯⎯⎯⎯

3. Male psychiatric patient to psychiatric nurse: "You remind me of a girl that I was in love with. She was the best thing that ever happened to me. When I get out of here next week, could I call you?"

*Response:* _____
_____
_____
_____

4. Male adolescent patient to young female HCP: "I've really flipped over someone around here. Do you know who it is? You!"

*Response:* _____
_____
_____
_____

5. Patient to receptionist: "Look, miss, I've been waiting to be called for two hours. You have called everyone who came after me and I'm still waiting. Don't you like me?"

*Response:* _____
_____
_____
_____

The communication of immediacy is detailed in the protocol presented in Exhibit 11–4.

**REFERENCES**

Carkhuff, R. R. *Helping and human relations: A primer for lay and professional helpers,* (Vol. 1), *Selection and training.* New York: Holt, Rinehart & Winston, 1969.

Gazda, G. M., Asbury, F. R., Balzer, F. J., Childers, W. C., & Walters, R. P. *Human relations development: A manual for educators* (2nd ed.). Boston: Allyn & Bacon, Inc., 1977.

**Exhibit 11–4** Protocol: Communicating Immediacy

| SITUATION: A nurse goes into the room of a 26-year-old depressed, reticent woman who has cancer. The nurse sits down and initiates the conversation. | | |
|---|---|---|
| *Helpee* | *Helper* | *Comments* |
| | "Do you mind if I sit with you for a few minutes?" | Since the helpee is quite depressed, the helper initiates the interaction (level 3.0). |
| "It's okay. (Silence) Why are you sitting there?" | "You're not used to someone just spending time with you, but I really want to, if you don't mind." | The helper responds at a 3.0 level, then initiates the relationship in general terms (level 3.0 immediacy). |
| "No, I'm not. Everyone else comes in, does what they have to do, and leaves. I'm glad you're here." | "Yes, it's very uncomfortable for them. They don't know what to say to you. I hope you will feel free to talk about your feelings with me." | The helper shows high level empathy (4.0), then initiates surface level immediacy (3.0). |
| "And doesn't it bother you?" | "It is uncomfortable for me but I know others are even more uncomfortable talking with patients who are seriously ill and fearful of dying." | Here the helper shares a personal feeling and initiates explicit discussion of the relationship. (Level 4.0 response on immediacy). |
| "It is so hard to believe that I might be dying. I need desperately to talk to someone." | (The conversation continues as the helpee feels comfortable now sharing all her fears about dying.) | |

# Chapter 12

# Problem Solving

Preceding chapters have described and illustrated a system for interacting with helpees that facilitated them in exploring their concerns, which in turn helped them further understand themselves and their situations. With improved understanding and a commitment to change, the helpees can be better prepared to take more appropriate action and/or seek more appropriate direction for themselves. In other words, an essential process that lays the groundwork for problem solving in the action phase of helping has been presented. This is represented by the block in the lower right-hand corner of Figure 4–1 in Chapter 4. The protocol in Exhibit 12–1 illustrates this process and a problem-solving method that may be used with it.

The helpee/patient in this case is a 55-year-old male with chronic alcoholism who was admitted by his wife for detoxification. The patient has worked for 20 years as a bookkeeper for a manufacturing company. In the past three years he has been admitted for detoxification on four occasions, twice within the last eight months.

During his detoxification, the patient has been receiving tranquilizers and IVs for nutritional deficits. In the course of treatment he begins to confide in one of the nurses. The example resulted after several earlier interactions and led the patient and nurse to plan a program of action.

## THE MATRIX SYSTEM

As the conversation ended, the helper turned to the matrix system (Exhibit 12–2) for selecting a course of action from among several alternatives. This system was developed by Dr. Robert R. Carkhuff and is described in *The Art of Problem-Solving* (1973).

The Carkhuff matrix involves a systematic way of choosing the preferred course of action from among several alternatives. The helpee's value system

**Exhibit 12–1** Protocol: Communication in Problem Solving

| | |
|---|---|
| Helpee: | Each time that I've been in here I vowed never to return. Yet after medical treatment I feel better and go back to work and right back to drinking. |
| Nurse: | James, you sound disappointed in yourself for not being able to stick to your vows. |
| Helpee: | Yeah, I am. Now I see that I need more than what they can do for me here. |
| Nurse: | You see that you need a different kind of help or treatment than what we provide. |
| Helpee: | Don't get me wrong. I appreciate what all of you have done for me. I'd have been dead long ago if you hadn't treated me. But I just can't go on like this and keep my job and my marriage. |
| Nurse: | You're grateful for our help but you're worried that unless you can stop drinking you might lose your job and your wife. |
| Helpee: | My supervisor told me the last time that if I didn't straighten up he could not continue to cover for me while I sobered up, and my wife told me when I was admitted this time that she couldn't take it any more. I can't blame them for feeling the way they do. |
| Nurse: | So what it adds up to is that you may not get another chance with your job and your marriage and you feel frightened by the prospects. |
| Helpee: | Uh huh, it all seems so meaningless doing the same thing day after day and coming home to the same thing day after day. I'm not sure what it is all about. I'm just drifting. I don't have any drive or energy and life has lost its appeal. |
| Nurse: | You seem to be grasping for something to give you a purpose and some motivation to reverse your drifting. |
| Helpee: | Yeah, I've really got to get a handle on things and get my priorities in order but I don't know quite where to begin. |
| Nurse: | You feel strongly about coming to grips with your predicament and you appear to be ready to work out a solution if you just had a starting point. |
| Helpee: | Do you have any ideas? |
| Nurse: | Well, we could start with a systematic evaluation of some possible options open to you. |
| Goals: | |
| | 1. Improve interest in work and marriage |
| | 2. Stop drinking |
| | 3. Increase energy level and improve physical condition |

**Exhibit 12–1** continued

Courses of Action:
1. Find and join a logotherapy group
2. Join Alcoholics Anonymous
3. Begin marriage counseling and/or attend a marriage encounter week-end
4. Change jobs
5. Get a legal separation
6. Join a health spa
7. Seek vocational counseling

is considered concurrently with the proposed courses of action. The helpee is asked to list values (those that pertain to the problem) and then label them with any unit from 1 to 10, with the value of the greatest importance being given the greatest weight. (These are arbitrary units and some other unit could work equally well.) It is not necessary to use all weights, and some values may be weighted equally.

In addition to the values, the helpee and helper generate reasonable alternatives to pursue in order to solve the problem. These may be labeled "courses of action." These alternatives also are ranked by the helpee from a double negative to a double positive, i.e., $--$, $-$, $-+$, $+$, $++$, to indicate the degree to which that alternative will enhance ($+$ or $++$) or decrease ($-$ or $--$) movement toward the particular value in that row of the matrix. The numerical weight assigned to the value is then multiplied by the rating assigned to the alternative and the product is recorded in the appropriate cell. The helper and helpee under consideration here worked out the matrix.

**INTERPRETATION OF MATRIX**

Inasmuch as the nurse/helper in this case believed that many individuals with serious problems such as alcoholism required multiple interventions for the most potent form of treatment (Gazda & Powell, 1981), the helpee was encouraged to participate in as many options as he could. The helpee decided to pursue the three top alternatives immediately.

Before he was discharged, the helpee, with the aid of the consulting psychiatrist, had located a logotherapist and was being considered for a logotherapy group (where he could work on his problem of lack of purpose/meaning in life), and had joined Alcoholics Anonymous. He and his wife had an appointment with the hospital chaplain to return for marriage coun-

**Exhibit 12–2** Matrix System for Choosing a Course of Action

| Course of Action: | 1. Logotherapy Group | 2. AA | 3. Marriage Counseling | 4. Job Change | 5. Legal Separation | 6. Health Spa | 7. Vocational Counseling |
|---|---|---|---|---|---|---|---|
| **VALUES** | | | | | | | |
| Work (8) | + (+8) | + (+8) | + (+8) | + (+8) | − (−8) | + (+8) | + + (+16) |
| Marriage (10) | + + (+20) | + + (+20) | + + (+20) | + (+10) | − − (−20) | + + (+10) | + (+0) |
| Money (7) | − (−7) | − + (0) | + − (0) | − − (−14) | − (−7) | − (−7) | + (+7) |
| Self-discipline (8) | + + (+20) | + + (+16) | + (+8) | − (−8) | − (−8) | + + (+16) | − (0) |
| Purpose (10) | + + (+20) | + (+10) | + + (+20) | + (+10) | − + (0) | + + (+10) | + (+10) |
| Health (8) | + (+8) | + + (+16) | − (+8) | + − (0) | − (−8) | + + (+16) | + (+8) |
| | +69 | +70 | 64 | +6 | −51 | +53 | 41 |

Source: Adapted from The Art of Problem Solving by Dr. Robert R. Carkhuff by permission of Human Resources Development Press, © 1973.

seling on an outpatient basis. He also had acted on the sixth alternative—he had contacted a health spa and had been scheduled for a physical examination.

With more serious problems, such as alcoholism, the helpee usually is deficient in more than one life skill. In the case of alcoholism, the person typically will have problems regarding purpose in life, work, marriage, and physical condition. Simultaneous treatment in multiple life skill deficits, referred to as Multiple Impact Training (Gazda & Powell, 1981), is the preferred mode of treatment/training. Exhibit 1–1 in Chapter 1 provides the helper with a schema for diagnosis. The self-report questionnaire (Appendix C) can be used to assist helpees in determining their deficits/strengths in the basic life skill areas.

**REFERENCES**

Carkhuff, R. R. *The art of problem solving.* Amherst, Mass.: Human Resources Development Press, 1973.

Gazda, G. M., & Powell, M. Multiple impact training: A model for teaching/training in life skills. In G. M. Gazda (Ed.), *Innovations to group psychotherapy* (2nd ed.). Springfield, Ill.: Charles C Thomas, Publisher, 1981.

# Chapter 13

# Facilitative Communication

Up to this point, three characteristics of communication have been studied: empathy, respect, and warmth. Health care professionals have learned that these conditions may be present in, or absent from, responses given by a helper and have learned to include these conditions in each of their responses. When a helper response has all three conditions, it is termed a "facilitative response;" a series of facilitative responses is called "facilitative communication."

It is facilitative because it assists the helpees, making it easier to discuss the problem with the helper. It encourages such persons to explore their feelings about it, makes it possible for them to gain more understanding of it, and builds a base relationship between helper and helpee.

## KEY ANALYSES IN THE LITERATURE

Talbot (1968) presents evidence that greater input from the behavioral sciences is needed in medical education. He notes that one in 10 persons in society suffers from significant psychological or behavioral problems. He concludes that any professional person who must interact with, manage, and help consumers of health services should be at least minimally effective interpersonally. This would include skills in communication, i.e., listening and responding to others with understanding and concern. He states that most physicians, in dealing with patients' emotional problems, base their approach on their personal experience rather than on professional preparation.

Blum (1960) discusses the various skills related to the management of difficult patients. He emphasizes the need for skills on the part of physicians to build and maintain a facilitative doctor-patient relationship. He stresses the need for doctors to be concerned about maintaining good rapport and preventing patient dissatisfaction because that leads to therapeutic failures and to a host of unpleasant personal consequences for the physician. In summarizing the problems, he states:

> Here then are the bitter fruits of breakdowns in the doctor-patient relationship: treatment failures, patients quitting their doctors, the majority of citizens are critical of doctors and medical care, patients are not paying doctors' fees, and fast rising rates of malpractice suits (p. xiv).

Rusk (1972) discusses the need to go beyond physical complaints when providing care for patients. He emphasizes dealing with patients in a warm, understanding, and respectful manner. Only in this manner, Rusk says, can the physician hope to change patients' behavior and attitude toward an illness with no organic cause, but he notes that this relationship is not limited to cases of an illness with a nonorganic cause. He asserts that all patients need and deserve a relationship in which they are treated with warmth, understanding, and respect.

Travelbee (1971) develops a theme of nursing as a profession involving caring. She feels that all nurses can learn to establish and maintain helping relationships with others. She defines nursing as "an interpersonal process whereby the professional nurse practitioner assists an individual, family, or community to prevent or cope with the experience of illness and suffering and, if necessary, to find meaning in these experiences." She stresses the importance for nursing personnel to learn effective human relations skills. She states:

> If nurses do not change by becoming increasingly involved in caring for and about ill persons, it is believed that the consumers of nursing and medical care will demand the services of a new and different kind of health worker. This health worker or "ombudsman" will serve as the representative, interpreter, and spokesman for the ill human being and his family. (p. 2)

To summarize Travelbee's position, if nurses do not convey care, respect, and warmth toward patients, patients will demand new health professionals who will communicate these conditions to them. A better alternative is for nursing and related health care personnel to learn the skills being demanded, either during their training or on an inservice basis.

Kron (1972) discusses communication problems and needs in nursing. She emphasizes the importance of communication skills in nursing and discusses reasons why breakdowns occur and how they may be prevented. She defines communication as interpersonal relationships and states that "the basic aim in communication is to establish and maintain harmonious and productive relationships among people." According to her, the "lack of good communication is probably one of the greatest weaknesses in hospitals today." Disagreements occur between employer and employee, nurse and nursing assistant, and patient and hospital staff members—harsh words are spoken or implied, and feelings are hurt. Misunderstanding usually occurs, she says, because someone does not fully attend to what another person is communicating. Kron believes that patients usually suffer the most from this breakdown in communication.

Walsh and Yura (1971) point out that effective supervisory nurses are those who not only have greater skills and expertise in technical areas of nursing but who also have the ability to understand their own actions and those of others. In addition, they are able to express this insight or understanding in a helpful way to the persons concerned. Supervisory nurses must be sensitive to the ways people communicate with each other.

Here is an example of a conversation between a helpee and a helper in which the latter uses facilitative communication. This interaction is between a student nurse (helpee), reporting for the first time to the orthopedic floor for clinical training, to a nurse (helper) on the floor.

Helpee: "Well, here I am. I'm Doris Jones. I'll be here this week."

Helper: "Good morning. I'm Ms. Goodwin. We've been expecting you."

Helpee: "I'd be glad to help out in any way I can."

Helper: "Thanks. We're pretty busy, so we could use some help, but we won't work you too hard the first day."

Helpee: "I've really been looking forward to being on this floor—I think I'll enjoy it a lot."

Helper: "You have been viewing working in orthopedics as a real positive experience. I hope you do enjoy it."

Helpee: "I've enjoyed all the departments I've been in so far; everything is so interesting and the whole experience has been just wonderful."

Helper: "That's great. It makes all the difference in the world when you can feel comfortable during your clinical work. I guess you see some of just about everything that goes on around here."

Helpee: "Yes, at least I will by the time I finish training. That kind of worries me, though. If I had to decide between two jobs, I'm not sure I could make up my mind."

Helper: "I guess it is a hard decision to make, especially since several areas appeal to you. I have had experience in most phases of hospital work. Maybe we can take some time off and talk about different jobs before you leave this floor."

Helpee: "I'd like that. I hope we can."

In this interaction, Ms. Goodwin responded with empathy, respect, and warmth. What effect did this have on Doris? Apparently Doris felt at ease and sensed that Ms. Goodwin cared about her and would not in any sense be punishing to her. By the fifth time Doris spoke, she "opened up," that is, she revealed further feelings and concerns. She probably would not have admitted her uncertainty about her career if Ms. Goodwin had not allowed her to feel comfortable. Ms. Goodwin earned the right to offer additional help by giving facilitative responses.

Everyone has defenses that they use to protect themselves from being hurt. They may be thought of as walls of protection so that things other people say or do will not hurt. They usually are a healthy, normal mechanism of the mind and psychological system. At the same time, however, they form a barrier between persons. As long as this barrier is between one individual and another, the first person cannot fully know and understand the second and is limited in the extent of helping that individual.

This model of communication for helping tries to get helpees to take down defenses to the extent necessary for purposes of helping and for the improvement of their interpersonal relationships. The model seeks to provide conditions in which helpees can comfortably choose to lower their defenses. The intent is to provide conditions in which they can feel comfortable being themselves. If they can do so, they can reveal their true inner selves. Caregivers then can help them understand themselves better. The method for providing those conditions is to communicate initially with facilitative responses.

Other communication models propose that the helpers' role is to climb over or break down the helpees' walls of defense, even though this may make the latter uncomfortable or may occasionally result in considerable harm to some of them. In facilitative responding, caregivers follow the lead of the helpees. By reflecting the helpees' communication in a spirit of genuine caring, health care professionals do not add to the helpees' communication, but do contribute something vital to their experience— the experience of being attended to fully. This itself is very therapeutic.

With some individuals, the defenses are so strong and rigid that the helpees cannot lower them even though they try. It may be necessary, then, for helpers to use stronger methods of helping to remove barriers. In other instances the defenses should not be penetrated because the psychic balance of forces within the helpees is precarious. In such cases, the appropriate role of lay helpers is to support helpees in obtaining competent and adequate professional care.

## IDIOSYNCRATIC CREDITS

One of the fundamental precepts of this model is the establishment of a base relationship through facilitative communication before action dimensions are used. An exception to this rule involves helpers who have what is termed "idiosyncratic credit" with the helpee. Idiosyncratic credit means that the helpee grants privileges because of who or what the helper is.

There are four major reasons why idiosyncratic credit may be given to a particular helper:

1. Degrees, title, vocation: Labels such as nurse, doctor, president, judge, minister, attorney, coach, man-of-the-year, champion, palm reader can be factors. These all mean different things to different persons but each of them commands respect from many. With that respect they provide the opportunity for those who carry the label to become active with persons who respect them.
2. Common experiences: The phenomenon of giving credibility to and acting upon the suggestions of persons whose background is similar to one's own is well-established and partially accounts for success of self-help groups such as AA and Synanon.
3. Association: Being part of a team or organization that is respected enhances the respect given its members. Members of a professional health care team are given credit for extensive expertise and are granted privileges that persons outside the team do not have.
4. Reputation: Some individuals, because of their perceptual skills and good sense, become known as persons whose advice is worth taking and discover, perhaps to their own surprise, that others seek them out for their opinions. Some popular newspaper columnists, because of their acceptance by a wide readership, often are successful in giving advice abruptly and pointedly. Individuals who might say the same thing face to face might find themselves in a lot of trouble. A level 2.0 that is accepted and used by the helpee becomes a level 4.0 (see the Global Scale in Chapter 14). Idiosyncratic credits often make the difference of whether a response is level 2.0 or level 4.0.

Even though the base may be given initially, it ultimately must be earned. For example, an individual might go to an unknown physician on the strength of the person's M.D. credentials. The individual will grant the physician the authority once to apply that professional expertise as a result of the doctor's idiosyncratic credits. But the individual will not return unless satisfied with those professional services. The physician must earn future opportunities to help.

## THE USE OF QUESTIONS IN HELPING

One of the most prevalent forms of communication involves the use of questions. This method probably is more common among health care professionals than among the lay public because those experts often are diagnostically oriented. This section is included so that the health care professionals can evaluate themselves on their use of questions and can learn more appropriate ways to communicate when indicated. First, to be considered is when the use of questions is indicated in interpersonal communication, especially as it relates to the whole spectrum of health care services.

### Appropriate Use of Questions

#### 1. To Obtain Identification or Other Information

These data may involve case history information such as types of previous illness, diseases, inoculations, and surgery; or details necessary for the business office such as address, phone number, name of guardian, and insurance coverage. Even though the information appears to be rather straightforward, some of it could be embarrassing to the helpee.

For this reason the preferred method is to have the helpee complete the form to the extent possible before the helper checks it for completeness and accuracy. In many instances, even during a physical examination, open-ended questions that elicit spontaneous helpee self-disclosure may be preferred over direct questions that allow the person to weigh how to answer the question to please the helper the most, regardless of accuracy or authenticity.

#### 2. To Clarify

When the helpee is being vague or evasive, a well-placed question may be useful for clarification. The health care professional may be able to choose a word that best describes a vague feeling in order to test a hypothesis when a helpee is having difficulty describing the feeling. For example, the helpee may be asked if a pain in the chest is sharp, piercing, and localized, or dull and encompassing. Specificity is especially important in defining a problem and in describing a plan of action or steps to be taken in problem solving. (This is discussed under the concreteness dimension in Chapter 10.)

### 3. To Pinpoint

There are many occasions when a health care professional must be very specific about the information received from the helpee-patient. For example, during a physical examination the caregiver may need to know exactly when and where applied pressure produces pain. In case of emergencies, such as a potential delivery, it may be vital to know the precise time interval between labor pains. Direct questions probably are the best means of obtaining specificity of feedback.

## Inappropriate Use of Questions

Perhaps the greatest misuse of direct questions is the tendency to rely on them to carry on a conversation. The use of direct questions may have numerous deleterious effects on the relationship between a helper and a helpee. For example, such use may:

### 1. Create a Dependency Relationship

The use of direct questions places the helpee in a dependent relationship. The helpee assumes that the answers will lead to the helper's providing some kind of solution and therefore begins to expect more from the helper than from self. This is especially true when the helper gives good advice because it places the helpee in the position of seeking other experts (or the same one) when new problems develop.

### 2. Put Problem-Solving Responsibility on the Helper

When the helper assumes the role of expert by asking direct questions, this conveys to the helpee that if they are answered the caregiver will offer a solution. Unfortunately, the helper also begins to make a similar assumption and may wind up responding to this unspoken agreement even when it may not be in the best interest of the helpee. In this sense it is the helper's solution, and the helpee may or may not be able to apply the result to the problem. Obviously in certain medical situations the helper must assume the role of expert and prescribe for the helpee, but what is referred to here is not the same nature as a prescription or medical procedure.

### 3. Reduce Helpee Involvement in Solving the Problem

A helpee who becomes the passive responder to direct questions does not actively seek solutions and becomes lazy insofar as not taking the initiative in problem solving is concerned.

### 4. Reduce Helpee Acceptance of Responsibility for Behavior

Perhaps the greatest harm that can occur from the use of direct questions is the helpee's tendency to put the responsibility on the helper for behavior resulting from the problem solving. If the attempt at problem solving is successful, the helpee does not accept credit and if it is unsuccessful does not accept blame. The success of a democratic society depends upon people's assuming responsibility for their behavior. The tendency to rely on experts and/or to blame them for helpees' behavior therefore is ultimately self-defeating for helpees as well as for the system or society.

### 5. Reduce Helpee Self-Exploration

Frequent use of direct questions tends to interfere with the helpee's self-exploration in depth because the caregiver unwittingly has taken on this task. When the helper controls the direction of the problem-solving attempt, especially early in the process, the helpee is discouraged from volunteering what the person may think is relevant. Voluntary self-disclosure, if not hindered by frequent direct questions, is more likely to be related to the issues the helpee perceives to be important. Once the response set of helper questions followed by helpee answers is established, it becomes difficult to turn over the initiative to the latter.

### 6. Produce Invalid Information

Almost every direct question has within it what the preferred answer should be. Since most helpees want to be liked and respected by their helpers, they try to oblige by listening between the lines, seeking to determine what the caregiver wants to hear. When they give such responses, they may communicate information that is not entirely accurate. The helper thus begins to make diagnoses based on inaccurate information.

### 7. Produce Unrealistic Helpee Expectations

It is important for the helpee to have confidence in the helper but it is even more important that the individual develop self-confidence. The helper's use of direct questions often communicates the idea that all the helpee has to do to solve problems is to answer the questions and a recipe for a solution will be forthcoming. By being reactive during the interview phase of problem solving, the helpee does not learn how to assume the proactive stance necessary if the person is to follow through with a program of problem resolution.

## 8. Produce Helpee Resentment

Many helper questions are asked out of curiosity rather than because they have direct bearing on the situation. These probes generally create resentment within the helpee. It is difficult to build an interaction around questions because a helper rarely can ask more than a dozen relevant ones; therefore, the longer the interaction, the more likely that the questions will become progressively more irrelevant. Facilitative responses give something (empathy, respect, and warmth) to the helpee. They provide an atmosphere in which the helpee is comfortable. In contrast, questions demand something and therefore may be threatening to the individual. The helpee may fear being pushed into areas the individual is not ready to deal with, and respond only superficially or seek to shift the conversation to another topic.

## 9. Create a 'Lazy,' Inattentive Helper

A helper who feels that the helpee can always be asked for clarification of a statement or feeling often pays less attention to the person and thus misses many cues. In other words, the caregiver does not attend fully to the helpee and relies on the individual for assistance, thus falling into the role of the person who is supposed to be aided. The extent to which the helper has to ask questions is a benchmark of the degree to which the expert is in tune with the helpee or is, in fact, capable of assisting. The greater the number of questions, the less likelihood that the helper can assist.

These nine conditions relate to the helper's use of direct questions. Open-ended questions usually do not have the same effect because they encourage helpee involvement and self-exploration. Therefore, the potential helper should develop expertise in the use of open-ended questions and statements. Some examples:

Could you describe some things that you have considered doing?

What kinds of things have you tried?

I assume that you have considered a number of things that you could do.

What would you predict would happen if you tried _____?

I assume that you have some ideas as to the reaction if you tried _____.

In what other kinds of situations do you find yourself feeling_____?

Others on your shift must have similar reactions if _____is so demanding.

I wonder if this is something that *always* happens? (Or sometimes or never.)


## Effective Facilitative Communication

Facilitative communication, then, is preferred during the early stages of a helping relationship because it allows the helpee to be comfortable and to reveal the person's self to the helper. The discussion that follows reviews what facilitative responding is and does, and summarizes the major reasons why it is effective.

1. A facilitative response is one in which the helper verbally and non-verbally communicates that the professional has heard what the helpee said and is attempting to understand how the person feels.
2. The necessary components of a facilitative response are: (a) empathy—reflecting accurately and fully the helpee's surface feelings; (b) respect—communicating acceptance of the helpee as a person; and (c) warmth—showing attentiveness and caring through nonverbal behaviors.
3. A facilitative response is similar enough to the helpee's statement that the two could be interchanged. The helper's response communicates the content and affect of the helpee's statement with accuracy and equal intensity. The helper does not add anything to what the helpee has said but also does not leave anything out.
4. Facilitative communication begins with thorough listening, but listening and repeating by rote are not sufficient. Equally essential are the acts of reading the helpee's nonverbal messages, sending appropriate nonverbal messages while listening, synthesizing the communication received from the helpee, and making mental notes of important items or hunches for possible future use. The complexity of these tasks demands the most intense, conscious involvement and participation of which the helper is capable.
5. Facilitative responding provides a nonthreatening atmosphere in which the helpee feels fully accepted and feels free to self-express in any

manner the person chooses. In this atmosphere a relationship of mutual trust and caring can develop between helper and helpee. This is referred to as a base relationship because it provides a foundation upon which meaningful dialogue on significant personal matters can occur.

6. Facilitative responding puts a boundary around the helper's role. The process defines what the caregiver can do to be effective, and thereby identifies what is ineffective. The helper, then, is alerted to avoid inappropriate or premature behaviors such as judging, advising, imposing, criticizing, confronting, dominating, ridiculing, or belittling.

7. Facilitative responses assist the helpee in getting a complete and accurate self-picture. In a mirror, people can see things about their physical bodies that they cannot see otherwise. In a similar way, facilitative responses serve as a mirror of the helpee's psychic self. When the helpee's statements are reflected back, as an empathic response does, the person may "see" and/or "hear" those views more clearly. In so doing, the individual tests the validity of perception, memory, and judgment. The helpee muses, "Is that really true; really how I feel; really what I believe?" The individual may discover contradictions within those statements, or omissions in what the helpee has said or believes. The helpee may decide that some of those assumptions or expectations are unrealistic. Facilitative responding gives the helpee an opportunity to correct misstatements and to clarify matters not sufficiently explained to the helper. The experience of self-exploration leads to better and more complete understanding of the situation and of self, both of which are necessary prerequisites to growth and problem solving.

8. Most people rarely have the experience of being understood by another. How often do they know, without doubt, that a person they are talking with is giving them full attention? Facilitative responding is a way of demonstrating to another person that the caregiver is listening with full attention. This is one of the greatest compliments that can be given a person.

## EXAMPLE OF FACILITATIVE COMMUNICATION

The dialogue in Exhibit 13–1 is between a 19-year-old female nursing student (helpee) and a counselor (helper) in a mental health clinic. The helper's statements are facilitative—that is, they communicate high-level empathy by reflecting the helpee's surface feelings and the content of her

**Exhibit 13–1** Protocol: Facilitative Communication

| Helpee (19-year-old female nursing student) | Helper (mental health clinic counselor) | Comments |
|---|---|---|
| "I really don't know why I came to see you. I don't know why I'm here at all. The doctor over in physical health just said I should make an appointment at mental health. There's nothing wrong with me." | "You don't visualize yourself as having a mental problem." | Matching predicates. Helpee uses word *see*. Helper uses word *visualize*. |
| "No, I never have considered having any mental problem. I told him, I'm just having trouble staying awake in class." | "You feel like you're in the wrong department for your problem." | Reflection of content. |
| "Well, I don't know. He said it could be emotional, falling asleep in class; but I just don't know. I've only been falling asleep this quarter. Even when the class is interesting I can't stay awake." | "Oh, you've never had this problem before and you wanted to come talk to somebody about it." | Inaccurate reflection. |
| "Well, he told me to come here, I didn't think I needed to. He kind of thought it could be a family problem, because I've had some pretty bad family problems lately. But I can't understand why that would make me go to sleep in class." | "You can't see any relationship between the two." | Matching predicates. |
| "No, my family has always been fighting. I never have known any sort of good family life." | "You must feel that this is a physical rather than an emotional problem." | Goes beyond interchangeable response. |
| "I don't know. The last three of four days is the first time in my life that I've thought that there might be anything wrong with me mentally." | "You've had a difficult time with your family." | Goes back to previous response, misses present feeling. |

**Exhibit 13–1** continued

| | | |
|---|---|---|
| "Yeah, well, everybody in my family fights. We've never been able to have close relationships. My father and mother just got separated in September." | "And this problem of falling asleep in class just started this quarter." | Tries to relate onset of problem to parent's separation. |
| "Yeah, I never had any trouble until this quarter. You see, I'm a good student. I have a 3.5 average." | "You don't see that your mother and father's separation could have affected you this way." | Matching predicates. |
| "Well, I don't know. I think my father is better off, to tell you the truth." | "You believe it's better that your parents are separated." | Reflects content. |
| "Well, I kind of feel guilty on account of it, but I think they are better off. My father is sure happier." | "You feel you failed your parents in some way as a result of this separation." | Goes beyond an interchangeable response. |
| "Well, not really. My five brothers and sisters and I got together and decided that if that is what our parents wanted to do, we would try not to make them feel guilty about it." | "Still, this is a difficult time for you with your parents getting divorced." | Softens previous response when helpee doesn't accept it. |
| "Yeah, well they aren't divorced, just separated. My father has an apartment he's living in. I have a 17-year-old sister who has a nervous condition and I think it's because she has to live with my mother." | "Your brothers and sisters agreed on the separation but you don't feel like it was the best thing." | Goes beyond interchangeable response. |
| "Well, I don't know. I guess I didn't realize until I came to school that there were families that were really happy. Maybe that sounds strange, but that's the way it has been. My father is a pretty good guy. I think mother had a lot to do with the situation we are in now." | "You believe that your mother caused the unhappiness in your family." | Responds to content. |

## Exhibit 13–1 continued

"Some of it, anyway. Like with my 16-year-old brother who lives with her now. He has this terrible temper. In fact, the last time I was home his car wouldn't crank and he got out and hit the windshield with his fist and broke it. Now you know that's not normal. I think it has to do with living with her."

"You think that the younger kids would be better off living with your father."

Goes beyond interchangeable response.

"I'm not sure. He's an electrical engineer and he just opened his own business. He works all the time, but I think he works because he's all alone. I don't know how he could take care of them. But what can I do? I'm off at school."

"You haven't been able to do much to help them because you've been here at school. It sounds like you might be feeling some guilt because of that. Could that be?"

Goes beyond interchangeable response.

"Yeah. But then I shouldn't because I've never accepted one dime from them. I've worked every summer and saved money; I'm working now and paying my own way. I really shouldn't feel guilty but I do. Even when I don't go home on weekends I feel guilty about it."

"You feel like the family situation is causing your sister and brother some real problems and you should be there to help them."

Goes beyond interchangeable response.

"Yeah, but I don't know what I could do. I thought I could come over here and you could tell me what to do. I know I have never felt like this before."

"Are you close to your sisters and brothers?"

Asks irrelevant question.

"I'm closer to my sisters than my brothers. In fact, my sisters and myself are going up to visit my older sister this weekend."

"You're going to have a 'joint conference.'"

Reflects content.

**Exhibit 13–1** continued

| | | |
|---|---|---|
| "Well, I'd like to talk to them about it but my younger sister will be there and she has this nervous condition. I need to talk about that, but I know I can't talk about it in her presence." | "You would like to discuss this with them, but you don't want your little sister to get upset." | Reflects content in such a way as to tap into feelings. |
| "That's exactly right." | "You think she can't handle it because of her nervous condition." | Reflects content from previous statement. |
| "Well, I just don't think I should talk right in front of her about that." | "She couldn't take that. And you think this is what is causing her nervous condition, this family situation." | Reflects content. |
| "I think so. The whole family seems to be messed up, now that I'm outside looking at it." | "You feel that if you were back at home you could kind of balance the situation; you could give your brother and sister some of your time and attention." | Goes beyond interchangeable response. |
| "I don't know. When I think about things, I think about being away from them rather than with them. If I could have my way without feeling guilty, I'd rather be away from them." | "You wouldn't miss them?" | Reflects content with a question; open-ended. |
| "Not much. We're not very close. We never have been able to communicate. In fact, here at school I've never felt comfortable in a one-to-one relationship. I have this group, we run around together. There are six of us. Three guys and three girls. We don't ever pair off; I mean we don't even think how we would pair off if we wanted to. That kind of worries me too. Maybe that's something we could work on." | "You feel that you are different from other people because of your family situation." | Plays it safe on responding to "different" but doesn't attempt specificity. Doesn't encourage follow-up with support of her "maybe that's something we could work on." |

**Exhibit 13–1** continued

| | | |
|---|---|---|
| "Yeah, I do. I never have before but I do now. It's just really an odd family." | "Maybe if you talked to other students, who have had family problems, that would help." | Recommends a counseling group when, for the present, individual counseling seems most relevant. |
| "Maybe it would. I tried to talk to my roommate. She is the only person I have ever tried to talk to about this. I tried that last night but that wasn't very successful. I don't know where I could run into people like that." | "We have several small groups of students who get together once a week to discuss personal concerns. One group of six students centers their attention on family problems they each have. I meet with them, but the important thing is the caring for each other that takes place." (Helper goes on to explain the purpose of the group and invites the helpee to join the open-ended counseling group.) | |
| "I feel better just talking to you about it. Yes, it does sound like it would be a good experience to be in that group. I would like to." | | |

statement; they communicate acceptance of and belief in her (high-level respect); and they communicate caring (high-level warmth).

Caregivers should compare the helper's response with the helpee's preceding statement; in most cases it will be a paraphrase of the statement. It might be thought that this would slow down the conversation but it does not; in fact, it has the opposite effect. The example shows that the helpee volunteers extensive information without being asked for it, an indication that she feels comfortable talking with the helper.

Of interest is the helpee's movement toward greater understanding of her situation as the interaction progresses. This is the goal—providing conditions in which the helpee can use her existing skills and capacities and acquire new skills that will lead to resolution of her problems, increased personal satisfaction with life, and stronger resources for dealing with future conditions.

Attention should be paid to what is happening as the interaction proceeds. Health care professionals might ask themselves such questions as, "How did the helpee feel about that helper response? What relationship exists at this moment between helpee and helper? What, if anything, has changed since the beginning of the interaction?" Impressions and observations should be recorded in the column at right. Sample observations already have been inserted.

## EXPERIMENT IN HOLDING ATTENTION

This experiment demonstrates two of the reasons why facilitative responses are effective. The caregiver picks a simple object in the room, for example, a chair, table, or picture and asks someone to signal when 30 seconds elapse. The helper should concentrate on the object until the signal is given. This should be done before reading any further in this section.

Was the caregiver able to keep attention on that object continuously? Probably not. If the individual was like most people, other things crept into the person's thinking to distract from the task.

Being attentive is difficult even under simple experimental conditions, and most persons have a tendency to drift in and out of attention. If it is difficult for an individual as a helper, it probably is equally difficult for the helpee to maintain attention. Therefore, the caregiver should make it as easy as possible for the helpee to focus attention on what the helper is saying.

Facilitative responding does just that. It assists the helpee in keeping attention on what the caregiver says because: (1) it repeats the message in different words, and (2) it deals with what the helpee has just said, which is the subject of most importance to that individual at the moment. How can a helpee be anything but interested in what a helper says when talking about what is most important to the helpee?

**REFERENCES**

Blum, R. H. *The mangement of the doctor-patient relationship*. New York: McGraw-Hill Book Company, 1960.

Kron, T. *Communication in nursing*. Philadelphia: W.B. Saunders Co., 1972.

Rusk, T. N. How to help when the problem is not really physical. *Consultant*, 1972, *12*, 59–60.

Talbot, N. Concerning the need for behavioral and social science in medicine. In J. Knowles (Ed.), *Views of medical education and medical care*. Cambridge, Mass.: Harvard University Press, 1968.

Travelbee, J. *Interpersonal aspects of nursing*. Philadelphia: F. A. Davis, 1971.

Walsh, M., & Yura, H. Super-vision. *Supervisor Nurse*, 1971, *2*, 19–23ff.

# Chapter 14

# Rating Facilitative Communication

The study of empathy, respect, and warmth used simple systems for rating the extent to which the helper was communicating that particular condition. This chapter presents another system for rating helper effectiveness, the Global Scale, which has four levels. This scale requires the helper to put it all together in the sense of being aware of the communication of empathy, respect, and warmth simultaneously.

Exhibit 14–1 summarizes the characteristics of communication at each level of the Global Scale. Communication at levels 1 and 2 includes the Ineffective Communication Styles given in Chapter 15 as examples of poor and damaging communication. Level 3 is the facilitative response covered in Chapter 13. The fourth level is introduced in this chapter.

The Global Scale defines each of the levels. Users should read the scale, then the examples that follow that illustrate each of the conditions defined by the four levels.

## ILLUSTRATION OF THE GLOBAL SCALE

*Example Case*

Female HCP to coworker: "I'm really in a bind for money. It looks like every time we get ahead, something happens and we have to spend all our savings. It really is beginning to bother me a lot—always having to skimp, having to go without things that everyone else has. I like my job here, and I like the people I work with, but it looks like I'll have to find a better paying position pretty soon."

*Levels   Helper Responses*

1.0     1. "Mary Foster quit last week and took a job in an insurance office. She's making $100 a month more than she got here, and it's easier work."

**Exhibit 14–1** The Global Scale for Rating Helper Responses

---

*Level 1*

**Not Helpful: Damaging** (Makes the other person sorry to even have talked with the helper.)

A response in which the helper:

ignores what the helpee is saying,
ridicules the helpee's feelings,
seeks to impose personal beliefs and values on the helpee,
dominates the conversation,
challenges the accuracy of the helpee's perception,
communicates absence of warmth nonverbally,
or uses problem-solving dimensions in a way that damages the relationship.

*Level 2*

**Not Helpful: Ineffective** (Slows down the conversation; other person plays it safe.)

A response in which the helper:

communicates a partial awareness of the helpee's surface feelings,
gives premature or superficial advice,
responds in a casual or mechanical way,
reflects total content but ignores the feelings of the helpee,
offers rational excuses for withholding involvement,
fails to communicate warmth nonverbally,
or uses problem-solving dimensions in a way that impedes the relationship.

*Level 3*

**Helpful: Facilitative** (Encourages the other person to say more.)

A response in which the helper:

reflects accurately and completely the helpee's surface feelings (empathy),
communicates acceptance of the helpee as a person of worth (respect),
and clearly communicates warmth nonverbally.

---

**Exhibit 14–1**  continued

*Level 4*

**Helpful: Additive** (The other person learns more about self and becomes more able to implement self-help in the future.)

A response in which the helper:

accurately perceives and responds to the helpee's underlying feelings (empathy),
demonstrates a willingness to be a helper (respect),
intensely communicates warmth nonverbally,

or

appropriately uses one or more of the transition or action dimensions to:

assist the helpee to move from vagueness to clarity (concreteness),
reveal the helpee's perceptions in their entirety (genuineness),
describe similar experiences and feelings (self-disclosure),
point out discrepancies in the helpee's words and/or actions (confrontation),
or talk about present feelings between self and helpee (immediacy).

*Discussion:* This response is rated low because it ignores the helpee and what she has said about her situation. The response is irrelevant. It is as though the helper had said, "I don't want to talk about what is happening to you; let's talk about something more pleasant."

1.0    2. "Don't talk like that. Things have always worked out for you eventually."

*Discussion:* This ridicules the helpee's feelings. It is just as though the helper had said, "There is something wrong with you because you feel that way."

1.0    3. "Oh, you should stay here. After all, having the opportunity to serve others is more important that what you are paid."

*Discussion:* The helper seeks to impose personal beliefs onto the helpee. A helper does not have to agree with every helpee or need to ignore personal values; at the same time, those values should not be imposed on another, and it generally is not productive to discuss differences in values until a base relationship is established.

1.0    4. "We had the same situation several years ago. We were living in a house trailer and it burned down. We couldn't get anything out of our insurance company. We had to live in an expensive apartment we couldn't afford. Then my husband broke his leg and was out of work. We had to go live with my parents. Then . . ."

*Discussion:* This person wants to be the center of conversation. At the slightest opportunity, the would-be helper launches into a long history of personal experiences.

1.0    5. "You're really not so bad off. You have as much money as anyone here."

*Discussion:* This is rated low because it challenges the helpee's perception of the situation. Whether true or not, the helpee believes it probably will be necessary to change jobs. The helpee may hear this response as saying, "What your eyes and ears are telling you is not true. I know more about what is happening to you than you do."

1.0    6. "You talk about skimping and then almost in the same breath you talk about taking the family out to eat in fancy restaurants. That doesn't make sense."

*Discussion:* This response uses the problem-solving dimension of confrontation prematurely. If this information is part of the problem, the helpee probably knows it and will only be agitated to have it pointed out. This response probably would result in termination of the relationship and leave a residue of bad feelings.

2.0    7. "That's too bad. I guess you're upset."

*Discussion*: This is rated 2.0 because it communicates only a partial awareness of the helpee's surface feelings. "Upset" is an accurate affective discrimination but it is incomplete. The helpee is saying more than that.

2.0    8. "I'd hate to see you leave. I don't know what to tell you since it's such a complicated decision."

*Discussion*: This is a polite attempt by the helper to decline to enter a helping relationship. For some reason the helper does not desire to communicate with the helpee and effectively terminates the interaction by claiming incompetence to handle such a complicated matter.

2.0    9. "Have you thought about getting a loan from the credit union?"

*Discussion*: This response gives premature advice. A suggestion such as this is simply hit or miss at this early stage of the interaction. The response really is saying what the helper might do in that situation. This action might be completely inappropriate for the helpee. Usually the helpee also will have thought of the alternatives that the helper presents off the top of her head.

2.0    10. "Oh, I'm sorry to hear that. I do hope things get better."

*Discussion*: This response is rated level 2.0 because the helper replies in a way that sounds mechanical. It is something that takes no investment of the helper's self to say, and it actually means little because it is so general.

2.0    11. "You can't get ahead and stay ahead so you need to get a better paying job somewhere else."

*Discussion*: This response reflects only content, with no mention of feelings. The helper might have heard all of what the helpee said but communicated only the content and none of the affect.

2.0    12. "Well, sometimes things get worse before they get better. Right now you are on the low end of things. A lot of people here feel like you do but we just have to put up with it."

*Discussion*: This uses the problem-solving dimension of concreteness at an ineffective level; that is, the helper is not concrete. The response is abstract and uses worn-out generalizations. The helper's communication is the opposite of concrete. This makes it more difficult for the helper to clarify her feelings and ideas.

2.0    13. "I went through the same thing last year, but after I thought about it for a while, I decided it wouldn't be worth it. We have some pretty good fringe benefits here."

*Discussion*: This uses the problem-solving dimension of self-disclosure in an ineffective way. Although it responds to what the helpee has been talking about, it puts the attention on the helper. This will discourage the helpee from continuing and thus will impede the interaction.

3.0    14. "It's pretty upsetting when you are never able to get ahead financially. You're uncertain whether or not you should stay. You might have to find a job that will provide a little more money."

*Discussion*: This response is rated 3.0 because it is accurate and completely reflects the helpee's surface feelings. The helper is communicating to the helpee, "I am attempting to understand what you are feeling," without acting on a first impression. The helpee is being listened to and responded to from "where she is" at the moment. When the helpee feels that she has been clearly heard and accepted as she is, she will be likely to volunteer to pursue the issue in greater depth.

The Global Scale demonstrates that at level 3.0 the response includes minimally helpful levels of empathy, respect, and warmth. But, just as there are many ways to give damaging and ineffective responses (levels 1.0 and 2.0), there are several ways to give additive responses (level 4.0). An additive response goes beyond what the helpee has expressed—it adds to the helpee's store of self-information and information about the relationship with the helper and other persons.

In the level 4.0 response the helper shares something of self with the helpee. The first kinds of additive information that the helper uses are the higher levels of the facilitative dimensions; in other words, the helper responds with level 4.0 empathy, respect, or warmth. Examples of responses of the level 4.0 facilitation variety appear in this chapter; the other types are explained in Chapters 7, 8, and 9.

The facilitative response (level 3.0 on the Global Scale) is the preferred level of responding during an early portion of an interaction, as explained in Chapter 13. An additive response always should be preceded by at least one facilitative reply. In the case of an initial response at level 4.0 (such as examples 15–17 that follow), it first must contain a good level 3.0 statement followed by one with level 4.0 empathy, respect, or warmth.

In an extended interaction it may not be possible to identify each of the facilitative dimensions in every 4.0 response but they should have been present in the context just prior to the additive material. It is rare that a helper will attempt to give a level 4.0 response as the initial reply to a helpee's first statement. Thus, the following responses probably would not be used at this stage of the relationship. (The additive portions are italicized.)

4.0    15. "Never being able to get ahead and stay ahead financially is a strain. You have to skimp, and then every time you get ahead you get set back. You feel pretty discouraged about it all right now. *I get the idea, too, that maybe you're feeling like a failure as a manager of your money—that you can't manage as well as other people can.*"

*Discussion:* This response is rated level 4.0 because it gives back all that the helpee had stated, and more. The first two sentences are level 3.0; the last sentence suggests a possible underlying feeling, which is level 4.0 empathy.

4.0    16. "You are having to struggle to get along financially. That's bad enough, but on top of that, now it looks as though the financial situation may be pushing in on you in another unpleasant way—you may have to quit this job you like to get one that pays more. *It sounds as though you might be asking yourself, 'Why does it have to be this way? Why me?'*"

*Discussion:* Again, the response is rated level 4.0 because it contains the facilitative dimensions at level 3.0 plus one of them (in this case, empathy) at level 4.0. A comparison of responses 15 and 16 shows that different underlying feelings have been suggested. Since one of the two is likely to be more accurate than the other, the risk implicit in level 4.0 responses is obvious. When the helper inaccurately suggests an underlying feeling, the flow of communication with the helpee usually is restricted or retarded; when underlying feelings are perceived and expressed, the understanding and flow of communication usually is increased.

4.0    17. "It sounds like you are under a lot of stress about this, and at this point there is a lot of uncertainty about the outcome. *I'm not sure whether this is something you want to talk about more, but if you would like to, I would be glad to spend some time with you.*"

*Discussion:* This response is rated level 4.0 because it includes 4.0 respect in addition to level 3.0 empathy and warmth.

## RATING HELPER RESPONSES ON GLOBAL SCALE

It is very important to be able to distinguish between levels of communication. The ability to perceive such differences is a prerequisite to responding appropriately. The next four cases involve a number of responses. Health care professionals should study them until they can distinguish readily between the levels. It should be remembered that written responses can be open to varying interpretations, based upon the absence of intonation and other nonverbal factors; thus, there may be disagreement over some.

*Case 1*

HCP to HCP: "Dr. Short jumped all over me in the O.R. this morning. He asked for a hemostat and I handed him a forceps. I guess I'm just dumb."

*Levels   Helper Responses*

1.0    1. "Oh, you know better than to say anything like that. You're one of the smartest nurses around here."

   *Discussion:* This response challenges the accuracy of the HCP's perception.

1.5    2. "Don't feel bad. He treats everyone that way."

   *Discussion:* No harm is intended but the response nevertheless is between hurtful and ineffective.

2.0    3. "If you keep your instruments laid out properly, it's a big help."

   *Discussion:* This response is superficial advice.

2.0    4. "The surgeons have all that training and they are so knowledgeable that when they make you feel dumb, you just accept it and you begin to believe it's true."

   *Discussion:* This generalizes rather than personalizes.

2.0    5. "Tensions run pretty high in the O.R. People pop off when they don't need to."

   *Discussion:* This is a casual or mechanical response.

3.0    6. "It must have been embarrassing to make a mistake like that. Especially since the doctor became angry."

   *Discussion:* This response is facilitative in that it includes feelings and content.

3.5    7. "It sounds like it was extremely unpleasant, not only when it happened but also now, as well."

   *Discussion:* This also is facilitative but goes slightly beyond what the helpee said.

*Case 2*

HCP who is about to transfer to another unit, talking with another HCP: "Next week I'll be in pediatrics. I'm really looking forward to it. I've been told the staff is just wonderful."

1.0    1. "Have we been so bad?"

*Discussion:* This ignores the communication from the helpee.

1.0    2. "I thought we'd been pretty nice."

*Discussion:* This response ignores what the helpee is saying.

2.0    3. "I hope things work out well for you."

*Discussion:* This is a casual or mechanical response.

2.0    4. "I hope it is as pleasant as you expect it to be."

*Discussion:* This lacks a feeling word.

3.0    5. "It's really great to have that to look forward to."

*Discussion:* This is a facilitative response in which feelings are communicated by equaling the intensity of the helpee.

4.0    6. "You're always enthusiastic about what you do, aren't you? It's not just this but it's your basic attitude toward life."

*Discussion:* This is facilitative but it goes slightly beyond what the helpee said.

4.0    7. (Hugging helpee) "They'll like you, too, just as we have. Your enthusiasm around here has been a lot of fun for us."

*Discussion:* This response is additive—level 4 warmth.

4.0    8. "You are quite excited about what you will be doing next week. I guess it is sort of reassuring to hear good reports from others about their experiences in that department."

*Discussion:* This response also is additive—level 4 empathy (reassuring).

*Case 3*

HCP in pediatrics to another HCP: "The nicest thing happened to me today. Karen, the little girl in 401, named her doll Connie, after me. It's really fun to have a patient who likes you that much. It's unusual, too."

1.0    1. "I thought she went home yesterday."

*Discussion:* This ignores what the helpee said.

1.0    2. "Yeah, I know what you mean. I had two dolls named after me in one week. I'll never forget that."

*Discussion:* Helper dominates the conservation.

1.0    3. "That's a good sign. It means she is feeling better. Maybe she'll be able to go home soon."

*Discussion:* This ignores what the helpee said.

2.0    4. "Yes, that's really nice. Is this the first time this has happened to you?"

*Discussion:* This response lacks a feeling word.

2.0    5. "That's great. You've done a lot for her and she responds with this symbol of her affection for you."

*Discussion:* This is a good response but lacks a surface feeling word.

3.0    6. "It sure is nice when that happens. You know you are doing something right when a patient does something like that."

*Discussion:* This is a facilitative response that communicates feelings and content.

3.0    7. "Yes, it gives you a great feeling to find out that you're doing a good job and that it's appreciated."

*Discussion:* This also is facilitative, communicating both feelings and content.

4.0    8. "It's so much fun when something like this happens. You wish every patient could be that nice. You wish it could happen like this more often."

*Discussion:* This response is additive—level 4 empathy.

*Case 4*

HCP to supervisor: "Working for you is a real pleasure. One of the things I admire about you is that you do not hesitate to jump in and help any of us when we are in a bind."

1.0    1. "Oh, I'm not that different from the other supervisors around here. It's just a matter of who you get used to."

*Discussion:* This ignores the helpee's communication.

2.0    2. "I know how you feel when the workload is heavy because I have been in your situation and know what it can be like."

*Discussion:* This lacks a feeling word.

2.0    3. "It sounds like you have had a bad experience with supervisors in the past and that makes your experience here just that much better."

*Discussion:* This also lacks a feeling word.

3.0    4. "Thank you for the compliment. I hope we can continue to work together as an effective team."

*Discussion:* This is a facilitative response that equals the helpee's intensity.

3.0    5. "It's a nice feeling to receive a compliment like that. Thank you."

*Discussion:* This also is facilitative and includes feeling and content.

## EXAMPLES OF GLOBAL RATINGS

The helpee, an HCP, invited another HCP to eat lunch with her. She chose a table for two in a corner of the cafeteria. After some casual conversation, she leaned closer to the helper and, in a confidential tone, began to speak (Exhibit 14–2).

## INEFFECTIVE AND EFFECTIVE INTERACTIONS

Protocols are included (Exhibits 14–3 and 14–4) to illustrate ineffective helper responses followed by the same helpee/helper situations in which the caregiver effectively uses the dimensions of a helping relationship described in this manual. The different effects that the various levels of helper responses have on the helpee should be compared. The discussion sections of each protocol focus attention on the significant elements of the interactions. Examples for further study are included in Appendix E.

**Exhibit 14–2** Protocol to Illustrate Global Ratings

| Helpee | Helper | Discussion |
|---|---|---|
| "I haven't said anything about this to anyone, but Bob and I are having a terrible time. He is in college and it seems like we never have any time together any more. He's in class all day and studying or at the library every night. I have to go to bed early since I got changed to first shift and have to be at work at 6:30. I don't know what to do about it." | "It makes a lonely life for both of you. Your job and his school work keep you apart. You're wondering what you can do to change this undesirable situation." | This response is rated level 3.0. |
| "Yes, I want to change it, but there doesn't seem to be a way. He has to keep up with school and I have to work. I tried to change shifts but I couldn't. I'd do anything to help our marriage." | "You've thought a lot about solutions, but it seems to you that there's no answer. You really feel stymied." | This response is rated 3.0. |
| "There has to be an answer. Bob and I are getting to be like strangers." | "You're growing apart. If things keep going as they are, you could end up with no marriage at all. Yet you feel powerless to change it. You feel like you're about to panic." | This response is rated level 4.0 because it communicates the helper's perception of underlying feelings, described in words "powerless" and "panic." These represent emotions that the helpee had not verbalized but were implied in what she had said. It is important to be as accurate as possible when communicating underlying feelings. |
| "Yeah, I get an overwhelming feeling that time is running out on our life together." | "You've tried every single avenue that you can think of?" | This response is rated level 4.0 because the helper is attempting to get the helpee to be more concrete (specific). This statement serves to ask the helpee to review what she has done to this point. This makes it possible for the helper to pursue productive leads and avoid alternatives that the helpee already has rejected. |

**Exhibit 14–2** continued

| | | |
|---|---|---|
| "Well, maybe I haven't tried everything. But I tried to get on evening shift and couldn't. Of course, Bob can't change his schedule, and I can't just quit working." | "I can't help feeling that maybe there are other things you could do, that there are other options for you." | This response is rated level 4.0 because of the high level of genuineness. The helper communicates her in-depth perception that the helpee is not doing all for herself that she might. |
| "I just don't know . . ." | "Every marriage is different, so what worked for Roy and me might not be exactly right for you, but I remember going through circumstances something like what you describe in the early years of our marriage." | This response is rated level 4.0 because of the helper's appropriate use of self-disclosure. Note that the helper allows for the possibility that individual circumstances may be different. She also tests the helpee's interest in hearing some more about her experiences. |
| "Really? I didn't think *you* ever had any problems." | "Oh yes, when Roy first started his business he worked 16 hours a day. I found that by learning more about what he was interested in, I could share more of his world, and this helped us become closer." | The helpee feels less isolated, learning that she is not the only person in the world who has had that problem. It encourages her to learn the strong person she picked out as a helper had survived the same problem. Again, level 4.0 because of self-disclosure. The helpee has shown interest so the helper continues. |
| "Well, I don't know much about what Bob does. He's studying finance, and that's so complicated." | "You're right about its being complicated. But I noticed in the paper that the bank is offering a short course about investments. It's especially for wives, to explain things in simple terms. There is no charge, and it's in the evening. It might mean a lot to Bob for you to make that move toward understanding his interests a little more." | This response is rated level 4.0 because the helper gives useful information that the helpee does not have. At this stage in helping, the problem is defined clearly enough for specific actions suggested by the helper to have a high probability of being accepted by and useful to the helpee. |

**Exhibit 14–2** continued

"Oh, I just couldn't do that. I'm afraid I couldn't learn all that stuff."

"You say you'd do anything to help your marriage. Here is one thing you could do but you don't want to do it. That makes me wonder."

This response is rated level 4.0 because it points out discrepancies in the helpee's words. The helpee has given contradictory messages to the helper, who takes the opportunity to point it out to her.

"I see what you mean. Maybe I haven't been willing to do all I could. Would you help me look into this bank thing?"

"Sure. This isn't going to solve your problems completely but it's a step in the right direction. At least it's something worth trying. You know, it makes me feel good that you wanted to talk to me. I'm glad that we have been able to accomplish something. I'll be interested in knowing what happens."

Confrontation generally is uncomfortable for the helpee since inconsistencies are brought to recognition. That is why it is necessary to establish a strong base relationship before confronting. The base relationship serves to support the helpee during the discomfort of confrontation. In this case the helpee was able to accept the information. The latter part of this response is rated level 4.0 because of the use of immediacy. The last sentence increases the likelihood of the helpee's implementing what she has learned during this interaction.

"I feel better about things. Thanks for listening and talking. It's been a big help. You've made me realize there are more things I can do to help myself than I thought."

The measure of success of a helping interaction lies in the helpee's subsequent behavior. The helpee's closing communication indicates that this interaction probably has been helpful.

## Exhibit 14–3 Protocol: The Ineffective Helper

| Patient (a 45-year-old female helpee) | Female Nurse (helper) | Discussion |
|---|---|---|
| "I'm glad you came in. I'm really feeling down. I'm miserable. Just lying here in pain, wasting my time." | "Is there something I can do to help you rest more comfortably? Yesterday you thought a small pillow under your back felt better." | This statement is taken as a request for action, and a particular action is suggested. There is no response to the affect. |
| "Well, thank you for offering, but that wouldn't change things. I'm as comfortable as I can be right now. What's really got me upset is that I take all these tests but still the doctor isn't coming up with anything helpful. He came in about an hour ago and said he can't find any reason for it. That's what's really got me upset." | "You know, your back is a very complicated part of your body and it's not at all unusual for diagnosis to be difficult. The doctor is doing everything that can be done." | There is a definite request for listening in the helpee's statement but the helper chooses to ignore the feelings and respond in a general, vague way that deemphasizes the severity of the helpee's expressed concern. |
| "But that's not enough. I came to the hospital to get help, not excuses. The doctor has run all those tests and hasn't found anything. Now it's almost as if he was telling me my back shouldn't be hurting. How can he say that when I can hardly walk?" | "I know you're in pain and I'm sure he knows and cares about that, too. He doesn't have all the results from the tests back yet. You know the radiologist hasn't yet looked at yesterday's x-rays." | Without knowing what the doctor has told this patient, the nurse seems to be trying to reassure her and thus terminate the interaction. The reference to the pain is communicated in a mechanical way. |
| "Really?" | "He's going to do that later this morning." | Communicates "I can't tell you any more until later when the results of the tests come back." |
| "I wonder why the doctor himself didn't tell me that. He was asking me about emotional problems and, you know, he's got a lot of nerve. Nobody in my family has ever had mental problems." | "He has to explore all possibilities." | A serious concern on the part of the helpee has been verbalized in spite of the prior ineffective responses. Again, however, the helper ignores these and responds in a trivial way. |
| "That's not a possibility." | "You wouldn't want him to overlook something that might be important." | The helper does not communicate that she heard the helpee. She denies the accuracy of the helpee's perception. |

## Exhibit 14–3 continued

"I don't want him to insult me, either. Do you know a better doctor? Better than he is?"

"He's the best in the city. He has an excellent reputation."

The helper is now on the defensive and is far away from what the patient is really trying to communicate.

"I'm lying up here in the bed and he's telling me there's nothing wrong with my back. I think I ought to get another doctor."

"Maybe you don't realize this, but people come from all over the state to be treated by Dr. Bordon. He's excellent in his field."

A continuation of the defensive nurse communication. This attempt to establish the doctor's reputation will not make the patient's back feel any better.

"Not in my book. You never heard anybody say that their back problem was all in their head, have you? That's ridiculous."

"Yes, I've seen that many times. That is not at all unusual. You'd be surprised if you knew how many persons in this hospital are here just to have their imagination treated."

The patient is scared and the nurse is simply reinforcing the fear. This information is certainly appropriate, but in the present context it is premature.

"You sound just like the doctor."

"Actually, there's nothing at all to be embarrassed about because of the doctor's questions. He's very thorough and if he's asking you about something you can be sure that there are good reasons for it. He has had a tremendous amount of training."

The patient is communicating, "I didn't get any satisfaction from the doctor so I thought I would talk to you. You are no more help than he was and now I feel worse than ever." The nurse again tries to establish the doctor's reputation.

"I've heard about persons who were put away in mental institutions just because the doctor got it set in his head that there was something wrong with them mentally and really it was something else entirely. They get sent away and never come back."

"You surely don't think that is going to happen to you, do you?"

The patient expands on her fear and again the helper ignores it. Her response is in disbelief to something that is very real to the patient.

"Well, I can't move. I can't defend myself. I'm lying here in bed and can't move and the man is telling me I'm crazy."

"Did he actually say that?"

Again discrediting the helpee.

## Exhibit 14–3 continued

"Well, he could have said it. He might as well have said that. He said, 'Have you ever had any emotional problems?' I know what that question means; he thinks I'm crazy."

"You see, that's a routine question. Almost all the doctors ask that question of almost all of their patients. You don't need to feel that you have been singled out because he asked that question."

This is appropriate information to give and should serve to ease the patient's mind. The nurse appears capable of handling technical material but she lacks perception of feelings.

"Well, that makes me feel a little better, at least. I was afraid that he was going to say I've got to go see a psychiatrist, or have one come to see me."

"I imagine that if he thinks that would be worthwhile you'd want to do what he suggests, wouldn't you? After all, you came here for expert treatment and if that's part of it I expect you'd want to take advantage of it. Doctor knows best."

The nurse is responding as if she has won this battle. And it is a battle that comes across as a very strained conversation. She could as well have said, "Nurse knows best."

"You know as well as I do, if I talked to a psychiatrist everybody in town would know about it before I got home."

"Oh, everything that happens here at the hospital is kept confidential, especially with the psychiatrists. They are very careful not to let any information go outside the walls of this hospital. You have nothing to worry about there."

Again, the nurse is very competent with information as long as feelings are left out.

"Well, that's encouraging. I guess my back did begin to get worse when I was having trouble at work. But I didn't think anything about it."

"You're certainly fortunate to have Dr. Bordon on your case. You just take him seriously and do whatever he says. He's the finest orthopedist in this state. He's going to get you feeling better."

He had better because this nurse has not had much luck. Doctors are important but so are the nurses. The nurse is not assuming any responsibility for the process here. Either she feels thwarted in her attempt to communicate with this particular patient or else she is attempting to terminate the interaction. In either case she is selling herself short. By responding in the affective domain, both nurse and patient could have felt better about the interaction.

Consider the dialogue in Exhibit 14–4.

**Exhibit 14–4** Protocol: The Effective Helper

| Patient (a 45-year-old female helpee) | Female Nurse (helper) | Discussion |
|---|---|---|
| "I'm glad you came in. I'm really feeling down. I'm miserable. Just lying here in pain, wasting my time." | "Is there something I can do to help you rest more comfortably? Could I adjust the bed, or would you like a small pillow under your back again?" | This statement is taken as a request for action, and kinds of action are suggested. There is no response to the affect. |
| "Well, thank you for offering, but that wouldn't really change things. I guess I'm as comfortable as I can be right now. What's really got me upset is that I take all these tests but still the doctor isn't coming up with anything helpful. He came in about an hour ago and said he can't find any reason for my pain. That's what's really got me upset." | "It's the uncertainty, then. Just waiting to find out what the problem is, that is hard." | The helper immediately recovers from the incorrect assumption that the request was for action and keys in on the patient's feelings. |
| "Yeah, I was kind of excited when I came here. I'd been bothered for a long time and I thought I would finally find out what was causing it. Then when he came in and told me he couldn't find any reason for it, I said, "Oh, no. All this time is wasted. I wonder what the problem really is?" | "So you're wondering what the problem is, what the treatment is going to be, and what will need to be done to take care of it. It's scary not to know what lies in the future." | Again, the nurse responds in a manner that will elicit further patient exploration of the concern. The patient is experiencing being listened to and is responding with a lot of verbalization. |
| "Yes. I'm a little bit afraid that the doctor's not going to be able to find out what's wrong with me and it will always be this way, and I just don't think I could stand it." | "It sounds like you are beginning to question the doctor's ability to help you, that you're not sure that he can do anything for you." | This is a high-level response that goes beyond what the helpee has been able to express. Helpers should be fairly sure that such a response is accurately additive before attempting it at this early stage of the interaction. |

## Exhibit 14–4 continued

"Well, it doesn't look like he is. You know what he told me today? I don't know if he talked to you about it or not, but it's almost as if he's given up on my case. He asked me today if I had ever had any emotional problems. It's like he says, 'Well, this has been a hard case and if I can't find anything wrong I'll just write it off as all in the head.' "

"Dr. Bordon is a very thorough specialist and it is not at all unusual for him or one of the other doctors to ask a question like that. Actually the question is quite routine."

Here the nurse has temporarily left the feeling level and has interjected information. It is quite appropriate at this point since her expertise can clarify a point that has been distorted by the helpee.

"Hmmm. Well, like I told him, 'No, I don't have any emotional problems, and my family has never had any.' So I thought that would end it but it didn't seem to. He sort of implied that that wasn't the end of that line of questioning. It's got me upset."

'It's pretty scary to you to think that part of your problem might be due to emotional reasons—the ideas in your mind could cause you trouble in your back. Especially when nothing like this has ever happened in your family."

This represents a resumption of the facilitative responses to the patient. She communicates to the patient, "I hear what you are saying and I'm attempting to understand how you are feeling."

"That's right. I just never even heard of anybody having such a thing. I'm wondering if—I've been thinking a lot about it—and it's hard for me to accept. I wonder what people in the community would think."

"You think that there's a real stigma attached to seeing a psychiatrist. You'd be embarrassed if your friends knew about it."

This is a continuation of the nurse's acknowledgement of the patient's concern. It is evident that a helper must find out the nature of a problem before helping someone deal with it; this is precisely what is happening in this interaction.

"Yeah, I would be embarrassed. Even if I did have some problems I needed to talk about, just think what people in the community would say. They'd all know about it, probably before I got home."

"Everything that is done in this hospital is kept confidential. The psychiatrists are particularly careful to make sure that nothing goes outside the walls of this hospital."

Again, the nurse has appropriately interjected information to help clarify a point of which the patient is not aware.

"Well, that's encouraging. I don't particularly like the idea of seeing a psychiatrist but if that's what Dr. Bordon thinks is best, I guess I'll do it. I'm here to try to find out what's wrong with me."

Both dialogues reach essentially the same conclusions but it is interesting to note the differences in length (or time) of interaction between the two.

# Chapter 15

# Responding with Information

Health care professionals are called upon daily to interact in a professional way with patients. Though these interactions may seem routine to the practitioners, the experience of receiving health care is not routine to the patients. Caregivers' attention, attitude, and the information they provide are very important to the patients. In the next two paragraphs, helpers should try to sense the way in which patients may look to them for strength and reassurance.

## UNSPOKEN THOUGHTS FROM A PATIENT TO A HEALTH CARE PROFESSIONAL

I am a patient. Needing professional treatment is a discomforting experience for me because I do not fully know what is going on. Usually I know more about me than anyone else in the world. It is rare that another person can tell me something about me that I do not already know or understand. Now, however, I find myself in a situation that is an exception to this rule. I believe that because of your position, your knowledge of your profession, and your accessibility to my health records, you know more about me than I know about myself. Therefore, when you speak I listen and I probably will remember a lot of what you say.

I am eager to find out as much as I can about myself from you. The more I can find out about myself, the more secure I become, and the more comfortable I feel about my position as a patient. Not only are your words important to me but how you say those words and what you do while you talk to me are equally important. If you withhold yourself or your information about me from me, you make me feel like a child. I feel less secure. If you do things for me without any input from me or if you take me for granted as you do your duties, I feel powerless.

An essential task of all health care professionals, then, is to help patients feel less like patients and more like capable, worthwhile human beings. The HCP must say and do things that will help patients feel they have control over their lives, that they are not children, and that they are not powerless. This sounds like a huge assignment, and it is more easily said than done, but it is a task that can be carried out. This chapter deals with some familiar topics and describes the application of the basic principles of good communication to those situations.

## WAYS TO GIVE INFORMATION

Giving information usually is a simple task but there are several ways of dispensing it, some of which are more helpful than others. Information must be given in a way that makes it usable to the person who receives it and leaves that individual with a willingness to hear and apply the information. Words such as "arrogant," "pushy," and "know-it-all" have negative connotations but these are impressions that caregivers sometimes leave as a result of giving information in an ineffective way.

Another way of giving information is for caregivers simply to provide it cheerfully and then continue the activities in which they were engaged. This way of responding is more helpful than harmful and often is appropriate in interpersonal relations, especially in the health care field. A third way of responding assumes that asking for information may imply more than simply a need for it. It might be a way of getting attention so that other, more important matters might be discussed. The second and third methods, in some combination, are sufficient for effective interpersonal interaction. Helpers consider time factors, professional ethics, prior knowledge of the helpee's situation, and nonverbal messages and modify their responses accordingly.

When a helpee's communication is categorized as a request for information, caregivers usually are concerned only with that particular statement, so that each one has to be evaluated separately. This allows helper flexibility to change in midstream and go from action to information to listening when indicated, in the same conversation. Giving information alone sometimes is sufficient, as is giving action or just listening. To feel good about the effectiveness of an interaction, it is important to be sensitive to what is happening verbally and nonverbally, both on the surface and at underlying levels. Much of an interaction must be interpreted in terms of the context of the situation, but broad determinations of orientations (listening, action, information, and inappropriate interaction) usually can be made on the basis of a statement by the helpee.

Examples of the different ways of providing information are given in the following:

Health care professional to health care professional: "Do you think these progress notes are good enought to suit Mrs. Stringer?"

## Ineffective Responses

*Example:*    1. "If you did your best, does it matter?"
2. "You've been doing progress notes for years."
3. "You know as much about doing progress notes as I do."

*Comments:* These common response types neither answer the question nor attempt to go beyond the surface concern. Although they probably were given with good intentions, they are ineffective in terms of communication. The helpee gets the message very clearly that the caregiver did not hear this concern. This kind of response, except in extraordinary circumstances, will terminate the interaction.

## Minimal Responses

A minimal response in this situation would be to look over the progress notes and only answer the question, to deal only with the content of the helpee's need.

*Example:*    4. "Yes, I think they are okay."
5. "Maybe you could be clearer in your description of the patient's anxiety attack."

*Comments:* Making one of these responses would be doing all the helpee had requested and would leave the door open for further interaction, if desired.

## Maximal Response

A maximal response does more than simply respond to the question; it involves responding to the affect verbalized or implied in the problem statement, as well as to the content. Classifying the helpee's request as in Chapter 4, it would be categorized information and understanding/involvement by the helper. This kind of need is not always present but caregivers should be able to recognize it if it is present.

*Example:*  6. "Yes, I think they are okay. It sounds like you are concerned about what Mrs. Stringer thinks."

*Helpee responds:* "Well, sometimes I get the feeling that she thinks I am incompetent. You should hear some of the comments she makes to me when no one else is around."

*Comment:* A maximal response should be made only when the helper feels sure that the helpee has an underlying concern and is ready to talk about it. If the caregiver is not sure, the response should deal only with the content. It should be remembered that the minimal response sometimes can accomplish just as much as the maximal but might take longer to work through.

## Giving Information Before It is Requested

Often the health care worker will recognize a need for information without being asked. Several nonverbal clues can signal the need for information: the quizzical or puzzled look in which the brow is knit; the look of surprise, often characterized by raised brows, the open mouth, or even a short gasp; the blank look or absence of agreement following the delivery of information, and hesitation in speaking or taking action. Any of these may portray confusion or lack of understanding. It is appropriate, under these circumstances, to offer such assistance as:

"Is there any way I can help you?"

"Do you understand?"

"If you have questions, I'd be happy to talk with you."

On other occasions the caregiver will have information for which the patient has no way of anticipating a need. It is essential to keep the patient well informed of the schedule in moving through treatment; if not, everything that happens (or does not happen as the individual thinks it should) will add to the helpee's discomfort and increase anxiety. Concretely, this means that caregivers should tell the patient in general terms such things as what is going to happen, when it is going to happen, how long it will take, and how much it will cost, as the situation requires. For example:

1. If a doctor in private practice gets behind schedule, patients should be informed of how the delay will affect their appointments. Details of the cause need not, and usually should not, be given. Most persons will accept a delay graciously if it is explained.

2. When a patient is left alone in an examining room, the person should be told what is going to happen next and given an estimate of how soon it will occur.
3. A patient never should be left without being told what to expect to happen next.
4. Procedures should be explained briefly, as, "This sample of blood will be sent to the lab for a routine check."

It must be remembered that what may be routine for the caregiver could be a unique event, and likely an anxiety-provoking one, for the patient. Several other specific situations involving giving information are covered in Chapter 19.

## Preoperative Procedures

The most important staff behavior in terms of preoperative procedures is communication to the patient concerning the nature of what is about to happen. The more of the procedure that can be shared, the narrower the more knowing/less knowing gap becomes. This kind of information usually is given in a structured way and is personalized by responding to each patient's style of reacting to what the caregivers are saying. For example, there are not very many different ways to communicate the fact that a patient will have no food for 16 hours before surgery, but each patient will respond to that statement in a different way. After explaining the reason, caregivers could make one of the following responses, depending on the appropriateness:

"It looks like you are concerned about tomorrow."

"You seem to be getting a little nervous."

"I guess my telling you this makes you realize that the time for your operation is here."

"I can tell that you are not confident about this."

The age or educational level of the patient does not determine psychological readiness for surgery. A seeming calmness and receptivity can turn out upon investigation to be a facade. The best thing to do is to invest some time to hear the patient and attempt to understand the individual's position. If that is done, the patient can do the rest.

## Orientation of New Patient to the Health Care Facility

The most important consideration during orientation should be an awareness of the patient. Many times patients will not ask questions about things they do not understand. They are new to the hospital, so they usually have no rapport with any of the staff members. This lack of rapport can be a barrier to desirable interaction because important areas of potential patient exploration or information might be overlooked. Patients might feel over-whelmed by all the information they are trying to process. They might be generally anxious about hospitalization or there might be a specific point that needs to be clarified. Nevertheless, it should be a staff responsibility to be alert to both verbal and nonverbal signals from patients that more attention is needed. This task involves responding to the affective messages that the patients are sending. For example:

HCP:      "Are there any questions, Mrs. Walker?"
Patient: "I think I understand everything."
HCP:      "When we were telling you about the x-rays scheduled for to-morrow, you seemed a bit agitated."
Patient: "Well, it's just that last time I was in the hospital, in St. Louis, the technician made me wait for two hours in the waiting room before he made the x-rays. I almost caught pneumonia."
HCP:      "I can see, then, how you could be concerned about the x-rays. We don't have a waiting room here. Our procedure is for you to stay in your room until the technicians are ready for you, and then they will take you right down."
Patient: "Oh, that's a relief. That was the worst experience I have ever had."

Simply by noticing the patient's affect, probably nonverbal in this case, the HCP was able to elicit a concern from the person. Then, by responding to it and giving appropriate information, the caregiver saved the patient unnecessary worry.

## Handling Questions from Patients on Their Condition

There may be standard procedures in some hospitals for dealing with this topic. Many times doctors prescribe ways of responding to this inquiry from their patients. For example, a nurse might say, "Dr. Roberts re-quested that we refer all questions about his patients' conditions to him. I'll be glad to leave him a note on your chart so he'll be sure and talk to you about it the next time he comes in." This limits a nurse's range of responses considerably, but it is the exception and not the rule.

The pat reply, "Ask your doctor," as many nurses were taught to re-spond, no longer is an adequate response. Even in hospitals where health care professionals are not allowed to talk about a patient's condition, an excellent opportunity exists to respond to the person's feelings. If health care professionals other than the doctor are allowed to discuss a condition, it should also be done in a way that communicates understanding as well as information. For example:

> Patient: "My doctor brought another doctor with him when he came to see me today. I wonder what that means?"

Alternate HCP responses:

1. "I guess it was frightening when they both walked in and you were expecting only your own doctor." (The nurse gave no information about the patient's condition, but responded to the individual's feelings.)

2. "He was a new resident and he accompanied Dr. Roberts all morning. I guess it was frightening when he didn't explain that." (The nurse gave no information about the patient's condition, but did supply some other information or explanation. Again, the helper responded to the patient's affect.)

3. "Dr. Roberts wanted to check everything thoroughly, so he decided to bring in a specialist to consult with him. I guess it does frighten you when you don't expect two doctors." (This implies there is more than routine concern about the patient so that this response alone probably would not be adequate and would require more extensive dialogue.)

All three examples represent adequate responses in terms of effective interpersonal functioning but each reflects a different kind of involvement. The point here is that even with restrictions imposed by ethics or by organizational regulations, it is possible to be a helpful person. It takes some involvement and investment, however, to make a difference.

## "Talking Down" to Patients

Most persons receiving health care have restricted freedom of choice. Their normal range of decisions has been preempted by doctor's orders, by the routine and regulations of the office or hospital, and by their own unfamiliarity with the situation. "Talking down" to patients, or belittling them, increases their feelings of powerlessness. The health care professional must make every effort to treat the patient like a responsible person. It is important to remember, too, that belittling can be done nonverbally as well as verbally. Examples of "talking down" are:

*Verbally:*

"Let's take your medicine."

"Now, are you going to be an ornery patient?"

"We wouldn't want the doctor to be unhappy with us, would we?"

*Nonverbally:*

Patting the patient on the top of the head.

Doing something for the patient that the person should do.

## Explaining At-Home Procedures to Patients

This procedure generally is a matter of imparting information. An important point to remember is the range of patient abilities that will be represented. Their individual differences are practically endless so the "routine" procedure of explaining at-home treatment is not routine at all. Rather, it must be tailored to the individual patient. This is not a difficult task if caregivers:

1. Assess the patient's ability to understand instructions.
2. Begin explaining procedures at that level of assessment.
3. Make certain the patient is comprehending by asking relevant questions to assess the degree of understanding.
4. Make any adjustments necessary from information received from assessment of patient understanding.
5. Be aware of the patient's reaction to what is being said. If there are verbal or nonverbal signs of fear, confusion, or misunderstanding (e.g., a moan, frown, or quizzical expression), stop the explanation and respond to the affect. Affirmative nods or a verbal "yes" or "I see" allow the explanation to proceed.

These will help ensure that patients understand both what they are to do and the importance of doing it. If they do not follow through on the plan, that is their choice and the caregivers need not blame themselves if they have done their part well.

## When the Patient Is Not Verbal

A patient who is not verbal raises many possibilities, some of which would require additional professional intervention and some that could be considered transient or situational. A health care professional, however, can hardly go wrong by responding to the patient's nonverbal behavior. If the responses do not produce verbalization, appropriate referral sources should be considered. The response to nonverbal behavior would, of course, differ from individual to individual and depend on the circumstances. The following are examples of responses by a health care professional:

1. "You seem to be pretty agitated today."
2. "You look like you might be a little angry about something."
3. "I can understand how you might be upset after what happened yesterday."
4. "You're mad at me and I would like to discuss it with you."

## CASES TO CONSIDER

Each of the following cases represents a request for information. Some may have more obvious underlying feelings or concern than others. Health care professionals should read each situation carefully and think about what they might say, producing both a minimal and a maximal response to each case.

1. Patient to HCP: "Are you allowed to tell me how much I am being charged for those sleeping pills?"
2. HCP to HCP: "I'm planning to take the registry exam again next month. Since you passed it the first time, I thought maybe you could give me some advice."
3. HCP to HCP: "I was wondering if you could introduce me to some people in town. It sure is lonely here."
4. An HCP in the hospital notices an elderly man in street clothes wandering, apparently aimlessly, through the corridor.
5. HCP to HCP: "Have you noticed how I start stuttering when a doctor asks me a question?"
6. An HCP in a clinic sees a man waiting in an examination room and realizes he has been there alone for 40 minutes. He appears angry.
7. Patient to HCP: "Everybody tells me what I should do here. Nobody ever fills me in on why I have to do it. Could you tell me why I need to take that white liquid every morning?"
8. A nurse in a GP's office receives a call from the doctor saying that he will be detained for two hours. The waiting room is full.
9. Patient to HCP: "Can you tell me if there are scholarships available for nursing school? I want to go but my parents can't afford to send me."

10. HCP in the ER observes the parents of a child who is receiving treatment conversing in low tones, with nonverbal signs of worry and restlessness.
11. Patient to HCP: "Can you get me something to read on depression?"
12. HCP to HCP: "Mrs. Bradley asked me about her condition today. I hated to lie, but she is so nice I just couldn't tell her the truth. Has that happened to you?"
13. An HCP with a GP in private practice is sending a patient to a hospital for an EKG as part of an annual physical.
14. HCP to HCP: "Do you think I will get the efficiency award this year for the changes I've made on this ward?"
15. Patient to HCP: "Is it possible to get a drink of booze here? I'm used to having a cocktail every night before supper."
16. HCP to HCP: "How much personal information about ourselves should we give a patient? Sometimes it's hard to avoid it when you get in a conversation."
17. Patient to HCP: "Is it too late to learn to eat different kinds of foods that won't make me gain so much weight? I've always heard that you can't teach an old dog new tricks."
18. Patient to HCP: "I'm worried. Does the medicine I'm taking ever cause hallucinations?"
19. HCP to HCP: "I'm not sure of my job performance. I'm afraid to ask anyone but you. I think you can level with me without much threat."
20. Patient's daughter to HCP: "The nurse last night was infuriated at our minister because he stayed two hours after visiting hours. For mother, he represents the only hope she has and I think in light of that, he should be allowed to stay beyond visiting hours. Don't you agree?"

# Chapter 16

# Responding with Action

Health care professionals do not function in the counselor role most of the time but rather are action oriented in carrying out the duties of the job. Most of the action involves doing something for patients or intervening in their lives in some way. These are actions that follow a patient's request or the caregiver's assessment of need, and are represented by the "Takes Appropriate Actions" block of Figure 4–1 in Chapter 4. Facilitative communication is related to these interventions and treatments because:

1. It is necessary to ascertain what the action should be and to establish acceptance of it.
2. It is supportive and restorative in its own right and in that sense is, itself, an "action."

Still, health care professionals are involved in doing something for or to patients a greater proportion of the time than in communicating with them. All communication with patients can be facilitative and thus contribute to their psychological comfort. This section discusses the application of the general principles of facilitative communication to the carrying out of services and treatments.

A request for action may be either overt or implied; that is, patients may request that some action take place or health care professionals may decide to take some action. In either case the caregiver behaves in an action-oriented way regardless of whether or not this step would be premature otherwise.

In many cases of this type, the action (i.e., taking charge of the situation) precedes all or most facilitation. This is the exception to the rule of using facilitation to build support in order to earn the right to be action oriented with the patient. There are many examples in health care that require the professional to take action right now and discuss it later. A good way to think about the appropriateness of this situation is in terms of the dimension of expertise. Situations that arise can call upon the professionals' expertise or information that, if patients also had, would make them be better off. Other situations might involve professionals' expertise or information that, if not implemented immediately, could put patients' health or life in jeopardy.

This is not to say that health care professionals have license to "do to" patients what they feel is right but that there are times when action should precede facilitation or when facilitation alone would be inappropriate. For example, when a professional discovers that an IV has infiltrated, the expert's primary responsibility is to see that it is restarted promptly. Admittedly some interaction might well take place at the moment of discovery to ease the patient's mind about the situation but an extended interaction would be inappropriate unless someone else was handling the IV problem. Of course, the incident might be followed with additional information, listening, or further action, depending upon the circumstances. Each situation or response is evaluated separately.

The following interaction is an example. Mr. Williamson has turned on his call light for the fourth time in two hours. The caregiver knows he really is in pain but has given him everything that the physician ordered for pain. The professional even administered a placebo the last time he called. The caregiver hates to go back in but must. Mr. Williamson says: "I know you must think I am a complainer, but I can't stand much more. Take whatever steps you have to to do something for me." First, a quick response in appropriate: "Mr. Williamson, I know you are really in pain. I will do what I can."

This response acknowledges that the HCP has heard the patient, takes him quite seriously, and has indicated that something would be done. Time has not been wasted in saying this. The second phase in handling this situation involves actually taking the appropriate action. Typically this would involve going up in the chain of command (to nursing supervisor) or calling the patient's physician and communicating concern. There are a number of ways to handle the situation at this point, but an action orientation is indicated.

Occasionally a situation may arise that requires the health care professional's taking the initiative in protecting the best interests of the organization and other persons. In such a situation, action often takes precedence over dialogue. The caregiver knows what to do under these conditions. Two different situations are examples:

**Example A**

A nurse returning from lunch rushes into the office and says, "The maintenance men left a ladder against the side of the building and there is a small boy climbing it—I'm afraid he'll fall off!'"

*Response:* Take the action that will most quickly get a responsible person to the scene, at which time it is assessed for the best course of action.

*Discussion:* Of course in this situation, action, (i.e., remedying the danger situation) precedes any other activity.

## Example B

A man in a gray work uniform says to a clerk in the hospital pharmacy, "I'm from the pest control service. I'm supposed to spray in your storage room."

*Response:* The clerk replies, "The pharmacy is a restricted area, so I will need to clear this with the office of the building maintenance superintendent. Excuse me just a moment while I phone."

*Discussion:* No employee should allow entrance to any nonpublic area containing drugs, valuable materials, confidential information, or equipment unless the person has authorization to do so from a supervisor. Posing as a maintenance or office machines repair person is a common method of deception used by unlawful individuals. If in doubt, it is prudent to check up.

## CASES TO CONSIDER

In each of the following situations, health care professionals should think (1) what they would say and (2) what they would do. They should ask whether the action they were thinking of would be likely to terminate the interaction and whether they thought there was an underlying reason for the request.

1. Patient to HCP: "Last night the nurse on the third shift chewed me out for complaining about the noise in the hall. I want to report her to the supervisor."
2. Patient to HCP: "I don't want to complain to my roommate about his cigarette smoke but I think it would be better if I moved to another room."
3. HCP to HCP: "Would you mind looking over my progress notes on Mrs. Sims and telling me your comments?"
4. Male patient to HCP: "Would you get a male to do my bed bath? I'm uncomfortable having a female nurse do it."

5. HCP to HCP: "I saw the new respiratory therapist slip something into his pocket this morning while he was in the medicine room preparing his treatments. I think he was stealing narcotics."

6. HCP to HCP: "Would you give me a hand with these meds? It seems like I always agree to help others with their work and then my own work does not get done."

7. Patient to HCP: "Would you bring me some bourbon? I always have one before going to sleep—it's like a sleeping pill."

8. Patient to HCP: "When my brother comes here to see me after work today, would you stop him in the hall and tell him I'm asleep. He's about to drive me crazy."

9. New HCP to supervisor: "Would you post the regulations for lunch break? Everybody seems to be operating by a different set of rules and it's confusing."

10. Patient to HCP: "I like you because you don't make me feel like I'm completely helpless just because I have a broken leg. Would you get me a magazine from the gift shop before you get off work?"

11. Patient to HCP: "Nurse, quick! Help me! I'm having another gall-bladder attack."

12. Patient to HCP: "I'm beginning to feel myself falling to pieces again. Can you do anything?"

# Chapter 17

# Responding to Inappropriate Communication

Responding to inappropriate communication may be the most awkward relationship situation to handle with confidence, especially with coworkers and with friends. This is because, by definition, health care professionals are dealing with a gray area of right and wrong. A's definition of "inappropriate" may be different from B's in a particular situation.

Five categories of communication are considered inappropriate, or at least frequently can be inappropriate: (1) rumor and gossip, (2) inordinate or chronic griping, (3) excessive dependency, (4) invitations to be involved in hurtful activities, and (5) hostile humor. Regardless of the type of inappropriate communication, the alternative responses are similar. They range from being punishing or damaging through silence or passivity to the preferred response of a warm but firm refusal to engage in inappropriate behavior.

The best way to respond to inappropriate communication is the same for each type: politely decline to take part in it. This response may not appear attractive at first glance. It is difficult to carry out and it carries with it the risk of being rejected by the other person. It is, however, the response style that will give the most favorable results over time; other response styles only perpetuate inappropriateness.

No answer anyone can give will suddenly change the helpee's communication patterns. But caregivers can establish a relationship of trust and caring that may, over time, permit them to influence the helpee. They can model good communication, give information, and encourage the individual to seek intensive help with the problem should that be indicated.

Probably more than in any other communication situation, the way in which the response is delivered (the nonverbal component) is critical. When caregivers decline to continue an inappropriate interaction, it is easy for the helpee to read an attitude of condescension, superiority, or arrogance into their response. The patient may want to do so to avoid feeling scolded for behavior that the helpee knows is inappropriate. The following suggestions will help health care professionals formulate and express an effective response.

### KEYS TO THE 'POLITELY' PART

Caregivers must remove condemnation and punishment from their nonverbal style. Their tone of voice should be calm and easygoing at the beginning. Their faces should be neutral. They should not smile during the "decline" statements. They should maintain direct, but not piercing or hostile, eye contact.

Helpers should keep the conversation going in a positive way to show their interest in and acceptance of the patients, perhaps by shifting the conversation to something they are interested in or asking an open-ended question. An appropriate conversation should be started. If this is not done, there is likely to be an awkward silence, and rejection of their behavior may seem to them as rejection of their personhood. On the other hand, professionals should not jump in so quickly or so lightly as to deny the point they just made and should not seem apologetic about the "decline" part.

Helpers should include anything they can that is genuinely supportive of the helpee as a person or that supports appropriate behavior.

### KEYS TO THE 'DECLINE' PART

Health care professionals should keep this part brief. They should not use harsh words such as "dumb," "awful," "troublemaker" and thus antagonize the other person. That would be inappropriate, of course.

Caregivers should speak thoughtfully, not rush their response, and use words that give a clear, definite rejection of the behavior without implying rejection of the person.

With this approach, caregivers seek to deal firmly with the inappropriateness and gently with the person. Even so, it may result in a bit of embarrassment for the person with the inappropriate behavior—the natural consequence of doing something out of the norm. Helpers should let the patients live with that and hope they learn from it. There is some risk with this approach but the potential for harm is greater if it is not used.

This seems like a sensible approach for several reasons:

- It rejects the behavior.

- It seeks to prevent hurt to innocent parties, organizations, and the person who is being inappropriate.

- It affirms the inappropriate person for behavior that is worthwhile.

- It models appropriateness.

- It involves minimum risk.

It's not easy, but it beats the alternatives.

Examples and discussions of the five types round out this chapter. While these situations may not occur in what usually are thought of as helpee-helper relationships, that terminology is used, referring to the person whose communication is inappropriate as the helpee. The person who habitually communicates inappropriately may not be asking for help but probably is in need of it. Perhaps the health care professional can become a helper.

## 1. RUMOR AND GOSSIP

Rumor is an opinion or statement without known authority for its truth. Rumors are not necessarily spread with the knowledge of their inappropriateness or inaccuracy but it seems inevitable that even "neutral" rumors quickly become distorted as they move from person to person. For example, the innocuous report, "There was a lot of talk in the staff meeting about vacation days but I don't know if there is anything in it for us," can quickly become, "All the departments but ours are getting an extra week of vacation next year." Sound ridiculous? Perhaps, but it is not difficult to recall actual situations in which an innocent remark quickly became absurdly different or, worse yet, vicious and harmful.

Rumors often begin with no names linked with them. This soon changes, probably as a result of carriers' trying to make the story more believable as they pass it along. This considerably increases the damage that can be done to specific persons, groups, or organizations.

Gossip is a rumor of an intimate nature; the focus is on the character or behavior of a person. Gossip may open with lines as blatant as, "Did you hear the latest about . . .?" or with a feeble attempt to be subtle, "You know, I'd be the last person to say anything against anyone, but . . . ." For most persons, the need is not to know how to recognize gossip but to know how to avoid becoming a part of it.

Nobody wants to become the victim of gossip so people may be afraid of cutting off a gossiper because they do not want to make that person angry and thus themselves become the subject of gossip. People may unwittingly reinforce the person by their silence and may even accidentally become carriers.

The helpee situation in the next example has five responses that illustrate ineffective ways of responding to rumor or gossip, plus an effective response.

## Examples of Rumor Responses

HCP to HCP: "Listen to this. You know that snippy little redhead in the lab? The one who was so crabby when you got down there late with the specimen yesterday? Well, she's finally going to get what's coming to her. Guess what they found out she's been up to?"

| *Response is polite but does not decline* | *Discussion* |
|---|---|
| 1. "What?" | The helper seems eager to hear more. |
| 2. "Who cares? She's not worth my time." | The helper also is inappropriate, though not to the speaker. |
| 3. "I wouldn't know anything about that." | Passive acceptance that invites more. |

| *Response declines but is not very polite* | *Discussion* |
|---|---|
| 4. "Thelma, you're always scraping up something and there's usually nothing to it anyway. If we gossip about her, it will be like putting ourselves on her level. So I'd rather not even hear about it." | This is disrespectful and punishing to the helpee; it is almost certain to damage the relationship. |
| 5. "I'm pretty busy right now so I would rather not talk about it." | This brusque, cool approach may not damage the relationship, but neither does it move it toward constructive behavior. |

| *Appropriate response* | *Discussion* |
|---|---|
| 6. "I guess you want to help me keep informed about what's going on around here, and I appreciate that, but this seems like something I really don't need to know about. By the way, I understand you're thinking about going to Hawaii. Are you?" | The helper attempts to be warm and respectful and to avoid sounding superior yet shows acceptance of the helpee as a person without condoning the inappropriate behavior. Even the use of hearsay shows that talking about people is okay if it is affirming. |

## 2. INORDINATE OR CHRONIC GRIPING

Inordinate griping is exaggerating a small complaint; chronic griping is continued complaining about something that cannot or need not be changed. Griping or complaining in any form is unpleasant to hear. It may signal a significant and legitimate complaint and if so it should be attended to with the helper's best and most facilitative efforts.

On the other hand, if the griping is found to be inappropriate, it should not be supported. It may result from deficient personality adjustment, and if so be outside the scope of the helper's domain. In that case, the best option is to accept the person as a person, support behaviors that are appropriate, and ignore as much as possible the inappropriate and unpleasant parts of the conduct.

## Example 1

| *Helpee* | *Helper* | *Discussion* |
|---|---|---|
| "Lousy, miserable, rainy weather again. This is the second rotten day in a row." | (1) "On days like this, I'm glad to have an inside job." (Or) (2) "I guess if we're busy with our work, we won't be affected by what's outside." (Or) (3) "It sounds as though this weather is changing some of your plans for you." | The helper changes the subject by stating something positive. In the third example, the helper sees the helpee's behavior as out of character and thus reflecting what might be an underlying situation. |

**Example 2**

| Helpee | Helper | Discussion |
|--------|--------|------------|
| "Every time we have a staff meeting it's the same old thing—they keep harping on us to cut down on costs, turn lights out, stuff like that. I get tired of hearing them complain." | "I've heard you say that before—that you get tired of the repetition. You've said it several times lately, I believe." | The helpee is doing the very things that are complained about. The helper probably would enjoy pouncing on this—pointing out the discrepancy sharply—but refrains in the hope that the helpee will discover it. If not, on to more direct, but still polite, confrontation. |

Helpers are not likely to be able to stop the inappropriateness but they do not want to use behaviors that reinforce it. With persons with certain personality formations, punishing the inappropriate behavior reinforces it. The HCPs' goal should be to relate to the individuals in a way in which the helpers good communication is modeled, the attitude toward the inappropriate behavior is clear, and neither side has unpleasant feelings about the other.

## 3. EXCESSIVE DEPENDENCY

A common occurrence in health care is the development of relationships in which helpees become dependent upon the helper for the meeting of needs in areas of their lives in which they should be functioning adequately on their own. This often occurs from worker to supervisor, from one spouse to another, and from patient to health care worker. There is considerable opportunity for the last-named because helpees actually are dependent upon helpers in many ways: for advice, for treatment (if hospitalized), for the basic necessities of life, and in a psychiatric setting even for protection of self.

These kinds of dependence are legitimate, although they should be controlled to prevent the fostering of overdependence. In the absence of such "real" needs, however, dependence is considered inappropriate. Health care professionals need to know how to assist helpees in moving from dependence to mature independence and interrelatedness.

Dependency usually arises from fear. The helpees believe they can't deal with an impending situation so they seek to be sheltered by the helper or to remain helpless so the object of the fear can be avoided. Fears that commonly arise with patients include the following:

1. suffering because of making a poor decision
2. inability to work
3. concern about others' opinions, especially among trauma victims and psychiatric patients
4. loss of financial support
5. inability to function without drugs or other regular treatment
6. estrangement from friends or family

Dependency may arise from a natural need for attention and grow into a neurotic dependence with hospitalized patients because their options for expressing themselves are restricted. Patients find that their ego needs can be met by being cared for and may fear that their old ways no longer will be successful so they resist giving up their dependency upon the health care professionals. Their behaviors may regress to those of an earlier stage of their illness or of an earlier period in their lives.

The process of helping the dependent person uses the skills analyzed in earlier chapters. Particular aspects are summarized as follows:

1. The helper, through facilitative communication, should find out what the situation is, then assist the helpee in exploring and understanding it, its roots, and its implications.
2. The helpee who reveals exaggerated or unfounded fear probably will disclose more fear and other issues during further facilitative communication.
3. The helpee who discloses "real" fear must have an intervention program devised. The patient should be given support, information, and as many success experiences as possible to restore confidence in the ability to cope with the feared situation. The caregiver should start with what the helpee can do and progress gradually toward the goal behavior. The helpee should be assisted in working toward changing the situation or in obtaining help in changing it, as indicated.
4. The helpee's dependency may be learned as a result of long illness. The patient loses some self-reliance and becomes comfortable in the dependent role. The person may be weaned away from dependency gradually by being given responsibility for tasks formerly done for the individual.

5. The helpee should be prepared for the transition from the patient role to one of greater independence. For hospitalized patients, this should be part of predischarge instruction.

## 4. INVITATIONS TO HURTFUL ACTIVITIES

This category includes suggestions for avoidance of the encouragement or solicitation of participation in activities that are potentially harmful to other persons or the organization. This would include acts that are illegal, unethical, of questionable judgment, risky to the safety of others, or encourage an inferior level of performance. These situations may carry a high potential for serious problems.

Helpers must decide whether the talk is idle chatter or something concrete and estimate the effect it may have on others. This will guide the style of the response. If the inappropriateness does not significantly threaten anyone's welfare, it may be dealt with by seeking to understand the helpee and trying to facilitate self-understanding. If risk to persons or property is involved, protective action must take precedence over facilitation. Still, this usually can be done without alienating the helpee. The HCPs should deal with the person as warmly and respectfully as possible while expressing their views clearly and firmly. Their response may be to: (1) point out undesirable consequences that might occur and/or (2) offer alternative actions that are appropriate, and (3) clearly state or imply what behavior would be appropriate.

If helpers are aware of inappropriate behavior of a serious, or potentially serious, nature they owe it to their organization, coworkers, and patients to take steps to prevent possible damage. This may mean talking with supervisors about it, a step that may take courage and may carry with it the possibility of making the helpers unpopular with the other individuals or coworkers, but for the long-term success of the organization there is no alternative. Examples of two types of cases are:

### Example 1

Two HCPs are working late to get caught up on paper work.

| Helpee | Helper | Discussion |
|---|---|---|
| 1. "Well, if we're going to bust our backs doing this extra work we at least ought to be comfortable. I've got some beer in the car. I'll have one here for each of us in two minutes." | "Thanks, but you can include me out." | Declines politely. |

| | | |
|---|---|---|
| 2. "You like beer, don't you?" | "I wouldn't be comfortable breaking the rule." | Explains. |
| 3. "Oh, come on. Don't get pompous." | "Maybe it seems that way, but just the same, no thanks." | Refuses to get angry. |
| 4. "Well, look. It sort of puts me on the spot to drink if you don't." | "That's a decision only you can make, although I hope you won't." | Expresses disapproval clearly, without taking control of the helpee. |
| 5. "I won't." | "How about we hit this work hard and then stop at the corner tavern on the way home?" | Communicates that there is friendship and there are no hard feelings. |

## Example 2

| *Helpee* | *Helper* | *Discussion* |
|---|---|---|
| 1. "Fritz hustled a bottle of NO out of the supply room for a party at his place Saturday night. You should come over." | "It's nice to get invited but there are a couple things about it that do not appeal to me." | Affirms what can be affirmed but voices disapproval of the other. |
| 2. "You're overreacting." | "NO is not something to play with. Plus, I should think you would have some reservations about supporting someone's stealing from the hospital." | Spells it out. |
| 3. "Hey, it's no big deal." | "Again, thanks, but it doesn't fit with where I'm at." | And hopes that the helpee decides that it's not where the person is at either. |

## 5. HOSTILE HUMOR

Everyone loves a laugh, but at what cost? Much humor grows out of hostility, appealing to the perverse selfishness that seems to be part of human nature.

Sarcasm and ethnic jokes seek to elevate the joker by putting down the person who is the butt of the gag. This style, no matter how clever, represents a primitive level of personal maturity appropriate at age 12 but grossly inappropriate for the health care professional.

Vulgarity usually is hostile in origin as well, often arising from a festering rebellion against authority. Whether its topic is sexual, scatological, or physical or mental handicaps, its tactic is to shock, to embarrass, to defy social convention. Thus it rips away, rather than builds up. Its long-term effect is to degrade its targets and its audiences. Vulgarity wishes the world to meet at its own level—the gutter.

It is not needed. As responsible professionals, health care persons can model more astute, more mature forms of humor based not on the mechanism of hostility but on such factors as surprise, exaggeration in the positive direction rather than exaggeration of the negative, and clever word play. The butt of a joke can be affirmed as well as put down. It's not as easy because much of the television humor in the last 15 years has been hostile and those who have been watching can easily make that comparison in their own minds.

Humor that affirms is more likely to bring a moderate chuckle than a raucous guffaw but it leaves listeners with satisfaction and no unpleasant aftertaste. Health care professionals should go for it.

# Chapter 18

# Anger: Friend and Foe

Anger is an unpleasant emotion that is here to stay. It is a result of problems and it can cause problems. It is common—if a person isn't angry, someone nearby is. It is strong, with the capacity to lead people into destructive behavior if they let it, yet it can be useful. It often is misunderstood.

Anger is a secondary emotion. It follows other emotions that may result from external forces that everyone faces:

1. *Losses* such as death of a loved one, physical impairment, or unemployment lead to feelings of pain, sorrow, grief.
2. *Threats* such as crime, war, or inflation lead to feelings of fear, anxiety, insecurity.
3. *Frustrations* such as those that result when individuals are blocked from having their needs met lead to their feeling helpless, weak, inadequate.
4. *Rejections* such as being pushed away by others is the most agonizing human experience and leads to feeling vulnerable, mortal, worthless.

These primary feelings easily turn to anger. When facing these normal conditions, some persons become angry easily and can not control their fury while others may not get mad or, if they do, can control it.

The difference lies with individuals' internal conditions. The following internal conditions are related to having anger in response to these external conditions and to difficulty in controlling it:

1. guilt, real or imagined
2. a sense of helplessness that may result from low self-esteem or from a lack of emotional or physical help from others

3. unrealistic expectations that may stem from excessive self-esteem or from having become accustomed to abusing power
4. aimlessness or lack of purpose in life

The emotion of anger has a strong physiological component, triggered by the autonomic nervous system. People respond as if under physical attack and the body prepares itself for fight or flight. The physical effects are well known: increases in heart rate, respiration, perspiration, and secretion of adrenalin, etc. These physical reactions often occur even though they are not needed and the gut reaction interferes with the processes of thinking and, of course, communicating.

Individuals do have a choice about what they do. Although the body may be signalling "fight" or "flight" and the mind is bewildered, they are capable of choosing from among the four alternatives:

1. expression of the anger feeling in rage—volatile, explosive release
2. expression in resentment—holding the feeling within, stifling it, denying the direct outward expression of it
3. indignation—keeping the feeling but using the energy to take constructive action against the conditions that cause the feeling
4. resolution of the feeling—reducing or removing the causes.

Rage and resentment are destructive and rarely acceptable options. Indignation, used rationally and judiciously, can be very beneficial in correcting injustices or advancing worthwhile causes. Resolution is the course followed most frequently.

Resolution begins with "first aid" techniques to buy some time while the physical activation subsides. In this phase, people can find many of the familiar tricks and gimmicks of folklore useful. Counselors would say to such individuals:

1. Remind yourself that even though you feel angry you are still in control of your behavior.
2. Turn your attention to something else. The tried and true method of counting to 10 is one way but almost anything will do: recite the alphabet backward, count backward from 200 by 7s, concentrate on using your sense of touch to investigate a nearby object that you long have taken for granted. The principle is to divert your attention, at least temporarily, from the anger-provoking stimulus to anything neutral.
3. Relax your breathing. Take a deep breath, hold it a second, release it slowly through your mouth.

4. Separate yourself from the scene of conflict, even for a couple minutes, if possible.
5. Maintain positive thoughts. Visualize yourself in a pleasant, relaxed scene.
6. Use music. Listen, play, or sing.
7. Channel the energy into something constructive. Rake the yard or write a report, jump vigorously into a project—physical if possible.
8. Do something you enjoy.
9. Talk with a friend.
10. Talk with yourself. Out loud, even. Yes, that's helpful and it's safe if no one's around. It's useful because it helps you bring the circumstances into perspective. Writing down your thoughts will do the same thing.
11. Relax. Give yourself a neck rub, put your feet up, take a short walk, use systematic muscle relaxation—whatever you can do in the circumstances and that has worked for you in the past.
12. Laugh. True laughter, incompatible with anger, will drive anger out.
13. Cry if you need to. When you repress feelings that need release you are putting those very feelings into control of yourself.
14. Measure the issue. Is it worth being angry about?

Obviously, circumstances dictate what individuals can or can not do. Usually they will be able to do a couple of these, enough to give them the breather they need.

Many persons become complacent after having done some "first aid" things and do not go on to the "cure" phase. That's a bad mistake. If the roots of anger remain, they will sprout again, and probably soon. Strategies for cure may include intensive counseling, possibly even psychotherapy, but there are many things people can do to help themselves. They can:

1. Learn to be aware of their anger and to accept it as a legitimate emotional experience, even though wishing to be rid of it.
2. Undo, to the extent possible, any damage done to others.
3. Decide whether a response will be to be free of angry feelings or whether it might be more constructive to keep the feeling and use the energizing effect to enhance an indignant protest against the forces that cause the feeling.
4. Find and analyze the sources of anger. This is where talking with others is particularly important. An "anger diary" is useful; carry a 3" × 5" card for a couple of weeks, making notes on what is happening each time anger rises. Or write "anger" at the top of a pad and put down words that come to mind with free association. Either of these

exercises will generate material that individuals (and friends or counselor) can explore for clues to the sources of anger.

5. Look beyond the precipitating event that triggered the feeling. The
   probability is high that emotional pressure had been building for a
   long time.
6. Make a firm commitment to themselves, and perhaps to others, that
   they will not be controlled by anger and will not express feelings in
   rage or resentment.
7. Plan constructive actions: (a) talk with persons they are angry with;
   (b) confront when necessary; (c) have a group meeting of persons
   involved, if appropriate; (d) forgive those who have hurt them; (e)
   get whatever outside help might be useful.
8. Rehearse their plan and carry it out.

Everyone has had the experience of receiving an attack of anger from
another person without warning and for no apparent reason. Two elements
are present in most such instances: (1) a precipitating situation or incident,
and (2) a readiness on the part of an individual to become angry. The
external and internal conditions that lead to the readiness may be multiple
and obscure to the receiver. Being aware that many such conditions affect
everyone at all times, and most certainly underlie expressions of anger,
should help individuals respond to the attacker rather than to the angry
behavior.

The following 10 points outline the aspects of communication that are
unique to responding to an outburst of anger. These considerations and
helpee behaviors precede using the eight dimensions of the interpersonal
skills model in its regular manner. When those conditions are met, helping
can begin. Counselors would advise individuals in such cases:

1. Know and understand your own response to anger. Anticipate the
   ineffective responses you might be inclined to give. Use the model,
   as applied in the exercises dealing with an angry person, to respond
   effectively.
2. Remember the dynamics of anger. Frequently an attack comes from
   a person who is unhappy because of events or needs not related to
   the precipitating incident. As soon as you show the angry person
   that you are trying to understand those needs, you have a friend.
3. Allow the person to talk and let angry feelings spill out. When the
   anger is allowed to flow, it usually dissipates quickly. The angry
   person is not going to feel good or be receptive to your help until
   the bad feelings are communicated and understood. It is futile to
   try to force logic or information on a person who is filled with strong

emotion—at that moment, it simply is not possible for the individual to use it.

4. Accept the individual's right to be angry, with acceptance as a person of worth, even though you may not agree with the stated reasons for being angry. You always must allow the other person the freedom to be wrong.

5. Be very careful in your reactions. The angry person is not functioning with optimal accuracy so anything you say or do is likely to be misinterpreted. This means that your communication must be particularly effective. You'll have the best chance of success by following these suggestions: (a) show nonverbally that you are listening; (b) nod affirmatively, pay close attention, do not crowd the person or give any motion that might be interpreted as anger on your part; (c) react calmly but with clear meaning. If it seems appropriate to speak, you might say something like, "I'd like to listen to what you want to say," or, "This must be very important; please let me know more about it;" (d) Say only enough to show your acceptance of the person in the angry condition and your attention to the individual.

6. Look for a quick solution to the precipitating incident and, if there is one, give it. If, for example, the person is angry because a fellow worker did not assist in some task, help out if your duties permit you to do so. This is "first aid" for anger, not a cure for the causes.

7. Respond to the angry person's feelings when the individual is ready for you to speak. Communicate verbally and nonverbally to the helpee that you recognize how important the situation is. Show that you want to understand how the person feels, and why. Do not be superficial or trite; your communication of caring and concern must be as intense as was the helpee's anger.

8. Admit it, fully and willingly, if you have been part of the problem. If you do not, no restoration is possible and the problem can only become more serious. Do not deal with the individual's feelings when you should be taking action. If, for example, the person is angry because you are not doing something that you are responsible for doing, do not sit around and listen to the anger, get up and do your job.

9. Seek something about which you can compliment the other person, or something about which you can agree, but do not use this as a technique. It can bring you and the person close together only if you are genuinely seeking to develop your areas of common interest.

10. Communicate helpfully at all times. This adds pleasure to the lives of others who, in turn, will communicate more helpfully with still other persons.

# Chapter 19

# Other Communication Situations

This book has sought to help health care professionals to acquire general principles of communication that can be applied to many different types of situations both on and off the job. Specific applications and variations were considered in the previous four chapters. This chapter considers three additional situations that occur frequently and are very important.

## 1. ACCEPTING COMPLIMENTS

Many persons respond to a compliment by denying or minimizing the achievement or characteristic being praised. For example: (compliment) "You really gave a good report in staff meeting this morning." (response) "Oh, I was so nervous I couldn't talk, and I lost my place, got my papers mixed up, and I couldn't answer all the questions, and . . . ." This response challenges the validity of the giver's statement (the receiver thus communicating low-level respect). It has almost the same effect as saying, "If you knew what you were talking about you wouldn't have said that."

Compliments usually are genuine; when they are not, it is obvious. Individuals should accept a compliment as they would accept any other gift from a friend. If it makes the recipient feel good, the person should say so. For example, a person says to a coworker, "Delores, it's hard to put this into words, but I want you to know it is really a privilege to work in the same department with you. You care about the rest of us and about how we feel. The things you have said and the way you have been have meant a lot to me." An appropriate response would be, "Thank you. It means a lot to hear you say that. It makes me very happy."

The most meaningful compliments often come as a surprise, which makes them difficult for the helper to respond to easily. But since the person who has given the compliment has revealed genuine feelings, the recipient also can do so in the response. For example, "I don't know how to thank you for saying that. I'll always remember it." People should do everything they can to deserve a compliment, and when they are fortunate enough to get one, they should enjoy it.

## 2. SUPERVISOR-EMPLOYEE COMMUNICATION

In the ideal employment situation the needs of both worker and organization are met in mutually satisfying ways. Good communication among members of the entity is the first step toward this goal.

The optimal supervisor-employee relationship is the same as that defined earlier between helper and helpee. In this relationship the supervisor understands the employees' goals and needs (empathy), values their opinions and considers their needs as important (respect), and creates a pleasant working environment (warmth). This in no way conflicts with the attainment of organizational goals or the maintenance of discipline within the work group. It also does not preclude the supervisor's use of the authority that has been provided to help attain the performance for which the manager is held responsible.

The relationship between supervisor and employees should be congenial, show mutual caring without undue familiarity, be personal but not show favoritism, and be relaxed but purposeful. From this relationship the supervisor can be as directive as the situation requires while allowing employees all the freedom and flexibility in the performance of duties as their competence allows. Good communication builds a relationship that strengthens the supervisor's ability to achieve the best efforts of the team because the members are satisfied with the relationship.

Supervisory relationships can be considered in four phases: meeting, knowing, enabling, and directing. These are somewhat sequential but like the facilitative, transition, and action stages that they resemble, are intertwined.

The tasks of the meeting phase are for the supervisor to learn about the employees' experience, aptitudes, and skills; to help them become oriented to the job; to create expectations for instruction and feedback processes that the manager will use; and to establish expectations about work attitudes and quality of performance. This usually is a short phase occurring at the beginning of the relationship.

Skills include the ability to give information clearly; to model appropriate action; to listen; and to communicate empathy, respect, and warmth. Basic friendship skills are used. Generally a personnel office helps with some of these tasks.

The effect of the meeting phases is that both levels obtain information about each other, size each other up, and lay the basis for the relationship. The employees are introduced to the job and become part of a work group.

The task of the knowing phase is to know the person. This means going beyond biographical and vocational facts to such intangibles as attitudes and motivation. Here the level 3 facilitative skills are particularly useful. The supervisor-employee relationship is strengthened. The supervisor learns the employees' capacity for doing assigned work and gains an understanding of how to improve that capacity. The supervisor finds out who the employees are: their attitudes and opinions; preferences for work, for fun and for people; and their motivators—what makes them tick. It also is important for supervisors to learn to accept characteristics that were disliked at first but that do not hurt the employees' work performance.

In the enabling phase, the supervisor uses the skills of giving encouragement and praise, pointing out performance problems or missed goals, giving advice and instruction frequently, and in other ways using the transition dimensions. The primary task here is informal. Later formal performance reviews will show what the employees need to change in order to be more successful on the job. These efforts all are directed toward helping the employees see how personal success comes by helping the organization advance by providing opportunities for staff members to grow professionally through work, and results in their working hard because personal needs are met through the job. This has benefits for productivity and effectiveness, especially over the long term.

In the directing phase, the supervisor enforces rules, sets deadlines, gives ultimatums, and takes disciplinary measures as appropriate. Here the action dimensions, especially confrontation, may be used. This includes dealing with inappropriate talk and responding to an angry person because in both types of cases the supervisor is being highly directive with the employee. The use of the directing phase dimensions usually results in some resistance, which is in proportion to how meaningful the relationship has been. This may strain the relationship, either temporarily or longer.

The supervisor's behavior, for the most part, is nondirective in the knowing phase and becomes increasingly directive in moving through the enabling phase to the highly directive behaviors of the directing phase. Nondirective, gentle supervisory behaviors of persuasion, encouragement, asking, listening, and cooperating are quite in contrast to the directive, tough, supervisory behaviors such as forcing, demanding, telling, and coercing. These, however, also are legitimate under certain conditions.

Using only gentle behaviors or only tough behaviors works for a while but good supervision requires the full range of actions. Optimal performance comes when the supervisor can concentrate on enabling employees to do their best but can shift to the gentler approach of the knowing phase or the tougher approach of the directing phase when either of those are indicated.

Some applications of the relationship model to supervisory-employee relations are illustrated next. These show various levels of supervisor skill—both effective and hurtful.

| Nurse | Supervisor | Discussion |
|---|---|---|
| 1. "I always get the most cantankerous patients—the ones nobody can get along with. It's always like that. You always give me the worst duty. I don't think I've done anything to deserve this kind of treatment." | "Have you taken Mr. Stinson down for his treatment?" | Level 1.0 because it ignores what the nurse is saying. |
| 2. "But you don't treat me fairly." | "You're imagining things. You know I treat everyone alike." | Level 1.0 because it argues about the nurse's perception. |
| 3. "I think we need to talk about this." | "My job is to decide who does what. Your job is to do it. Go!" | Level 1.0 because it rudely refuses to deal with the nurse's needs. |
| 4. "Please listen to this—I'm having a lot of trouble with Mr. Stinson." | "You say some of your patients are giving you a hard time today?" | Level 2.0 because it recognizes, half-heartedly, that there is a problem but ignores the feelings and the bigger problem. |
| 5. "I'm not sure I can keep going." | "Maybe you're not getting enough rest at night." | Level 2.0 because it is cheap advice. |
| 6. "That's not all there is to it. I can't sleep, true, but it's because I feel pushed around here by my work, and not supported by you." | "Right now you feel overwhelmed by all you have to do. But I think I hear some resentment toward me because you think I'm not fair with you, and you can't understand why." | Level 3.0 because it identifies the feelings and events, shows acceptance, and invites the nurse to say more because there is no condemnation for what has been said so far. |
| 7. "That's pretty much the way I see it. It has really hurt." | "It's been rough for you and it's been getting you down. Now that you point it out to me, I see that you are right— I have tended to give you more difficult patients but it has been because you are skilled in dealing with them, not for any other reason. Your work has been very good. I didn't realize that working with some of these patients was getting so unpleasant for you." | Level 4.0 because it takes responsibility (high-level respect) as well as identifying the nurse's feelings and needs. |

8. "Well, it wasn't the work so much, but I just couldn't understand why I got all the problem cases. It's a compliment in a way, I guess, but could you spread the load around a little more?"

"Yes, that's no more than fair, and I'll follow through. Please make sure we talk about this again two weeks from now."

Level 4.0 because it recognizes the nurse's complaint as legitimate, takes action, and shows genuine acceptance by being willing to be held accountable.

Suppose, however, that at statement 7 the supervisor believed that the complaint was unfounded. This would have resulted in a different, but equally appropriate, conclusion:

7a.

"The way things are today, and the way they have been, make you pretty uncomfortable. You say that it seems to you that I don't like you so I deliberately overwork you, yet it sounds like you're not completely sure."

Level 4.0 because it points out to the nurse a possible discrepancy in her perception. This is confrontation.

8a. "No, I'm not sure. I've always thought of you as being fair, a good person to work for. But when I look at what I'm doing, and see what others are doing, it does seem like I get the worst end of things quite often."

"I'm glad you've said that, if that's the way you see it. I appreciate your compliments. I think you are being treated fairly, but I want you to be as confident about that as I am. I want the two of us to talk about this briefly at 3:30. Right now it's best that you continue with your duties. How is that with you?"

Level 4.0 because it has high-level genuineness, immediacy of relationship, and brings it to closure with respect. It is directive without being pushy and makes a demand without being demanding.

9a. "Okay."

"Thanks."

Probably the most difficult task in supervision is talking with an employee about such things as deficiencies in performance of duties, infractions of rules, or undesirable interpersonal relationships. In terms of the communication model, such interactions use the initiative dimensions of confrontation. The acceptance of any confrontation depends upon (a) a good base relationship and (b) skillful use of the confrontation itself.

The confrontation occasion does not need to be extremely uncomfortable for either supervisor or subordinate. It can, in fact, be a time of constructive advance in skills and understanding for both parties. These suggestions can maximize the benefits of these occasions. The supervisor should:

1. Be careful not to get overly caught up in the crisis of the moment but keep the long-range relationship in mind.

2. Take care not to accuse prematurely, listen to the employee's story, be alert for new data that are relevant to the situation.
3. Give employees an opportunity to take the initiative in explaining and correcting the situation, follow the principle of allowing them to do as much for themselves as they are capable of doing.
4. Put the criticism and the problem area in perspective by discussing employees' areas of strength. To let employees mistakenly feel that they are doing nothing right is tragic but it happens frequently. Again, stay alert for the effect of the interaction on the employees.
5. Provide the best protection against remedial supervisory work by prevention of problems through clear task assignment and other preparation of employees to carry out their duties.
6. Avoid "hit and run" confrontation. Things rarely are as simple as they appear on the surface so allow for explanation of the problem and ample time for interaction.

The following dialogue illustrates an effective supervisor using her skills to resolve a problem. In this example, a supervising nurse, Mrs. Plummer, is talking with two of her team's aides, Gail and Anne. Their inappropriate behavior had been reported to Mrs. Plummer, who subsequently had verified it, and called them in to talk.

| Aides | Supervisor | Discussion |
|---|---|---|
| 1. | "The reason I wanted to see you two together is to discuss a complaint I had a few minutes ago from one of your patients." | Level 3.0: shows respect, is concrete. |
| 2. (Gail) "Okay, what is it?" | "It was about loud talking and laughing while you were making a patient's bed. You both know that I rarely get a report like that from one of your patients, but I need to talk with you about this." | Level 3.0: She explains the purpose of the conversation, then eases her criticism by pointing out, briefly, that the job performance usually has been good. |
| 3. (Gail) "I don't believe it, but who said it?" | "I guess you're surprised, and maybe you aren't sure I have my facts straight. It was Mrs. Moon." | Level 4.0: picks up underlying feelings. |
| 4. (Anne) "She's nothing but a complainer." | "We're here to talk about you, not her." | Level 3.0: Concreteness brings helpees back to the subject. |
| 5. (Gail) "What time? Real early today?" | "Yes." | Level 3.0: responds to request for information. |

6. (Anne, breaking in angrily) "She's been a troublemaker from day one. She's . . ."

7. (Anne, shouting) "The whole thing's a lie! We've hardly spoken to each other all morning!"
(Gail, timidly) "Well, Anne . . ."
(Anne continues) "Mrs. Plummer, you don't know what you're talking about. You never do!"

(firmly) "Anne, let me repeat that we are here to talk about your behavior."

"These are things you have strong feelings about, so we will talk about them in privacy. Gail, you can go on with your work for the moment. Anne and I will be in my office."

Level 4.0 concreteness.

Level 4.0: begins to speak when Gail breaks in, only to be interrupted by Anne. Mrs. Plummer must take firm control. She feels confident of her facts and of Gail's cooperation. She gives Anne the right to have and to express anger and wants to get more information about its causes. The rest of the conversation is between Anne and Mrs. Plummer.

8. "Excuse me for yelling, but there are some things I have to say."

"And, I assume, they are important for me to hear. I want to. So tell me about those things and then we'll also finish up with the matter of Mrs. Moon."

Level 4.0 respect: Mrs. Plummer chooses to follow Anne's strongest feelings—to go with Anne's agenda—first, but keeps it clear that the original topic is still important.

9. "It's not possible to work as a team if we never speak to each other."

"You know that some conversation is necessary."

Level 3.0 facilitative response. This encourages continued helpee exploration.

10. "The only time you ever talk to me is like now, when I'm getting chewed out."

"You want more from me than that."

Level 3.0. This response is concrete and also touches on the immediacy of relationship dimension.

11. "Yeah."

"Perhaps to be given more encouragement."

Level 4.0 for getting at underlying needs.

12. "Yeah."

"To let you know how you're doing, when things go well."

Level 4.0 for getting at underlying needs.

13. "That would be nice."

"And you should hear that."

Level 4.0 respect.

14. "I guess I need to."

"As I do, too."

Level 4.0 self-disclosure.

15. "I don't get any encouragement at home."

"It sounds like things are kind of rough there right now."

Level 3.0 empathy.

16. "Like you wouldn't believe."

"I hear a lot of pain as you say that. I don't know if you want to say more about it, but if you do, it would be all right with me."

Level 4.0 respect.

| | | |
|---|---|---|
| 17. "No. Not now, at least." | "You've identified something you want from me—more positive reports when you deserve them. I'll do that. I'll do my best to give you the praise that you earn." | Level 4.0 respect. |
| 18. "Thanks." | "Now we still need to talk about this report from Mrs. Moon." | Level 4.0 concreteness. |
| 19. (silence) | (pause) "Is there anything you can tell me about it?" | Mrs. Plummer does not jump in too early to fill up the silence. She wants Anne to take as much initiative as she can and will. |
| 20. "Well, she was right." | "You're saying that, yes, you and Gail were too noisy?" | Level 4.0 concreteness. |
| 21. "We did let things get out of hand. We stopped as soon as we realized we were bothering Mrs. Moon, but I guess once you have bothered someone you have bothered them." | "True, but I want you to consider if you and Mrs. Moon wouldn't both be more comfortable if you apologized to her." | Level 4.0 confrontation. |
| 22. "You've got to be kidding!" | "You know I'm not. Think about it, and think about it in terms of what our goals are in our work here." | Level 4.0 concreteness. |
| 23. "Yeah, I know what you mean. You are right, but . . . sheesh!" | "It won't be easy for you." | Level 3.0 empathy. |
| 24. "I'm not sure I can." | "Scary." | Level 4.0 empathy. |
| 25. "Yeah." | "What are you going to do?" | Level 4.0 concreteness. |
| 26. "I'll take a shot at it." | "Great! (pause) And in the future?" | Level 4.0 warmth and concreteness. |
| 27. "I'll keep my mouth under control." | "Good. And for my part, I'll try to touch base with you more often. I guess that's it." | Level 4.0 respect and concreteness. |
| 28. (stands up) "Thanks." | "And thanks for your cooperation. And if there are other things we ought to talk about, see to it that we do." | Level 4.0 immediacy of relationship and respect. |

29. "I appreciate that.
Maybe we will." (leaves the
office)

Even though Mrs. Plummer attempted to deal with both Anne and Gail together, she decided to send Gail back to work when Anne became very angry during the conference. Of course, at this point in the conflict resolution situation Mrs. Plummer has reached closure with Anne and her next task is to call Gail in and repeat the above process.

## 3. COMMUNICATING IN TIMES OF GRIEF

Grief is a complexity of emotions. The words anxiety, hopelessness, guilt, lonelines, sadness, and despair all describe aspects of it. While grief usually is associated with death and dying, it accompanies many other situations that are not uncommon in health care such as permanent physical impairment, job loss, amputation, deformed birth, wanting to have a child but not being able to, births out of wedlock, and mental illness.

Many helpers find it very difficult to communicate with a grieving person, particularly in the case of death or dying. For many persons in today's society, the discussion of death and dying has been taboo. In addition, people seem to be increasingly removed from the sight of death. Differing religious views concerning the meaning of death further complicate communication.

Many experienced health care professionals report that helping grieving persons does not become easier with practice. It requires keen perception and careful formulation of responses to meet adequately and accurately the needs of the grieving persons, who are focusing intense emotional energy upon their situation.

To be able to help a grieving person effectively, caregivers must understand their own views and attitudes as well as those of the helpee. Kubler-Ross (1969) enumerated five stages through which many persons pass in their relationship to dying. These stages also are evident frequently in dealing with grief from other causes. The descriptions of these stages include suggestions about appropriate measures for the helper.

1. The first stage is shock and denial. The dying person may have physical symptoms similar to those during fear.
2. The next stage often is anger—resentment over what is happening. In both of these stages the dying person may be very difficult to work with. Health care professionals may be resented because they represent and are a reminder of the problem. At all times, but particularly

during these stages, helpers need to be fully accepting of the person
and the behaviors. They should let the individual express any and all
feelings, even though they may be unpleasant. Unexpressed feelings
create more bad feelings.

3. After a time, the person may begin to bargain. Promises of good
   behavior or changed patterns of living may be made to family or to
   God. These may be entirely sincere and may give the person a sense
   of hope and encouragement. Helpers should be supportive but should
   not reinforce expectations known to be unrealistic.
4. After a time the person discovers that the hope was unfounded and
   becomes depressed, or experiences an overpowering sense of lone-
   liness. The caring expressed by spending time with the person is
   probably the most powerful act of helping possible during this stage.
5. The final stage is acceptance. The dying person then may be able to
   talk about and plan for the funeral and settle personal affairs. The
   individual may manifest a detachment from and indifference to sur-
   roundings and even to family. This may be a difficult time for the
   helpers because they may feel rejected by the patient or feel that
   efforts to prolong the person's life are not appreciated. Helpers should
   exercise every effort to avoid communicating indifference or resentment to the patient in any way.

For other persons this stage signals the beginning of reconstruction—a
time for picking up the things that remain and building with them. It is
appropriate for helpers in these circumstances to be supportive, to facilitate
the helpee's exploration of alternatives, and to otherwise assist the renewal
of functioning.

To the extent possible, the health care professionals should always maintain both physical and psychological contact with the grieving person. They
should take care to communicate with the person with their usual frequency. The individual should be allowed to have as much information
about and control over the situation as is possible without being detrimental
to morale. Health permitting, interaction with other persons and visits
from the family should be encouraged. The nature of these interactions,
however, must be appropriate to the needs of the individual at that time.
Appropriate physical contact often means more than any words in times
of grief.

At times, dealing with the family can be as difficult as dealing with the
patient. The protocol in Exhibit 19–1 illustrates the application of the
principles described above and of the appropriate use of the dimensions
of the interpersonal skills model in an interaction between a nurse and the
wife of a terminally ill patient.

REFERENCE

Kubler-Ross, E. *On death and dying.* New York: The Macmillan Company, 1969.

**Exhibit 19–1** Protocol: Effective Helper
(Responding to the Wife of a Terminally Ill Patient)

SITUATION: A 76-year-old man is hospitalized as terminally ill with carcinoma of the prostate. The following is a conversation between his wife and a nurse.

| Helpee (Wife of Terminally Ill Patient) | Helper (Nurse) | Discussion |
|---|---|---|
| (Stopping by room where nurse is drinking coffee) "Oh, the coffee smells so good. Would it be possible for me to get a cup?" | "Surely, come in and sit: I'll get you the coffee." (Returns with coffee) "The nights get awfully long, don't they?" | The nurse (helper) provides direct assistance through getting the coffee but more importantly opens up the opportunity for the helpee to talk about her ordeal if she chooses to do so. |
| "They sure do, and right now he's dozing so I just had to get out for a little while." | "Being with him through this is really hard on you." | The helper responds with empathy to the helpee. |
| "Oh, I can't stand to see him suffer so. He has gone down so fast since the doctor told him he had cancer. It seems like he just gave up." | "It sounds like you might regret that the doctor told your husband that he had cancer." | The helper keeps the focus on the helpee's feelings even though the helpee has shifted the content to her husband. |
| "I do. I didn't want him told—but he was told—and ever since then, he's just laid in his bed and gotten steadily worse." | "You can't help but be angry at the doctor for telling your husband something that seems to have hurt him, especially when you didn't want him to because you knew how your husband would react." | The helper responds to the helpee's underlying feelings of anger toward the doctor. |
| "That's true, but I know the doctor didn't know and he did what he felt was best." | "But that doesn't help the both of you now. Perhaps you're blaming yourself for not being more forceful and convincing with the doctor." | Here the helper reaches beyond the surface content and feeling and anticipates how the helpee may feel about her own part in the doctor's action. |

## Exhibit 19–1 continued

"I do feel guilty, but I don't know what to do now."

"You apparently felt able to handle the situation when your husband didn't know he had cancer but really feel helpless now that he's given up and apparently resigned himself to dying."

The helper responds to the helpee's new dilemma of not knowing how to handle her husband's reaction now that he knows the seriousness of his illness. The helper therefore opens up this idea of concern for further exploration.

"But I can't stand to see him die. I keep telling him that if he would try, he'd get over this."

"You really don't want to lose him and you are unable to believe or accept that you will."

The helper gets right to the point of the extreme difficulty the wife is having accepting the husband's death.

"I can't! I won't! It can't happen to us."

(Reaching out and touching the woman's hand.) "You know this is probably the hardest thing you will have to do in life and right now you can't see how you can possibly do it."

At this point the helper demonstrates her warmth by touching the helpee and responding to her disbelief and felt inadequacy.

(Silence, then begins crying quietly.)

(Says nothing; continues to hold woman's hand.)

The silent comforting of the helper is magnified by her holding the helpee's hand and being physically close as well as emotionally close.

"I love him so much. We married late; I was 40 and he was 56. I had never been married and his wife was dead. He had four children that were all grown and, of course, we didn't have any. And all my family is dead except for a brother."

"So he is really almost all you have and that makes accepting his dying especially difficult."

The helpee now feels free to disclose more about her relationship with her husband and thus she is able to show the helper the magnitude of her impending loss—the fact that she will be virtually alone after his death.

"Yes, but I knew it had to come. One of us would have to leave the other and we have had a wonderful 20 years together." (Pause) "I believe I'll go back now; he may need me. Thank you for the coffee and for listening. I feel better, at least for now."

The helper has done all she can at the moment. She has built a good base with the helpee, who freely chooses to close the interaction for the moment. She probably feels less alone with her problem and strengthened in her ability to face it.

**Exhibit 19–1** continued

SITUATION: Several days later—the same woman and the same nurse.

"You know, my husband wants to go home. He has always said he wanted to die at home in his bed—not in a hospital."

"And you are trying to decide what to do."

The helper senses and communicates to the helpee the helpee's indecision—her need to resolve this serious dilemma.

"Yes. I know he wants to be at home, but I want him to have everything possible and I know you can look after him better here."

"It is a big decision for you to make. Let's go in my office and talk about it. Let's see, some of your alternatives might be leaving him in the hospital, caring for him at home, or possibly placing him in a nursing home."

The helper enumerates some possible choices for the helpee as she moves the interaction into the action phase of the problem solving—considering alternatives.

"Oh no! I could never put him in a nursing home."

"OK, that leaves us the hospital or home, or perhaps some other alternative."

The helper learns quickly that the alternatives are essentially two: staying in the hospital or going home. Here the helper delimits the alternatives.

"He wants to die at home, but I don't know if he'll get the proper care he needs there or if Margaret (a close personal friend) and I can care for him."

"That is a very realistic concern. Taking him home will mean a big commitment and will really be hard for you and Margaret."

The helper is concrete and genuine, recognizing the extra effort that the helpee will have to make if she takes her husband home.

"Especially since I don't feel I'll be able to change my mind because I made a promise to him that I would let him die at home."

"And right now, there is no way for you to know what might happen—how long he will live, how much pain there will be, or even how death will occur."

The helper goes over the elements the wife must consider in her choice of taking her husband home. The helper is specific about the unknowns that face the helpee in her decision.

"That's right, and with only Margaret to help me, it really worries me. And actually Margaret will have to do most of the care because of my health, and she's not even family."

"So part of what bothers you is that you're not only making a commitment for yourself, but for someone else."

At this point the helper communicates the concern that the helpee has for her friend and the fact that she also is committing her friend to a difficult task.

"It really does, but I know Margaret will do it. We went through all of this with her husband several years ago."

"So you were helpful to Margaret then and she is ready to help you now. I have noticed that she has been with you all the time, almost 24 hours a day."

The helper communicates that she understands why the helpee would even entertain the idea of committing her friend to this ordeal.

## Exhibit 19–1 continued

"Yes, she's a great friend—closer than any family. I'm really lucky to have her."

"And she's lucky to have a friend like you."

As the wife focuses on her friend, the helper reassures her that she is deserving of such a good friend since, though not elaborated, the helpee evidently had suffered through a similar experience with her friend Margaret.

(Laughs lightly) "Well, I guess we could do it, but what about the doctors?"

"Well, Jane, you know there is very little they can do. He's getting his hormone shot once a week, and I could come and give that. The only other thing that they could do for him here is to give him some fluids intravenously later, and there is no reason we couldn't do that at home. We can give suppositories for pain and, if necessary, I can give him shots. I can help you and answer questions as they come up. The hardest thing is going to be that you will be nursing him 24 hours a day."

The helper outlines the feasibility of the helpee's wish and commits herself even further to help make it possible for the wife to implement her wish to take her husband home.

"Well, we're already staying with him all the time. He won't let us go. So I guess we might as well do it at home."

"I will help you all I can."

The helpee has made the decision and the helper supports it with her reassurance of assistance. (Of course, if the helper could not live up to her commitment, then it would be inappropriate to make such a commitment.)

"Well, when the doctors come around, I'm going to ask them to let him go home."

## Exhibit 19–1 continued

SITUATION: Several months later, same woman and same nurse.

| | | |
|---|---|---|
| "You have meant so much to me through this, and it has been so hard. But at least I'm letting him have his last wish—to die at home." | "That's a great feeling for you, too. At least you won't have to live with regrets that you could or should have done more, for you have given your all and that will comfort you the rest of your life." | The helper communicates to the helpee that she understands how much it has meant to the wife to provide her husband with his wish—to die at home. |
| "But we couldn't have done it without you." | "Thank you. I have gotten so much from knowing you, too—seeing people who will give so much to help someone they care about." | The helper was able to receive the gratitude and also return it for the benefit of both helpee and helper. |
| "Did you notice how little urine he had when you were in there?" | "Yes, I did, and you're worried about it." | Again the helper sees below the content of the wife's comment and zeroes in on the helpee's real feeling. |
| "You told us to watch it and let you know if it got below 1,000 cc's a day. And, you know, the last several days it has gone down each day. Yesterday it was only 400 cc's." | "You have been very observant. Now you want to know what we're going to do." | The helper allows the helpee to explore a painful possibility. |
| "Yes." | "Well, the low urine means he's dehydrated—not getting enough fluid—so we could give him some more fluids intravenously. But you know how he hates that." | The nurse shows respect by answering the helpee's question even though they both know what the sign means. |
| "I know. Every time you come over with that equipment he cries." | "I know, that's why I haven't done it this time." | The helper has made it easier for the helpee to make a painful decision of not prolonging her husband's agony. |
| "But what happens if he doesn't get the fluids?" | "Jane, I think you know. The fluids would keep him alive a little longer." | Once again the helper shows respect to the wife by answering a question to which the helpee already knows the answer. |
| "How much longer?" | "I don't know, but what we've got to consider is what you and he would want." | The helper is first honest and genuine and then opens up the issue for further exploration. |

**Exhibit 19–1** continued

| | | |
|---|---|---|
| "Well, I know he doesn't want the fluids, but I don't want to give up." | "You're afraid of his dying." | The helper taps the underlying feeling of helpee fear and moves toward immediacy. |
| "I am. I've never seen anyone die and I won't know what to do or what to say—or even to recognize when he is dying." | "Jane, there is little I can say or do to make this easier on you or him. His refusal to drink may be his way of self-protection from pain and probably even from an awareness of dying. Death will probably be quiet. He'll probably have a little trouble breathing first. I know you don't want to be here alone. Anytime you think it might be happening, you call me and I'll come right over." | The helper self-discloses in giving her own personal interpretation of what the husband's condition must be like. She then informs the wife of signs to observe and concludes by offering to come whenever she is called. |
| "You know I'll call you." | | The helper reassures the wife of her willingness to help even when inconvenienced. She conveys that she does not consider the helpee's dependence to be a burden on her. |

# Chapter 20

# Epilogue: The Happiness and Hazards of Helping

Being a helper can be extremely rewarding and the rewards are real, even though they often are intangible. Much of the payoff is in the enhancement of the health care professional's own life as the result of investing emotional effort in others.

Using helping skills makes caregivers attractive persons to be with because they have the potential to meet some of the needs of others rather than be a part of the problem. Sharpening their perceptual and communication skills makes them more aware of everything that is around them, both the pleasant and the unpleasant. It increases their appreciation of the pleasant and strengthens their power to change the unpleasant. Having skills to effect change and to cope successfully with difficult interpersonal situations increases their confidence.

Persons who have poor communication become targets for the hostility and frustration of others, but those with good communication do not attract this dissension. They not only are rewarded for their good communication, but have fewer unpleasant interactions for which they may need help. The use of good communication is self-reinforcing because it begets good communication.

At the same time, helping has its hazards. Health care professionals probably have discovered that perceiving another person's communication, accepting that person as is, and responding with accurate and genuine empathy is tough, demanding work. This can become burdensome if they do not keep their skills sharp and keep their role as helpers in perspective. There are some measures caregivers can take to minimize the stress of being helpers, with the result that the process of helping will be an exciting and productive activity.

First, it must be recognized that helpers need helpers. They are human, too, and subject to the same psychic and societal stresses as the persons with whom they interact. These stresses are neutralized or relieved for helpers through the same processes as for helpees; in other words, occasionally helpers becomes helpees. Everyone needs to have significant relationships with others to whom he or she can turn for facilitative interaction—for a recharge of the emotional batteries. It is, in part, this resource that helps caregivers become and remain sufficiently secure within themselves to be able to serve effectively as helpers. They should feel no sense of inadequacy or stigma if they, too, need the understanding, support, and prodding of a helper.

Health care professionals must learn to spot trouble when it is small. A benefit that often comes with learning to perceive the feelings of others accurately is greater awareness of things that cause caregivers to be uncomfortable. This makes possible early recognition of situations in which helpers may be vulnerable so they can take countermeasures. They must avoid those situations if possible and seek to strengthen their skills in dealing with them.

Caregivers should not try to be helpers when they cannot be. There are some instances in which their effectiveness as helpers will be limited. If they are significantly distracted by such factors as personal illness, financial worries, family needs, deep sadness, or change of job, they temporarily may not have the capacity for the intense involvement required for helping. They probably cannot help someone with a problem in an area that they have not resolved for themselves, nor is it probable that they can help persons they do not like. Difficulty in understanding the language of persons of another culture or subculture may create a barrier that retards or precludes helping. Under any of these conditions caregivers should postpone attempts to help. Instead, they should assist the person in finding another helper.

Caregivers also should rate themselves to keep their skills high. If health care professionals understand the principles of helpful communication presented in this manual and have command of the Global Scale, they can appraise their own level of communication as an interaction proceeds. This model for helping focuses on the helpee; thus, helpers are continuously evaluating the effect of their communication upon the helpee. As skills develop, HCPs will find this instant feedback more and more useful. It will enable them to increase their level of functioning and will broaden the range of helpees with whom they can be effective.

Finally, it must be remembered that helping is for the helpee. Helping is a privilege. Caregivers who are allowed to help enter another person's innermost self. Even though they stress the helpee's active self-help role, the person does become unprotected and vulnerable in the process. When helpees allow this, they give the highest compliment of which they are capable—they are trusting the caregivers completely. This places extreme responsibility on helpers to not take advantage of the situation, to not use the helpee to meet their own needs, and to maintain total confidentiality. Health care professionals who are not willing to be helpers for the sake of the helpees and only of such persons should not try to be helpers; they will not be effective.

Helping can enhance the life satisfaction of helpees and of the persons with whom they come in contact. Helping also can be an exciting and personally satisfying adventure for the helpers.

# Nursing Index of Responding

The Nursing Index of Responding allows nurses to evaluate their progress according to the communication model presented in this text. The index has been administered as premeasures and postmeasures for training groups directed by the authors.

Administration of an index as a pretest will help you by establishing a baseline that may be used to plan individuals' training programs. If their average score is 2.5 to 3.0 or better on the Nursing Index of Responding, this would allow health care professionals to move quickly into training in higher levels of the facilitative dimensions and into the transition and action dimensions of the model. They should use the Global Scale (as explained in Chapter 14) for rating responses on the Nursing Index of Responding. The key at the end of this index should be used as a pretest/training measure.

Administration of the index as a posttest permits evaluation of HCPs' growth. In general, they are expected to achieve a modal score of 3.0 or more on the Index of Responding at posttraining.

### NURSING INDEX OF RESPONDING (FORM N)

*Situation 1*—Patient to nurse: "I haven't worked for quite a while now. My bills are piling up, and the doctor says I might not be able to work as a carpenter again. Losing the sight in my right eye after the accident really presents problems."

*Response:*_____

_____

_____

_____

*Situation 2*—Nurse to nurse colleague: "I don't know what I'm going to do with my son. He isn't doing at all well in school. Yet he is bright and can do well when he wants to. Every time I mention his grades we get into a hot argument and I lose my temper and say hurtful things to him. He ends up hurting my feelings and storms out of the house."

*Response:*_____

_____

_____

*Situation 3*—Patient's mother to nurse: "I've been here in the hospital with my son since Friday. (Pause) The doctors don't give him much hope."

*Response:*_____

_____

_____

*Situation 4*—Patient to nurse: "The doctors just told me I can't go home tomorrow. They said they have more tests to do. That means being hurt over and over again. The doctors said I could go home next Wednesday. But I just don't know when I really will get home to look after mother."

*Response:*_____

_____

_____

*Situation 5*—Psychiatric patient to psychiatric nurse: "One reason I had to come to the hospital is that my husband and I are separated. My husband was always so good to me and I was always so mean. I wasn't ever satisfied. I always wanted more."

*Response:*_____

_____

_____

*Situation 6*—Nurse to supervisor: "I'm glad you got a promotion to Clinical Nurse III even if you won't recommend me for one. But I still see myself as a Clinical Nurse III because I do the work of one."

*Response:*_____

_____

_____

*Situation 7*—Patient's husband to nurse: "My wife was admitted before 4 o'clock, and now it's 8 p.m. She had no supper, there are no private duty nurses for her, and she doesn't have a call light. You call yourselves nurses, but you aren't taking care of my wife!"

*Response:*_____

_____

_____

_____

### KEY TO NURSING INDEX OF RESPONDING (FORM N)

#### Preface

For each of the seven stimulus statements of the Nursing Index of Responding (Form N) an example of the four different levels of responses is given. When this key is used in conjunction with the Global Scale, more accuracy in scoring/rating is possible. However, if the rater has not mastered the Global Scale, a comparison of responses with each of the four sample responses should provide a general indication of the person's level of communication.

The rater should realize that only one of numerous examples of each level could be included because of space limitations. To earn a level 4.0, there usually must be a previously established high level of rapport. Even then, it can only be speculated how the response would be received, and the authors would need to hear the respondent's answer to the proposed level 4.0 response to be sure it was utilized productively. A level 4.0 response includes responding accurately to the surface feeling and the content of the helpee and also going beyond to a deeper, unexpressed feeling/attitude.

A level 3.0 response must include at least an accurate reflection of the surface feeling of the helpee and preferably the content as well.

A level 2.0 response is one that is not quite accurate in reflecting the surface feeling and the content. It also may be represented by a question that is relevant to the helpee's request but is premature.

A level 1.0 response is one that is inappropriate by being punitive or insensitive, or by changing the subject.

## KEY
**Nursing Index of Responding (Form N)**
(Sample Responses for Rating Comparisons)

*Situation 1*

Assume the patient and nurse already have established a high level of rapport or mutual trust:

Level 4: "You're really feeling worried about how you will pay your medical bills, but an even greater worry is what kind of work you will be able to get if you have the use of only one eye. You may even be wondering if you will be able to work again, and if not, how you ever will manage."

Level 3: "You're pretty worried about paying your medical bills and what losing the sight in your eye will mean to your work as a carpenter."

Level 2: "You're not sure how you will pay your medical bills if you aren't able to work as a carpenter."

Level 1: "You don't have anything to worry about. A lot of people manage with more serious problems than yours."

*Situation 2*

Assume the nurse and colleague have a high level of rapport and mutual trust:

Level 4: "You want to do what is best for your son, but somehow you haven't been able to discover the way to confront him so that he can accept it and use it to improve his goals. You seem to be feeling guilty about losing your control and also angry at your son for his disrespect."

Level 3: "You're uncertain as to what to do to motivate your son to do better in school. You also seem very upset with him because he won't listen to you."

Level 2: "Your son isn't working up to his potential but you don't know what to do about it."

Level 1: "Why don't you try getting off his back."

*Situation 3*

Assume the patient's mother and nurse already have established a high level of rapport and mutual trust:

Level 4: "You're fearful that your son might die and you feel helpless to do anything about it."

Level 3: "You're really frightened because the doctors haven't been able to help your son."

Level 2: "Are you saying there is no hope for your son?"

Level 1: "Why don't you go down to the coffee shop and think about something else for a while."

*Situation 4*

Assume the patient and nurse already have established a high level of rapport and mutual trust:

Level 4: "Your trust in the doctors has been shaken because they have decided to keep you longer to run more tests. In addition to the pain of undergoing all the new tests, you have the additional burden of worrying about who will care for your mother. You must be feeling pretty overwhelmed by all of this."

Level 3: "It is very disturbing to you to learn that there may be something more seriously wrong than the doctors first thought. And you're also worried about the additional pain of the tests and who will care for your mother."

Level 2: "Why don't you tell the doctors that you can't stay for more tests until after you go home and get somebody to take care of your mother."

Level 1: "Don't worry, someone will take care of your mother."

*Situation 5*

Assume the patient and nurse already have established a high level of rapport and mutual trust:

Level 4: "You're really worried that maybe you have lost your husband because you were mean and too demanding of him. You seem to want a second chance to make it up to him. Perhaps we can still find a way."

Level 3: "You're fearful that because of your past behavior with your husband, he won't take you back. You seem also to be feeling pretty guilty about your behavior toward him."

Level 2: "Why don't you call your husband and tell him you're sorry."

Level 1: "You can't be that bad. Anyway, there are more fish in the sea if he should divorce you."

### Situation 6

Assume the nurse and the supervisor already have established a high level of rapport and mutual trust even though it appears to have been momentarily shaken:

Level 4: "I'm pleased that you approve of my promotion. I know that you are disappointed that I have not yet recommended you for the same promotion but I sense that you have confidence enough in my judgment to see that you are treated fairly."

Level 3: "You're pleased about my promotion but disappointed that I have not recommended you for promotion."

Level 2: "You believe that you do the work of a Clinical Nurse III."

Level 1: "You're just jealous of my success."

### Situation 7

Assume the patient's husband and this particular nurse previously have established a high level of rapport and mutual trust:

Level 4: "John, I know how worried you are about Helen. You want the very best care for her and you're angry because we don't seem to be showing enough concern for her well being. I'll find out why these things haven't been done and see that they are taken care of promptly."

Level 3: "You're really worried about your wife and angry at us for not doing more for her."

Level 2: "We have had a lot of emergencies this evening but they are under control and now we should be able to attend to your wife."

Level 1: "Look, sir, don't jump on me! I only do what my supervisor tells me to do."

# Sensory Modality Checklist

Discover your preferred cognitive style for learning and self-expression.

The Sensory Modality Checklist assesses the strengths of each of your major sensory modalities—auditory, visual, and kinesthetic.

There are ten incomplete sentences and three choices for completing each sentence. Some of the choices contain more than one option. If any one of those options seems typical of you, score that answer. All of the options do not have to apply to you.

Score the three choices by rating (3) to the answer most typical of you, (2) to your second choice, and (1) to the last answer.

## SENSORY MODALITY CHECKLIST

Score (3) to the answer most typical of you, (2) to your second choice, and (1) to the last answer.

1. When I want to learn something new, I usually:
   A ( ) want someone to explain it to me.
   B ( ) want to read about it in a book or magazine.
   C ( ) want to try it out, take notes, or make a model of it.

2. At a party, most of the time I like to:
   A ( ) listen and talk to two or three people at once.
   B ( ) see how everyone looks and watch the people.

---

C ( ) dance, play games, or take part in some activities.

3. If I were helping with a musical show, I would most likely:
   A ( ) write the music, sing the songs, or play the accompaniment.
   B ( ) design the costumes, paint the scenery, or work the lighting effects.
   C ( ) make the costumes, build the sets, or take an acting role.

4. When I am angry, my first reaction is to:
   A ( ) tell people off, laugh, joke, or talk it over with someone.
   B ( ) blame myself or someone else, daydream about taking revenge, or keep it inside.
   C ( ) make a fist or tense my muscles, take it out on something else, hit or throw things.

5. A happy event I would like to have is:
   A ( ) hearing the thunderous applause for my speech or music.
   B ( ) photographing the prized picture of sensational newspaper story.
   C ( ) achieving the fame of being first in a physical activity such as dancing, acting, surfing, or a sports event.

6. I prefer a teacher to:
   A ( ) use the lecture method with informative explanations, and discussions.
   B ( ) write on the chalkboard, use visual aids, and assign readings.
   C ( ) require posters, models, or inservice practice, and some activities in class.

7. I know that I talk with:
   A ( ) different tones of voice.
   B ( ) my eyes and facial expressions.
   C ( ) my hands and gestures.

8. If I had to remember an event so that I could record it later, I would choose to:
   A ( ) tell it aloud to someone, or hear an audio tape recording or a song about it.
   B ( ) see pictures of it, or read a description.
   C ( ) replay it in some practice rehearsal using movements such as dance, playacting, or drill.

9. When I cook something new, I like to:
   A ( ) have someone tell me the directions—a friend or television show.
   B ( ) read the recipe and judge by how it looks.

C ( ) use many pots and dishes, stir often, and taste-test.

10. In my free time, I like to:
    A ( ) listen to the radio, talk on the telephone, or attend a musical event.
    B ( ) go to the movies, watch television, or read a magazine or book.
    C ( ) get some exercise, go for a walk, play games, or make things.

Total all "A" choices _____Auditory
Total all "B" choices _____Visual
Total all "C" choices _____Kinesthetic

Look at the three scores you added for
Auditory, Visual, and Kinesthetic.

They will range from 10 to 30; together they will total 60.

The Auditory score means that you learn and express yourself through sounds and hearing. The Visual score means that you enjoy learning and expressing yourself with your eyes, seeing things written, colors, and imageries. The Kinesthetic score means that you learn and express yourself through physical, muscular activity and practice.

If the scores are within four points of each other, you have a mixed modality, which means that you process information in any sensory modality with balanced ease.

If there are five points or more between any of the scores, you have a relative strength in that modality as compared to the others. You may have two modalities that seem stronger than the other one. This means that you learn more easily and express yourself more naturally in the modality with the larger score(s).

There are, of course, no right or wrong choices of sensory modalities. This checklist is a criterion-referenced achievement scale, revealing the sensory modalities that you have learned to depend on and enjoy the most. You can practice to improve your skill in any modality with the goal of achieving a mixed and balanced modality of sensory strengths.

# Life Skills Self-Report Questionnaire

Name _____

Date _____

Instructions: Circle the numbers under the categories that indicate the degree to which the statements describe you.

1. Describes me rarely
2. Describes me occasionally
3. Describes me about half of the time
4. Describes me frequently
5. Describes me almost always
6. Does not apply to me

1. I am able to share my problems with significant others such as family members, friends, and hospital staff.  1 2 3 4 5 6

2. I am not able to carry on a meaningful conversation with others.  1 2 3 4 5 6

3. I look at the person with whom I am talking.  1 2 3 4 5 6

4. When I am upset I am able to express these feelings without verbally offending or physically hurting someone.  1 2 3 4 5 6

5. I am not able to say "no" without hurting others and feeling guilty about it.  1 2 3 4 5 6

6. I am able to identify the feelings of other people and respond to them so that they feel understood.  1 2 3 4 5 6

7. I know the necessary steps involved in getting information about and applying for a job suitable to my interests and skills.    1  2  3  4  5  6

8. I know my behaviors that have led to my losing jobs.    1  2  3  4  5  6

9. I am not satisfied with myself and the things I have accomplished.    1  2  3  4  5  6

10. I am satisfied with my reason for living.    1  2  3  4  5  6

11. I am able to set and carry out day-to-day goals.    1  2  3  4  5  6

12. I know my long-term goals.    1  2  3  4  5  6

13. I do not know which foods and drinks are good for me.    1  2  3  4  5  6

14. I eat foods and drink liquids that are good for my health.    1  2  3  4  5  6

15. I follow a physical exercise program to improve my mental and physical health.    1  2  3  4  5  6

16. I am satisfied with my sex life.    1  2  3  4  5  6

17. I know the things that upset me.    1  2  3  4  5  6

18. I can not identify accurately my different feelings or emotions.    1  2  3  4  5  6

19. I know how to relieve my anxiety and tension.    1  2  3  4  5  6

20. I am not able to express good feelings such as love, appreciation, and happiness.    1  2  3  4  5  6

21. I use alcohol or other drugs to help me deal with my anxiety and problems.    1  2  3  4  5  6

22. I have a good marriage. We have love and respect for each other.    1  2  3  4  5  6

23. I get along well with my children. They respect me and obey me and I love and respect them.    1  2  3  4  5  6

24. I get along well with my parents. They
encourage and respect my independence and
they are willing to help when I need it.          1  2  3  4  5  6

25. I do not get along well with my brothers and
sisters. We cannot depend on each other for
help when someone needs it.                       1  2  3  4  5  6

26. I use effective methods for understanding my
problems.                                         1  2  3  4  5  6

27. I know some effective ways of solving my
problems.                                         1  2  3  4  5  6

28. I am not able to take specific action to
reduce my problems so that they do not
overwhelm me.                                     1  2  3  4  5  6

29. I do not know how to enjoy being with a
group of people.                                  1  2  3  4  5  6

30. I do not criticize people in front of others.   1  2  3  4  5  6

31. I am not able to trust and have confidence in
others.                                           1  2  3  4  5  6

32. I am sure of my personal values and beliefs.    1  2  3  4  5  6

33. I am not able to live up to my values and
beliefs.                                          1  2  3  4  5  6

34. I know which community agencies to contact
when I need emergency financial, mental or
medical help.                                     1  2  3  4  5  6

35. I am willing to seek financial, mental, or
medical help from community agencies when
I have a need for them and I cannot afford
to obtain them from private sources.              1  2  3  4  5  6

## KEY

This key shows which items are to be included for each life skill area.

*Interpersonal Communications*
Items: 1, 2, 3, 4, 5, 6, 29, 30, 31

*Vocational/Career Development*

Items: 7, 8

*Purpose/Meaning in Life*
Items: 9, 10, 11, 12, 32, 33

*Physical Fitness/Health Maintenance*
Items: 13, 14, 15, 16

*Emotional Understanding*
Items: 17, 18, 19, 20

*Family Relationships*
Items: 22, 23, 24, 25

*Problem Solving*
Items: 21, 26, 27, 28

*Use of Community Resources*
Items: 34, 35

# Vocabulary of Affective Adjectives

This list of adjectives was developed to help the user find the most appropriate description of perceived feelings. No attempt has been made to order these words in terms of their degree of intensity.

By simply preceding many of these adjectives with appropriate adverbs, it is possible to control the intensity of the communication. For example:

You can feel *somewhat* angry with your instructor for embarrassing you.
You feel *quite* angry with your instructor for embarrassing you.
You feel *very* angry with your instructor for embarrassing you.
You feel *extremely* angry with your instructor for embarrassing you.

## PLEASANT AFFECTIVE STATES

### (Love, Affection, Concern)

| | | | |
|---|---|---|---|
| admired | congenial | generous | kind-hearted |
| adorable | conscientious | genuine | kindly |
| affectionate | considerate | giving | lenient |
| agreeable | cooperative | good | lovable |
| altruistic | cordial | good-humored | loving |
| amiable | courteous | good-natured | mellow |
| benevolent | dedicated | helpful | mild |
| benign | devoted | honest | moral |
| big-hearted | easy-going | honorable | neighborly |
| brotherly | empathetic | hospitable | nice |
| caring | fair | humane | obliging |
| charitable | faithful | interested | open |
| Christian | forgiving | just | optimistic |
| comforting | friendly | kind | patient |

265

## (Love, Affection, Concern) continued

| | | | |
|---|---|---|---|
| peaceful | respectful | thoughtful | unselfish |
| pleasant | responsible | tolerant | warm |
| polite | sensitive | truthful | warm-hearted |
| reasonable | sweet | trustworthy | well-meaning |
| receptive | sympathetic | understanding | wise |
| reliable | tender | | |

## (Elation, Joy)

| | | | |
|---|---|---|---|
| amused | exalted | humorous | serene |
| at ease | excellent | in high spirits | splendid |
| blissful | excited | inspired | superb |
| brilliant | fantastic | jovial | terrific |
| calm | fine | joyful | thrilled |
| cheerful | fit | jubilant | tremendous |
| comical | gay | magnificent | triumphant |
| contented | glad | majestic | turned on |
| delighted | glorious | marvelous | vivacious |
| ecstatic | good | overjoyed | witty |
| elated | grand | pleasant | wonderful |
| elevated | gratified | pleased | |
| enchanted | great | proud | |
| enthusiastic | happy | satisfied | |

## (Potency)

| | | | |
|---|---|---|---|
| able | durable | influential | spirited |
| adequate | dynamic | intense | stable |
| assured | effective | lion-hearted | stouthearted |
| authoritative | energetic | manly | strong |
| bold | fearless | mighty | sure |
| brave | firm | powerful | tough |
| capable | forceful | robust | virile |
| competent | gallant | secure | well-equipped |
| confident | hardy | self-confident | well-put- |
| courageous | healthy | self-reliant | together |
| daring | heroic | sharp | |
| determined | important | skillfull | |

## UNPLEASANT AFFECTIVE STATES

### (Depression)

| | | | |
|---|---|---|---|
| abandoned | despised | horrible | pathetic |
| alien | despondent | humiliated | pitiful |
| alienated | destroyed | hurt | rebuked |
| alone | discarded | in-the-dumps | regretful |
| annihilate | discouraged | jilted | rejected |
| awful | disfavored | kaput | reprimanded |
| battered | dismal | left-out | rotten |
| below par | done-for | loathed | ruined |
| blue | downcast | lonely | run-down |
| burned | downhearted | lonesome | sad |
| castoff | downtrodden | lousy | stranded |
| cheapened | dreadful | low | tearful |
| crushed | estranged | miserable | terrible |
| debased | excluded | mishandled | unhappy |
| defeated | forlorn | mistreated | unloved |
| degraded | forsaken | moody | valueless |
| dejected | gloomy | mournful | washed-up |
| demolished | glum | obsolete | whipped |
| depressed | grim | ostracized | worthless |
| desolate | hated | out-of-sorts | wrecked |
| despair | hopeless | overlooked | |

### (Distress)

| | | | |
|---|---|---|---|
| afflicted | dissatisfied | lost | suspicious |
| anguished | distrustful | nauseated | swamped |
| awkward | disturbed | offended | tormented |
| badgered | doubtful | pained | touchy |
| bewildered | foolish | perplexed | ungainly |
| blameworthy | futile | puzzled | unlucky |
| clumsy | grief | ridiculous | unpopular |
| confused | helpless | sickened | unsatisfied |
| constrained | hindered | silly | unsure |
| disgusted | impaired | skeptical | |
| disliked | impatient | speechless | |
| displeased | imprisoned | strained | |

## (Fear, Anxiety)

| | | | |
|---|---|---|---|
| afraid | fearful | jittery | shy |
| agitated | fidgety | jumpy | strained |
| alarmed | frightened | nervous | tense |
| anxious | hesitant | on-edge | terrified |
| apprehensive | horrified | overwhelmed | terror-stricken |
| bashful | ill-at-ease | panicky | timid |
| desperate | insecure | restless | uncomfortable |
| dread | intimidated | scared | uneasy |
| embarrassed | jealous | shaky | worrying |

## (Belittling, Criticism, Scorn)

| | | | |
|---|---|---|---|
| abused | derided | libeled | scoffed-at |
| belittled | diminished | make light of | scorned |
| branded | discredited | maligned | shamed |
| carped-at | disdained | minimized | slammed |
| caviled-at | disgraced | mocked | slandered |
| censured | disparaged | neglected | slighted |
| criticized | humiliated | overlooked | underestimated |
| defamed | ignored | pooh-poohed | underrated |
| deflated | jeered | put-down | |
| deprecated | lampooned | ridiculed | |
| depreciated | laughed-at | roasted | |

## (Impotency, Inadequacy)

| | | | |
|---|---|---|---|
| anemic | flimsy | insecure | unable |
| broken | fragile | insufficient | unarmed |
| broken-down | frail | lame | uncertain |
| chicken-hearted | harmless | maimed | unfit |
| cowardly | helpless | meek | unimportant |
| crippled | impotent | nerveless | unqualified |
| debilitated | inadequate | paralyzed | unsound |
| defective | incapable | powerless | unsubstantiated |
| deficient | incompetent | puny | useless |
| demoralized | indefensible | shaken | vulnerable |
| disabled | ineffective | shaky | weak |

| | | | |
|---|---|---|---|
| effeminate | inefficient | sickly | weak-hearted |
| exhausted | inept | small | |
| exposed | inferior | strengthless | |
| feeble | infirm | trivial | |

## (Anger, Hostility, Cruelty)

| | | | |
|---|---|---|---|
| aggravated | cross | hypercritical | rebellious |
| agitated | cruel | ill-tempered | reckless |
| aggressive | deadly | impatient | resentful |
| angry | cool | inconsiderate | revengeful |
| annoyed | corrosive | inhuman | rough |
| antagonistic | dictatorial | insensitive | rude |
| arrogant | disagreeable | intolerable | ruthless |
| austere | discontented | intolerant | sadistic |
| bad-tempered | dogmatic | irritated | savage |
| belligerent | enraged | mad | severe |
| bigoted | envious | malicious | spiteful |
| biting | fierce | mean | stern |
| bloodthirsty | furious | murderous | stormy |
| blunt | gruesome | nasty | unfeeling |
| bullying | hard | obstinate | unfriendly |
| callous | hard-hearted | opposed | unmerciful |
| cantankerous | harsh | oppressive | unruly |
| cold-blooded | hateful | outraged | vicious |
| combative | heartless | perturbed | vindictive |
| contrary | hellish | poisonous | violent |
| cranky | hideous | prejudiced | wrathful |
| critical | hostile | pushy | |

# Additional Stimulus Situations

The following list of stimulus situations is provided for additional study and/or discussion.

Nurse to nurse: "This hospital is so task-oriented that there is no time left in the day to talk with the patients. When we were in nursing school we were taught that it is good to just talk with the patients but apparently this hospital doesn't believe that."

RN to new RN: "We work on a team-leader concept, which means that I mostly supervise and the LPNs and aides have most of the interaction with the patients. That is okay, I guess, but I miss not being able to work directly with the patients."

Nurse to nurse: "I get frustrated a lot because of the patient load we have in this hospital. In nursing school we only had three patients at a time and we gave complete care. Here I have so many patients to look after I don't get involved with any of them."

Nurse to nurse: "I have had the feeling for the past several weeks that the reason I feel dissatisfied with my job is because it is so routine. It seems like the tasks are honed down to a point where I am doing nothing else. There is something missing."

Nurse to nurse: "I'm really upset. I have been practicing 'good nursing' just like I learned in nursing school. Now they tell me that I am spending too much time with each patient and as a result all of the work is not getting done. If they would just add another employee to our shift, things would be okay."

Nurse to lab technician: "You know when we went in to draw that sample of blood from Mr. Wilson all you said was, 'We need to get a WBC!' The poor man had never been in a hospital before so you know he did not have any idea what you meant."

Two aides concerning a new RN: "That Miss Sweetwater is really a loser! All week long we have had to tell her exactly what to do. You would think she would already know a little bit. She is an RN, you know, and she makes a lot more money than we do."

Nurse to nurse: "I think technicians could be trained to do many of the minor things we have to spend so much of our time doing. That would free us to spend more time with the patients. I think that is where we are most valuable—not filling out forms."

Nurse is on her way to give a stat medication. As she passes Mrs. Hamilton's room, she yells, "Nurse, *please* help me. It feels like I'm bleeding from my incision."

Student nurse to instructor: "I wish I didn't have to tell you this, but I guess I better. I really did something stupid. I was getting ready to give my patient an injection of Demoral ® and I stuck my own thumb. I think I got some in. What will it do to me?"

A student nurse entered the nursery and said to the head nurse, "Can I see the meningomyelocele baby?" The head nurse thought the infant's mother, who was just leaving the area, might have overheard so she severely criticized the student for the remark. The student has just come to you, as the instructor, and is nearly in tears. She says, "all I was trying to do was to learn something. What's wrong with that?"

Nursing student to instructor: "I don't want to spend any more time in geriatrics. I can't stand the way nurses up there treat their patients. It's terrible. They push them around like they were furniture."

Student nurse to instructor: "I think I would like being in orthopedics except the nurses up there always make me feel like I'm in the way."

You are a nursing instructor. You just found out that one of your students did not give a patient an injection that was scheduled for one hour ago. The student has just said to you, in a rather huffy tone of voice, "Well, you weren't anywhere to be found, and I didn't dare ask one of the regular nurses. So what else could I do but wait? You keep telling us we can't give injections without supervision."

You are a nurse and have just finished giving your patient an injection. There is a knock on the door. The patient says, "Who's there?" The answer from outside the door is, "It's nobody but the maid." Would you say anything? If so, what?

Your work station is near the emergency room. About an hour ago a 3-year-old boy was brought in. The boy, who had been playing in the driveway of his home, was run over by his father in his car. Fortunately, despite external appearances, the boy had no serious injuries. During the last 10 minutes, the mother has been waiting near your desk. Now she approaches you and says, "We just got word that our boy, Jamie, is all right! You can't imagine what a relief that is!" She then bursts into tears, standing facing you and moving slightly toward you. What is your response?

It is now a week later. The boy and his mother approach your desk and she says, "I'll never forget what you said to me last week; it was such a big help. I just had to stop by and say 'Thank you.' " You respond.

The mother continues, "We just came from some follow-up tests. It looks like Jamie is going to be just fine. In fact, I think he's almost forgotten about it. His father, though, he's really taking it hard. He hasn't been himself at all. He has hardly spoken to me since it happened—he just sits around and stares into space. It's not like him at all. I wish he would get over it—it worries me so to see him that way. I just wish he would get over it."

## Patient to Nurse

"A month ago I had everything I ever wanted. Now I just lie here and feel my world crumbling around me."

"My parents are so busy out saving the world that they don't ever have time for their own kid. In fact, they act like they wish I'd never been born."

"If my parents knew how I was living now, it would really freak them out."

"I sit here watching my son dying and there's not a thing I can do to stop it."

"I get so angry with my kids. I'm afraid I'm going to do something to really hurt one of them some day."

"Jimmy's so slow—is there any chance he'll ever be normal?"

"My son—on drugs? That can't be! There must be some mistake!"

"Sometimes I think if I had it all to do over again, knowing what I do now, I'd never have any kids."

"All you can be sure of in this world is that people are going to put the screws to you every chance they get."

"I gave my kids the best years of my life and now they seem to have forgotten me. They don't ever write; they don't ever call; they don't even seem to know I exist."

"I don't know what I would have done without your help. You're the first person in my life who has ever cared about me."

"I don't know what in the world I'm doing here. The doctors won't listen, the nurses won't listen—this place is a waste of my time."

"Why should I cooperate with you? I don't want to get well. There's nothing for me to go home to. I guess there wasn't much there to begin with."

"You needn't bring my baby in to me to feed. I don't feel like taking care of him. Anyway, I'm not going to be the one taking care of him when I get home—my mother is."

"I just don't know what to do. I've lived with my wife so many years and love her very much—but I love my children, too. Sometimes she makes me so angry; she goes around the house yelling at the children, telling them that they're driving her crazy, that she hates them and can't live in the same house with them. Sometimes I think the kindest thing for me to do for her and the kids would be to divorce her."

"I just separated from my husband a month ago. The kids seem to be doing OK. Every once in a while, though, they say things that let me know they miss him. It's so hard being alone, wondering if you've made the right decision, and knowing so many people's lives are being affected by your judgment."

"If every hour of my life was as special as the last 24 have been, I could go on living forever. I never knew life could be so good."

"I've always wanted a baby so badly. Now I'm seriously thinking about never having one. With all the filth, crime, violence, and overcrowding in the world, it seems crazy to think about bringing a baby into this mess."

## Nurse to Nurse

"Those people on welfare—they keep on having illegitimate children and expecting society to take care of them."

"Women who have abortions are murderers."

"I don't think there's anything on earth lower than a person who'll abuse a child."

"When a woman comes into the hospital to have an abortion, I feel it's my professional obligation to explain to her the moral implications of what she's doing."

"You're a pleasure to work with!"

"I never thought I'd live to see the day when I'd be glad to see someone die."

"I can't understand why the coordinators rotate us on other wards for the evening shift. It's stupid. I don't know those patients."

"I think people should be able to choose whether or not to have an abortion. Around here, though, that seems to be a minority opinion."

# Scales for Rating the Helpees

All scales that have been presented up to this point have dealt with rating helpers in their interaction with helpees. The three five-level scales in this section are used to rate the helpees. These scales look at the extent of helpees' desire for problem-solving. They are analagous to the commitment of helpers to helpees, which is measured on the Respect Scale, except in this case it reflects the commitment of the helpees to themselves.

The three presented are the Helpee Help-Seeking Scale, Helpee Self-Exploration Scale, and Helpee Action-Implementing Scale. These are designed so that helpees must be at high levels on the Help-Seeking Scale before they can be at high levels on the Self-Exploration Scale, and, likewise must be high on the Self-Exploration Scale before they can be high on the Action-Implementing Scale. Thus, the three scales roughly form a continuum of helpees' commitment to the process of their own problem resolution or personal growth.

The action dimensions should be used only after high levels of self-exploration have been achieved. Therefore, the scale of helpee self-exploration may be used as an excellent indicator for timing the introduction of action responses.

The three helpee rating scales are outlined in the following section and the levels are defined.

## HELPEE HELP-SEEKING SCALE

The Help-Seeking Scale is a measure of whether or not helpees want to be involved in a helper-helpee relationship. They are rated on this scale according to the strength of their desire for help.

Level 5: Helpee actively seeks help.

Level 4: Helpee accepts help when provided.

Level 3: Helpee is open to being helped, will consider entering a helping relationship.

Level 2: Helpee admits need for help but avoids entering a helping relationship.

Level 1: Helpee overtly refuses available help, or participates in helper-helpee relationships in order to qualify for benefits extrinsic to the aims of the relationship.

## HELPEE SELF-EXPLORATION SCALE

The Helpee Self-Exploration Scale is a measure of the extent to which the person is actively searching for new feelings and experiences. Helpees are rated on this scale according to the strength of their desire to self-explore.

Level 5: Helpee actively searches for new feelings and experiences (even if fearful).

Level 4: Helpee volunteers personally relevant material with spontaneity and appropriate emotion.

Level 3: Helpee volunteers personally relevant material but does so mechanically and with no feeling.

Level 2: Helpee responds mechanically and with no feeling to personally relevant material introduced by the helper.

Level 1: Helpee avoids all self-expression, is defensive, and provides no opportunity to discuss personally relevant material.

## HELPEE ACTION-IMPLEMENTING SCALE

The Implementing Scale is a measure of the degree to which the helpee participates in the determination of and puts into practice problem-solving or growth-directed behaviors. The course of action is defined as the steps helpees take toward solving their problems and includes training or psychotherapy, socialization, education, restitution, physical exercise, relaxation, or other efforts.

Level 5: Helpee follows the course of action to the extent that it exists. Helpee does everything known to be done for that situation at that time.

Level 4: Helpee accepts part of the course of action.

Level 3: Helpee considers following the course of action as it is evolving.

Level 2: Helpee is accepting of helper communication that is high on action dimensions.
Level 1: Helpee rejects or avoids helper communication.

# Index

# About the Authors

GEORGE M. GAZDA, Ed.D. is Research Professor of Education at the University of Georgia and Clinical Professor at the Medical College of Georgia. He is an internationally recognized authority in counselor education, interpersonal communication skills training, and group counseling. Dr. Gazda, a licensed psychologist, is a Fellow of the American Psychological Association, and past president of the American Personnel and Guidance Association. He is author or editor of ten books and has written over 150 articles for professional journals. He has done pioneering work in teaching counseling and interpersonal relationship skills to health care personnel, teachers, corrections officers, and other groups worldwide.

WILLIAM C. CHILDERS, Ph.D. is Adult Counseling Specialist at the University of Georgia Center for Continuing Education, where he conducts skill development workshops for health care personnel, counselors, teachers, and other helping professionals. Before this, Dr. Childers worked for six years in Respiratory Therapy for three hospitals in Georgia. He is coauthor of three books on human relations training and is interested in creating positive learning and helping environments through improved communications.

RICHARD P. WALTERS, Ph.D. spends half of his time as staff psychologist in the adult outpatient department of Pine Rest Christian Hospital in Grand Rapids, Michigan. He also serves as senior trainer for Pine Rest's Life Enrichment Center. In addition, a major part of his time is devoted to writing, teaching, and consulting. Dr. Walters conducts workshops for health care personnel, clergy, teachers, and other helping professionals. He is author or coauthor of six books and a number of articles on skill development in interpersonal relationships.